THE ASHES
OF WACO

AN INVESTIGATION

Dick J. Reavis

Syracuse University Press

To Sitting Bull
and the
Ghost Dance believers

Copyright © 1995 by Dick J. Reavis
All Rights Reserved
First Syracuse University Press Edition 1998
98 99 00 01 02 03   6 5 4 3 2 1

Originally published in 1995 by Simon & Schuster Inc.

Designed by Jeanette Olender

The paper used in this publication meets the minimum requirements
of American National Standard for Information Sciences — Perma-
nence of Paper for Printed Library Materials, ANSI Z39.48-1984. ∞™

Library of Congress Cataloging-in-Publication Data

Reavis, Dick J.
    The ashes of Waco : an investigation / Dick J. Reavis. — 1st
Syracuse University Press ed.
        p.   cm.
    Includes index.
    ISBN 0-8156-0502-1 (pbk. : alk. paper)
    1. Waco Branch Davidian Disaster, Tex., 1993.
    2. Koresh, David, 1959–1993.   3. Branch Davidians.
    I. Title.
    BP605.B72R43   1998
    976.4'284063 — dc21   97-46646

Manufactured in the United States of America

ACKNOWLEDGMENTS

Every serious journalist that I know is doubly in debt. He or she owes the bank, the credit card companies, an offspring, in-law, or parent. These debts we contract sometimes with great encouragement, and as a rule, we pay them as ingrates do: slowly, grudgingly, or not at all.

Our second debt as journalists is to professional patrons and story sources, the people who aid us in trying to answer questions that, often, the public doesn't want asked. These people run all sorts of risks on our behalf: embarrassment, exposure, the loss of a job, the pain of reliving moments from a tragic event. Debts like these are never forgotten—and can't be fully paid.

For this book, I owe, first of all, my agent Esther Newberg, and my editor Alice Mayhew, both of whom I believe took a gamble on me. When they funded my research, none of us knew what, if anything, we might learn.

I also quickly came into a debt to the writers Harry Hurt III and Carlton Stowers. Both had toyed with the idea of writing books of their own and graciously yielded when I told them that I had signed a contract. Stowers, bless his heart, turned over his files to me.

For more than a year, I contacted anybody who I believed might have saved anything in print, on tape or videocassette concerning what had happened in Waco. In this effort to recruit documents, I got very, very little help from the Justice Department and its child, the FBI. My Freedom of Information Act requests, like presumably all others, were delayed for six months at a time—though our laws compel public agencies to speedily comply. The Treasury's Bureau of Alcohol, Tobacco and Firearms, or ATF, was more forthcoming, but veterans of the affair, in both agencies, are even today gagged by bureaucratic fiat. In 1993, when the FBI and ATF published their formal reports on what happened at Waco, the government issued its last words on the subject.

The opponents, apostates, rivals, and surviving followers of David Koresh, and the scholars who probed his teachings after he was dead, are among the thousands of Americans who are not yet ready to see the affair interred. They gave me tapes and tracts and letters until I wondered if I could ever digest it all. Among the scholars, I want to thank Lynn Rainard, Ron Numbers, James Tabor, and Phil Arnold, and along with them, the apostate-autobiographer Marc Breault, the researcher James Trimm, deputy medical examiner Rodney Crow, and especially Mark Swett, who built an electronic library that all of us could use. Dennis Hokama of California also provided Koresh material that nobody else had. The Adventist Church Supply store in Alvarado, Texas, provided me with a ton of books, always efficiently and with good cheer. The Watchman Fellowship, a group dedicated to combating what it regards as cults, published exceptional materials on both theological and personal aspects of the Waco affair. My aunt Mary Crawford, faithful to her denomination, sent me a series of anti-Koresh letters and ultimately, a helpful book on the Oneida community.

Among Koresh's rivals are the faithful of the Mt. Carmel Center (DSDA) of Salem, South Carolina, and Charles Pace and the members of the Living Waters Branch of Righteousness, headquartered in Alabama. Several people associated with these two groups took the time to explain doctrinal differences to me, an outsider to most of the questions involved.

Besides Breault, Robyn Bunds and Joel Jones and several other friends-turned-foes of David Koresh spoke to me several times by telephone or in person. Steven Schneider's sister, Sue Johnson, and Ruth Mosher, mother of Sherri Jewell, met with me and stayed in touch throughout the time that I was researching.

Koresh's surviving followers, especially Livingstone Fagan, Clive Doyle, Jaime Castillo, Sheila Martin, Woodrow and Janet Kendrick, and Catherine Matteson, took the time to write or talk to me repeatedly over the course of eighteenth months. Ofelia Santoyo, Mary Belle Jones, Janet McBean, Margaret Lawson, Annetta Richards, Wally Kennett, Graeme Craddock, Paul Fatta, and Stan Sylvia also put their trust in me. People who have in some ways drifted out of the circle, like Kathy Jones, government witness Kathryn Schroeder, and Oliver Gyarfas, Sr., and his wife Elizabeth, likewise found my purpose important, as did three Waco figures who never knew Koresh—Dewey Millay, Ron Cole, and Mark Domangue. One man whose acquaintanceship was brief, Louis Alaniz, also helped greatly.

ACKNOWLEDGMENTS

In the course of developing this book—from credible sources whom I will not name—I ran across transcripts of the telephone conversations between Mt. Carmel and FBI negotiators during the fifty-one-day siege. No other journalist has read these materials, perhaps because no one has looked for them, or because their mass is daunting—or perhaps because their cover sheets bear the inscription: "This document has been produced in compliance with Rule 16, Federal Rules of Criminal Procedure, and is not for public distribution." My thanks go out to Peggy Chapman for helping me plow through these transcripts, whose contents will now be known to the taxpayers, the unwitting patrons of their compilation.

Most newspapers and broadcasting stations did not do the job assigned to the press in covering the Waco affair. I would like to single out Jim Pate of *Soldier of Fortune* magazine, Diana Fuentes of the *San Antonio Express*, and Ross Milloy of the *New York Times* as reporters who I believe broke away from the pack on this story, and who, when I needed help, helped me. Among stand-in journalists—whose work was especially important on this story—Carol Moore, Jack DeVault, and Jeff Brailey deserve praise. When all of my work was done, three old friends who are journalists—Suzanne Winckler, Joe Nocera, and Joe Nick Patoski—and an editor—Elizabeth Stein—helped me figure out what I'd written.

Part of the reportage in this book comes from attorneys associated with Koresh, Steven Schneider, and the eleven survivors whose trial was staged in San Antonio during 1994. To them, I won't give thanks: for the sake of the story, I've had to quote some of them in this book, and that's advertising enough!

In addition to the debts they can tally, track, and fix in time, most writers owe something—usually a lot—to a spouse. My needs for this book brought to life the lines of the blues song that says, "I asked my baby for a nickel, / And she gave me a twenty-dollar bill." Whenever I needed time, she also took on my household chores. My wife, Miriam Lizcano, and her boss, Jason Webster, were my first lines of assistance in writing this book.

TABLE OF CONTENTS

INTRODUCTION

On February 28, 1993, viewers across the globe glanced at their television sets, and were provoked or intrigued by the fresh, hot documentary footage that passed across their cool screens. In an attempt to arrest one man, Vernon Wayne Howell, aka David Koresh, federal law enforcement agents, dressed in combat gear, had assaulted a large wooden residence near Waco, Texas—scaling its walls, breaking its windows, throwing grenades inside. It was as if the agents had gone to war.

Equally startling, the inhabitants of the building, known as Mt. Carmel, had fired upon the lawmen. Videotape showed the federal raiders in a rout, loading their dead onto the hoods of civilian vehicles. Wounded, bloodied agents hobbled away gasping, arms across the shoulders of retreating comrades. Not only had a seeming war broken out in America, but the government appeared to have lost.

A thousand reporters and cameramen—the eyes and ears, and sometimes the brains of the nation—descended on Waco as fast as helicopters and Learjets could take them. To the assembled press, the government tried to explain. Its explanation was built on four concepts: Texas–Child Molester–Gun Cult–Crazies, its spokesmen said. While some agents explained, others cordoned the zone of conflict and cut the telephone lines that connected Mt. Carmel to the world outside. The press was denied access to the story beyond the barricades. It reported the rest of the action by telephoto lens, from a spot more than two miles away.

All four terms in officialdom's conceptual construct carried a negative charge, each worthy of intellectual scrutiny. But during the seven-week siege that followed the February 28 raid, the reporters were unable to analyze the conflict. A full deck of sources wasn't available. Federal officials, except for designated spokesmen, were gagged. Residents of the besieged building surrendered in trickles and spurts, but reporters couldn't reach them: as the Society of Professional Journalists would point out, "Court appearances were held secretly. Hearings were closed to the press. Key documents ranging from motions to government responses to arrest and search warrants were sealed." Just as in the American invasions of Grenada and Panama, journalists found that the news environment was so tightly managed that they could not fulfill their investigative role.

Yet the press had to produce. The whole world was hungry for news. " . . . During the long siege, reporters, some under pressure from their editors or news directors, were too often tempted to create or embellish news beyond the facts," the journalists' society would observe. The data that the press had to work with—the raw material for any embellishment or relay—were largely derived from facts and fabrications that carried the government's imprimatur. Under the circumstances, the press became an amplifier for bureaucratic spinmeisters.

The managed nature of the news was apparent in the terminology of press reports. The religious community at Mt. Carmel was called a "cult," and its chieftain became, quite naturally, "a charismatic leader" who ruled his followers by something called "mind control." The community's rambling wooden house became a "heavily-fortified compound," its concrete structures became "bunkers," its children "hostages." A nation stood by, watching to see if these children would be "rescued" from the care of their parents.

The scene that was unfolding could have been cast in England, before Quakers and Pilgrims fled to America, or in the colonies at Salem, or in the new Republic during the nineteenth century, when descendants of the Quakers and Pilgrims turned their suspicions on the early-day Mormons. It could also have been a continuation of the extermination of African and Native American faiths—aka "paganism"—since the days before the Republic was founded. The elements that these very American crusades had in common were, on one hand, a group of people with beliefs incomprehensible to the majority of the population, and on the other, police agencies whose operatives could not distinguish custom from law, idiosyncrasy from threat. The line between churches, which Americans believe should be protected from government interference, and cults, which most Americans hold in disdain, has nothing to do with the Constitution—whose First Amendment in theory shields both—and everything to do with the prejudices of a nation that has grown fearful of the diversity that made it nearly unique. The residents of Mt. Carmel were instantly convicted of sin and lawbreaking by the kind of gossip that unites remote hamlets and electronic villages alike.

At the time of the Mt. Carmel siege, I was working as a writer for an "alternative," or local newsweekly, a part of the New Times chain. Its publisher-editor wasn't interested in thoroughly investigating the affair, nor was I—until I found out that if I didn't do the job, no other writer would.

The realization that none of my peers were going to probe the story first dawned on me during a conversation with a friend who covered the Waco events for the daily press. She had spent several days on the scene, trying to work what her editors considered the edges of the story by interviewing members of the Davidian Seventh-Day Adventist movement, a group historically, geographically, and theologically close to the followers of Koresh. "These people are crazy! Nobody can understand what they say," she told me. I disputed her contention until she presented me with a pamphlet entitled *The Breaking of the Seven Seals: The Mystery Behind the Standoff at Mt. Carmel*. Looking into its pages I decided that my friend was qualifiedly right: no journalist that I knew could fathom what it said. Ignorant of the Bible and its interpretations, the document was a mystery to me, just as the writings of Mormon founder Joseph Smith must have been to the reporters who covered his death at the hands of a mob. But it seemed fundamental, if one were to write about the subject, to be able to view the conflict at Mt. Carmel from the minds of both parties involved, from the side of both the lawmen and the besieged. I resolved to learn something about the Bible and its interpretation, if ever the day came when I would write about what was happening in Waco.

On April 19, 1993—hereafter merely "April 19"—Mt. Carmel rapidly burned to the ground, folding the lives of 76 men, women, and children into its flames. A comparable tragedy had never been played out, live and in living color, over global TV. So electrifying was the footage that viewers got the feeling that If You Can See It, You Are There. The event was a national sensation, a great day for the press.

As soon as the flames were visible on camera, the government's spokesmen began explaining what was afoot, by adding two new words to the conceptual tools that they had already issued for grappling with the few bloody and now charred facts at hand: Texas–Child Molester– Gun Cult–Crazies–*Commit Suicide*, they—and even the President—said. The verb and its modifier had the ring of finality, and from the camera's perspective, so did the blaze.

Within forty-eight hours the press had abandoned Waco and moved on, as if the story had been only a visual event: no more besieged building, no more story. The reams of documents and the score of witnesses freed for inspection and interview after the finale—the countervailing arguments, the breathing ashes, the impenetrable Bible—were not of immediate consequence. The press did not probe what happened at Waco, as it does many instances of possible malfeasance, because it could not investigate the story while it was breaking—and because its members did not have the intellectual tools to make sense of pamphlets like the one that befuddled me. In an age dominated by electronic media, instant facts are paramount.

Congresspeople asked cursory questions in postmortem hearings—some of whose proceedings are still under wraps—and six months later, two federal agencies that had participated in the Little War at Waco published reports on their roles. When the reports were issued, the media cast a fleeting backward glance, summarizing what the two tomes said. It was as if, following the now-famous burglary of the Watergate Building, the press had accepted the Nixon administration's investigation of itself. Little effort was made to unravel the tale, wrapped in thick scriptures and wet with tears, that survivors of the conflict were trying to tell.

A year after the shoot-out, a handful of Mt. Carmel's survivors were tried as a group on conspiracy, murder, and firearms charges. A verdict favorable to the accused was reached by a jury, then subverted by high-handed judicial pranks, but this affair, like the assault and siege, was not dissected by journalism, in part because it collided with a hotter scandal: the pursuit and apprehension of O. J. Simpson, broadcast, as all news today must be, live over the screen. The Simpson drama provided news hounds and news junkies with sustenance for a year, and in the shadow of the deaths of Nicole and Ron, the Waco massacre was orphaned once again. It was not as accessible as the O. J. drama, both because the government refused to provide information, and because the information at hand was buried in biblical garb.

The job of finding out what had happened at Mt. Carmel ultimately fell to people outside the media's salaried circles, to scholars, defense attorneys, survivors, and self-financed, independent researchers—and to me. A few weeks after the fire, I began to look into the affair. Two months later, I quit my newsweekly job, to devote myself full time to the Mt. Carmel investigation, because my initial discoveries unsettled me. The people who had lived at Mt. Carmel were more akin to the Shakers and to the Oneida community—parts of today's Americana—than to the members of the Charles Manson cult. Mt. Carmel was a settlement older than its leader, and indeed, one that spanned generations. Its theological doctrines had been formed, disputed, and shared over decades by predecessor and sibling groups whose members had never owned a gun, had never been accused of sexual misdeeds, and had been guilty only of reclusiveness.

Mt. Carmel's leader, Vernon Howell—who in 1989 had changed his name to David Koresh—far from being charismatic, had in most senses been only a redneck from the suburbs of Dallas. His followers were not angry young rebels or runaways, as those of Manson had been, and drugs were apparently not a part of his community's life. While Manson's followers had reportedly confined their children to the crawlspace beneath a house, parents from Mt. Carmel swore that their kids were raised with love and care; both the reports of experts and the children whom I met seemed to bear out the claim. The surviving adults were not, as I had expected, Bible-beaters or street-corner preachers, either. They did not tell me to snuff my cigarettes, nor urge me "to accept Jesus Christ as your Lord and Saviour." When I asked why they didn't make such appeals, one of them told me, "Well, because what we believe is not so simple that we can explain it in fifteen minutes."

Truer words were never spoken. Not much that Koresh's survivors said could be fathomed without recourse to the Good Book. For six months, I buried myself in the Bible and its commentaries, trying to make sense of what I was told. By telephone, I took doctrinal lessons from a survivor in jail. I came out of this immersion with no more, and no different, religion than I had going in, though I must say that during the course of my research, I acquired a grinning respect for the poetry and vision of the Holy Writ.

From my conversations with survivors, from moldering audiotapes of sermons by Koresh and his forerunners, from pamphlets and books and press clippings ten, twenty, and even sixty years old, from video records of the siege, and from government reports, I began to form an understanding of the conflict that had been taking shape at Mt. Carmel for years, waiting for the destruction of 1993. The story cannot be laid out in any strict, chronological order: it is like a tornado, darting and swirling, and the sources that tell it are scattered in spots over its timeline, like tornado debris, a few here, a few there, with mostly empty spaces in between. But by sifting through this debris, the course of the twister can be seen.

Throughout this book, I rely heavily on two government documents, the September 1993 *Report of the Department of Treasury on the Bureau of Alcohol, Tobacco and Firearms Investigation of Vernon Wayne Howell, also known as David Koresh*—which I usually cite as "the Treasury report" or "ATF report," and the October 1993 *Report of the Deputy Attorney General on the Events at Waco, Texas, February 28 to April 19, 1993, Redacted Version*—which I cite as "the Justice report" or "FBI report." I cannot cite from the "unredacted" or unedited Justice report, because it has not been released, and may never be. In this book, I do not refer to "Vernon Wayne Howell also known as David Koresh," but instead to Vernon Howell, when I am citing the words or acts of the man whom we know as David Koresh *before* 1989, when he took the Koresh name. Cites to Koresh are cites that postdate his legal name change.

The book relies as well on documents that I refer to as "the Ranger interviews." In the days following the February 28, 1993, raid—afterwards in this book, merely "February 28"—the Texas Rangers, who were supposed to perform an independent investigation of the events, interviewed all of the federal agents who participated in the raid on Mt. Carmel. The Texas Department of Public Safety, or DPS, parent agency of the one hundred–man Ranger force, has declassified the interviews of only the dozen agents whom federal prosecutors slated to testify in the

San Antonio trial of the survivors' group. If you call the DPS's public information officer to ask for the rest of the transcripts of the Ranger interviews, he'll tell you that you'll have to sue to get them. This book quotes from the available or declassified interviews, and from the transcript of the testimony that the raiders gave in the San Antonio trial. My object in using these records is to tell, in the raiders' own words, what they believe happened on February 28. The more than fifty agents whose interviews have not been declassified cannot speak through my book, because they remain under a gag order.

In the course of my research, I ran across some 18,000 pages of transcripts from telephone conversations between Mt. Carmel's residents and government agents during the fifty-one-day siege. Every word spoken over Mt. Carmel's telephone during the siege is recorded in the documents, which have not been declassified. Our government's police agencies have established offices to implement the federal Freedom of Information Act, but the law ought to be known as the Stalling Act: the agencies involved say that these transcripts will not be available, through prescribed or proper channels, for four to five years.

I came to these records without resort to burglary, bribery, or any illegal act. Once I read into them, I found it hard to believe that no other longtime journalist was on their track. They are an essential source for any account of the Waco events, yet our press, which describes itself as "enterprising," "investigative," and "hard-hitting," either does not know of their existence—or doesn't care about the story.

My research now allows me to tell the fullest story yet told of what happened at Mt. Carmel. But it does not enable me to tell it all. Not even the survivors can give a complete version of the events: each can speak only for what he or she saw and heard, and in no case, for what went on out of view. The nine people who survived the fire at Mt. Carmel cannot, for example, say with any certainty how the fatal blaze started. None of them saw it begin.

The final account of what happened at Mt. Carmel can't be written until—and unless—our government comes clean. Access is still barred to dozens of documents and records, and to the memories of ATF agents and FBI men, under pretexts that run from lawsuits to fears of espionage. Yet an old American adage says that "Justice delayed is justice denied." A nation that prides itself on a free press should take to heart a computer-age corollary of the old saw: "Information delayed is information denied." For reasons that are open only to speculation, our government, founded to serve the people, is stubbornly denying us information about what public servants did and said.

MT. CARMEL CENTER

MT. CARMEL CENTER

FIRST FLOOR

N — NOT TO SCALE

Swimming Pool

Gymnasium

WATER TOWER

STAGE

UP

CHAPEL

W. Martin's Office

COMPUTER ROOM

FRONT DOOR

TELEPHONE ROOM

UP

COOLER

KITCHEN & SERVING PORT

UP

CAFETERIA

VINYL WATER TANKS

MEN'S QUARTERS

WINSTON BLAKE'S ROOM

TRAP DOOR

LARGE ROOM

Underground Bus

Tornado Shelter

MT. CARMEL CENTER

WATER TOWER

SECOND FLOOR

WALKWAY

Presumed Gun Room

Presumed Koresh Bedroom

Residential Tower

Jaydean Wendell's Room

DN

DN

DN

N

NOT TO SCALE

Chapter 1

MR. RETARDO

"My mother always thought I was a strange one."
—David Koresh

Vernon Wayne Howell was the illegitimate son of Bonnie Clark, a young woman who had been only fourteen when she'd brought Vernon into the world in 1959. Her turbulent affair with Vernon's father, Bobby Howell, had produced no lasting relationship, though it did give the infant a moniker, "Sputnik." His parents chose the nickname because of the child's apparent hyperactivity.

Bonnie, who had dropped out of school in Houston, Texas, because of her pregnancy, married another man as soon as her affair with Bobby Howell was over. But her marriage collapsed almost as soon as it was made. Her new man, Bonnie said, beat his two-year-old stepson.

After her divorce, Bonnie left Vernon in Houston with her mother and father, whom she refers to as "an alcoholic." She began a new life in Dallas. Her son didn't join her until he was five, after she had married Roy Haldeman, a former seaman and lounge operator. Based entirely on hearsay, David Koresh would claim that Haldeman had been a shady character back in Houston, but Koresh may have enlarged the tale. His mother recalls that at the lounge Roy operated, ". . . there was a lot of prostitutes that hung out around there, but they didn't work out of there." Vernon told the FBI that his mother had been a prostitute. She denies the charge: "I had some rich boyfriends, and we did a lot of partying and stuff," she expains, adding, "I don't think that my personal life is anybody's business." Haldeman denies the salacious (or more colorful) stories that Vernon told about him as well.

In Dallas and in Tyler, ninety-nine miles east, Bonnie Haldeman established a construction clean-up service; her husband was known as a carpenter who carried a union card. Vernon's life in their household, the Haldemans say, was merely a drab slice out of the routine of the Texas working class. Its backdrop was a florid East Texas lake, where Vernon and his grandfather went fishing on weekends, and the raw plains surrounding the Dallas suburbs of Richardson and Plano, where Vernon, like a lot of Texas boys, hunted rabbit, squirrel, and dove with a .22 rifle and a 410-gauge shotgun.

In working-class Texas households in those days children were spanked; they still are, and civilization doesn't seem to have suffered much from the practice. David Koresh would claim that when Roy spanked him, "he made me fly like a kite," and Bonnie, he said, had even beaten him in the view of the guests at his thirteenth birthday party. His detractors would later say that David Koresh took his revenge on children who lived at Mt. Carmel, and he probably did.

But if David Koresh felt any resentment about the way he was raised, it showed only when he spoke of the past. He wept when his maternal grandfather died in the early eighties, and late in the decade, his mother, stepdad, and half brother were guests at his invitation for months on end at Mt. Carmel. After he was wounded in the February 28 raid, thinking that he was dying, David Koresh picked up the telephone. "Hello, Mamma. It's your boy," he told her answering machine. "They shot me and I'm dying, alright? But I'll be back real soon, okay? I'm sorry you didn't learn the Seals, but I'll be merciful, okay? I'll see ya'll in the skies."

If, as his parents say, Vernon Howell had been just an ordinary kid, there were nevertheless dangerous oversights in the upbringing they gave him. Howell talked of his stepfather, Roy—whose nickname was "Rocky" and "the Rock"—as unfeeling and cold. Bonnie says that she doesn't know why Vernon dropped out of high school because "my own life was in so much turmoil at the time that maybe I didn't notice." And Vernon's only sibling, half brother Roger—six years his junior, the son of Bonnie and Roy—did not become just another pale member of the laboring class. Instead, he went to prison for burglary and drug offenses. The household that produced Vernon Howell was not a model of the virtues of family life.

Young Vernon was a special case, even inside a troubled family. Most people who knew him before he came to Mt. Carmel thought of him as only half-bright. Childhood friends had given him the nickname "Mr. Retardo," and sometimes he played the part. "There's not one grade in school that I didn't fail in," he bragged. "I already failed the first grade twice, so I failed the second grade." As he told the story, the opening day of the third grade was a day that, sadly, he'd never forget.

"So, we went to this special school," he explained. "And we got like three teachers to one small class, right? And the teachers are presenting to us, 'Well, now class, you're special students and we have more teachers to be able to help you' . . . you know, making us feel real good like, yeah, we're special students, right? . . . And so it came time for recess . . . and we got let out a little bit later than the other kids in the same school. . . . And these other kids in the school, they weren't special. They were regular kids, you know what I mean? So, here me and these special kids are coming out the side of the door to go to the swing sets and all that . . . and we're running as fast as we can . . . and all of a sudden you start hearing this, 'here comes the retarded kids!' . . . I mean you're, you know, 'here comes the retarded kids.' And it's like, I just stopped in my tracks. It's like the sun went down over my world. . . . That day was the longest day in my life. . . . So, my mom came to pick me up that evening . . . and I walked over to the car and I sat in the car and I burst out crying. I said, 'I'm in retarded class.' . . . She, she says, you're not in retarded class. You just have a learning disability."

During his year of remedial training, Vernon Howell learned the alphabet and the fundamentals of reading, which he hadn't known before. But he could not master writing. "If he was to write 'angel,' it might come out 'angle,' " former follower Robyn Bunds notes. ". . . He writes more or less phonetically. His spelling is not always the greatest . . . ," his friend Steven Schneider confessed.

When Vernon reached puberty, he did not rebel in the usual way. He was never arrested, his deportment grades were always good, he obeyed his parents around the house. Later, as David Koresh, he tried to create the impression that he had been more of a failure than he was. For example, he did not drop out of school during ninth grade, as he sometimes claimed; instead, he dropped out during the eleventh grade. "He was in class; he was an average student; he did nothing to warrant remembering," a school official reported. But in after-school hours, the young Vernon had been an adolescent obsessed.

"All of my early days," he recalled, "I could remember pictures . . . I couldn't understand reading or writing, but I could understand looking at a car or a motor, or anything I could put my hands on." Machinery fascinated him, probably more than other boys his age.

"I worked my butt off one time having a Tupperware party," his mother says, "to get enough points to buy Vernon a radio. Two or three days later, I went into his room, and there he had the radio all torn apart. He said that he just wanted to see what made it work."

Music also distracted him. On a guitar he found in an abandoned barn, and with a few lessons from a local music store, he learned to play the mostly country and western songs that were a part of his environment. In adolescence, he formed garage bands, whose short lives he blamed on the drug hobbies of other members.

Religion was his strongest—and most unexpected—concern. "I was raised in the Adventist Church, but I didn't know what I believed," Bonnie confesses. Earline Clark, Vernon's grandmother, took him to church often and his mother says that she took him from time to time. Both women note that from an early age, unlike other children, Vernon was rapt in the pews. Though he'd later make fun of their "dyed, fried and tied to the side" hairstyles, he also listened closely to TV and radio evangelists. Former junior high classmates complain that Vernon Howell lectured them from the Bible, and family members recall that he had memorized large tracts by the time he was twelve. It was at that same age, his followers point out, that little Jesus of Nazareth had amazed the rabbis in Jerusalem with his knowledge of the Law.

In 1981, when Vernon Howell, then twenty-two, came to live at Mt. Carmel, he was interested in theology. But he wasn't consumed. He had personal problems to solve. Something was on his mind, something that had happened between his adolescence and manhood. It plagued him. He talked about it for hours at a time, days on end—for years. Vernon wept, too. He cried both when he was alone, his former housemates say, and when he was with others, even during prayers and Bible sessions. He was suffering from an adolescent crisis of love. It was the sort of tragic situation that, had he been either more worldly or more sanctified, would have never come to pass.

Vernon was obsessed with his first love. "I came to God because of her," he declared in one of the first statements he made to the Mt. Carmel community. He'd met her in 1977, when he was eighteen and she was sixteen. It was the time of the Texas oil boom, and Vernon, a non-union carpenter, was flush: he was making payments on a brand-new pickup. During his off-hours he frequented a North Dallas arcade that was a hang-out for the students he'd known before he abandoned his schooling.

One night the young woman, then only an acquaintance, had approached him, asking for a ride home. Vernon was hesitant. "I didn't want nothing to do with her," he said later, "because . . . you know, she was very beautiful and everything and, you know, how sometimes you get in trouble like that."

"This is one of those experiences where, you know, good men fall," he warned when telling the story.

Vernon gave her a ride home, once, and their chat ended without consequence. But it was fateful the second time. On that encounter, when the couple arrived at the house where she lived with her father, she found that her dad was asleep. She invited Vernon inside. "So, we ended up talking and stuff like that and everything," Vernon said in a lighthearted way. "And one thing led to another and I tell you what . . . there should be a law against it, but you know how humanity is."

Vernon's baptism into sex didn't sit well with his Seventh-Day Ad-

27

ventist conscience. He had a reputation among his friends as an upright and religious young soul, and what he'd done didn't square. Besides that, the girl was a minor, jailbait. So, as he told the story, the following day he returned to her house, to apologize—"and I fell into it again."

This time, he was really dismayed, because, "you know, Mr. Cool and Mr. Religious ain't so hot." To put himself out of contradiction's reach, Vernon moved to the home of a family friend in Tyler. For two months, he had no contact with his first love.

Then one night the telephone rang. She was on the line. She was pregnant, she said.

The news shook Vernon. "Me, Mr. Retardo, going to have a baby!" he said to himself.

Howell had a deft and devious mind. He knew in an instant just what to say to her.

". . . My reaction was, I says . . . 'I'm sterile.' " He later claimed, "I heard that statement from a movie or something." She hung up the phone, and didn't call again.

But that wasn't the end of the story, because God stepped in. He had, in fact, been stepping in for quite a while. While imbibing Adventist doctrine in elementary school, Vernon had been puzzled. "Why did God write all this book if we're supposed to wait 'til we get to heaven to learn it?" he'd asked his teachers. Since they couldn't answer the question satisfactorily, he had taken it and other pressing matters directly to their chief. One afternoon he slipped out of his school and into the sanctuary of its church. There he'd bent on his knees to pray. "Dear Father," he'd said, ". . . I don't understand why I'm this way. . . . I know I'm stupid but . . . please talk to me because I want to serve you. . . ." Before long the Good Lord was addressing Vernon. By the time his first love called, Vernon Howell and God had been carrying on conversations for six years.

In the weeks following her confession, the voice of God spoke to Vernon again. According to the young man's understanding of the scriptures, he was already married to the girl in God's eyes; their first copulation had been the vow. Now God told Vernon to live up to his worldly duty. He obediently went back to Dallas, ready to make her his wife.

When Vernon telephoned her from Dallas, she told him that, with her father's permission, she'd gotten an abortion—and, oddly, that she wanted to see him again. Vernon couldn't understand why, but years later, he still recalled the praise that she'd given him that day. "She goes, 'You know, you were always so different from everybody else . . . like guys who'd smoke dope—you wouldn't take it. Guys would be drinking a lot of beers and you'd only maybe have a half of one, or one. . . . But you always seem to be able to, to be with everybody else . . . but . . . to be independent of everybody else and you didn't have to, to do what everybody else was doing to have a good time.'

". . .This girl had a head on her," Vernon concluded. "I never realized, I just thought she was another . . . beautiful, gorgeous girl, but she really had a deep mind."

Having shown him that she was "more religious than most of the religious girls . . . a good Christian without being a Christian," Vernon resumed seeing his first love. Her father wouldn't permit his daughter to marry, but before long Vernon was living in her bedroom—with her father's permission, Koresh claimed. According to the tale that he told, in the mornings her dad would knock on the bedroom door to remind him that it was time to head to work, her that it was time to get ready for school. In later years, Howell would sometimes tell the story with a certain amusement, pointing out that the Bible is full of tales of stranger marriages, sanctioned from on high.

Because Vernon thought that the Writ forbid it, Mr. Retardo and his girlfriend did not practice birth control, and sure enough, a couple of months later she turned up pregnant again. She wasn't happy, apparently because Vernon's professional status was less than enviable, and when he blurted out that he'd fathered her first fetus, her dad ran Vernon out of her life. The young Adventist was confused—it would be years before he'd understand—because it seemed that God's marriage plan had been derailed.

Vernon Howell slept in his pickup on the edges of Dallas suburbs for weeks after he left her house. As he was bedding down one night, God came around to explain. "This presence enshrouds me," Howell said, when recounting the event. "And I'm talking about [how] its authority encompasses me. And here I am zeroed in and all of a sudden I start

29

shaking and I'm scared to death. I mean, you would be scared if you was out in the field and all of a sudden two black guys came at you, wouldn't you?

". . . And here I am, looking at the sky, but all of a sudden it's like, it's like I'm being watched from every angle. And there's this, there's this being confronting me and it's like I have no place to run. . . . And this voice says to me, it says—it's not a voice such as, see, when I'm talking to you. . . . It's a voice that imparted a picture completely perfect in my mind. . . . And He says, 'You're really hurt, aren't you?' And, and, you know, nineteen years of my life flash in front of me, just like on a film. The whole damn aura of being.

"It says, 'You're really hurt, aren't you? You've loved her for about a year and now she's turned her back on you. And now she's rejected you.' And which, you know, that's, that's the climactic thing, because the, the most highest elevation of human completeness is, is marriage, right?

"And then the voice all of a sudden—it, it re—it reviewed to me all of these weird and strange and unique and enstrengthening experiences throughout my whole childhood and life. And it says, 'Don't you know that for nineteen years I've loved you and for nineteen years you've turned your back on me and rejected me?' And all of a sudden, every-thing is like, bang! It hits me all at once. Ah, what an ability to forget the reasons and purposes of life! . . . But the key note is this. God said he would give her to me later."

Just how God would do that became one of the theological puzzles that Vernon Howell would resolve after he joined the community at Mt. Carmel.

Chapter 2

SHOWTIME

"... The sad reality is this: they wanted a big one. They wanted
a spectacular one."

—David Koresh

As the morning sun inched into the rain clouds over the blackland
prairie on Sunday, February 28, Special Agent Sharon Wheeler braced
herself for the raid that was about to begin. Her agency, the Treasury
Department's Bureau of Alcohol, Tobacco and Firearms (ATF), was
launching the biggest and most important operation since the days
when it had been the Bureau of Prohibition. If the raid on Mt. Carmel
went as planned, it could make the acronym of Wheeler's agency as
well known as that of the FBI.

Thorough preparations had been made. Advance men—"Support
Coordinators," the ATF called them—had been in Waco, about one
hundred miles south of Dallas, for more than a month. They had set
up a command post at an airstrip northeast of downtown. More than
fifty agents and helicopter crewmen had moved into town the night
before, and for the evening of the 28th, the agency had reserved one
hundred fifty rooms for its troops in Waco's three leading hotels.

The ATF had also contracted an ambulance service, told hospitals to
make ready, and enlisted sheriff's deputies and Texas Highway Patrol-
men for back-up duties. The Support Coordinators had ordered coffee

and doughnuts, and even portable toilets, for the men and women who, within a few minutes, at about 9:00 A.M., would rally at the Bellmead Civic Center, some ten miles from their target, off in the countryside. Fresh from training and a sunup briefing at the Army's Fort Hood, some sixty miles southwest, the raiders were moving north on Interstate 35, in an eighty-vehicle convoy more than a mile long. A half-dozen snipers—"forward observers," the ATF called them—had already taken up positions, both in front of and behind Mt. Carmel, and the leadership of the burgeoning assault was converging on the command center, to suit up in combat gear.

Much of this movement was being filmed because documentation of the event was as important to the ATF as the action itself. The agency faced congressional budget hearings on March 10, less than two weeks away. Televised film of the raid—"a dynamic entry," the ATF called it—would, at the very least, establish a counterpoint to the sprinkle of bad publicity that its director, Stephen Higgins, had received a few months before. Dramatic footage of the raid might even air in a documentary serial like *Cops*. A raid on cultists would make a titillating episode; the ATF's routine work, such as enforcing the Contraband Cigarette Act, was far from that.

For a month, surveillance cameras with high-powered lenses had been rolling at what was called the "undercover house," a bungalow located about 200 yards from Mt. Carmel's front door. The video cameras recorded everything that came into view. The ATF had also filmed the raid's planning and training sessions, and it planned to record the action's finale on tape, though spokesmen would later say that on the morning of February 28, the surveillance cameras had "malfunctioned." A part of Special Agent Sharon Wheeler's job was to make footage of the raid and its preparation available to television news crews. She was a Public Information Officer, or public relations flack, for the ATF, and she wasn't alone. Special Agent Franceska Perot had been sent from the ATF's Houston office to assist her.

Their job, as Wheeler later told Congress, was to put a spin on the news. "You want to promote your agency in a good light, and ATF hired public information officers over the last two years, to do that, to show the agency in a good light. . . ," she testified.

But Special Agents Wheeler and Perot weren't called Special Agent because of their PR duties. So conscious of its image was the ATF that all its agents, office and field troops alike, were called Special Agents. The ATF had no agents, only Special Agents.

Even Special Agent Wheeler, who wasn't a part of the raiding team, was toting a camera. She filmed the operation's commanders as they dressed for war and climbed into the three helicopters from which they would view—and film—the action. The ground troops carried cameras, too, stuffed in their pockets and hanging off their uniforms, along with flash-bang grenades, nylon handcuffs, and ammunition. Preparations to film the assault had been so intensive that they'd inspired a code name for the operation. The brass called it "Operation Trojan Horse," but the grunts had named it "Showtime."

Showtime was the fruit of an investigation that had begun nine months earlier, after a United Parcel Service driver learned that the package he was delivering to Mt. Carmel contained dummy hand grenades. ATF officers, alerted by the local sheriff's department, followed the lead, and through shipping and sales records found that some 90 pounds of powdered aluminum had also been dropped off there. Powdered aluminum, when mixed with black gunpowder—also on a delivery invoice—can be used to make grenades, and grenades are on a list of "destructive devices" prohibited by federal firearms laws. But powdered aluminum and gunpowder can also be used for reloading spent rifle cartridges, a common and legal activity.

The grenades weren't the only items that attracted the agency's attention. A paper trail also showed that thirty-three-year-old Vernon Howell—who in 1989 had changed his name to David Koresh—and several other residents of the target, had recently spent some $40,000 on armaments, including 104 "upper receivers" for AR-15 rifles. The AR-15 is a civilian version of the M-16 rifle used by American forces in the Vietnam War. It is a semi-automatic weapon, that is, one that reloads itself but will fire only a single shot at the pull of the trigger. Automatic weapons like the M-16, by contrast, continue firing, round after round, until the operator removes his finger from the trigger, or until the gun's ammunition is spent.

The ownership of semi-automatic rifles was not legally restricted at the time, as was the ownership of automatic weapons. Fully automatic weapons—machine guns—may be lawfully purchased or made in the United States, but only when their buyer or maker obtains a clearance from local authorities, and pays a $200 per weapon registration fee. An ATF history explains the law this way: "Rather than ban outright the purchase of machine guns and sawed-off shotguns—the weapons of choice for the mobsters—Congress in 1934 simply imposed a tax on those weapons. Paying the tax required registering the weapon." In 1993, more than 234,000 Americans owned machine guns under the terms set forth in the law.

Since M-16s made from AR-15s are legal if properly registered, kits to convert the semi-automatics to automatic fire are also legal items of commerce, as ostensible replacements for worn components. Furthermore, there is no federal or Texas statute against stockpiling arms; anyone who can legally buy one weapon can legally buy a hundred, or even a thousand of them.

Judging from credit card records and shipping invoices, the ATF investigators believed that Koresh or someone else at Mt. Carmel might have converted, or might have made plans to convert, AR-15s to automatic fire by matching legal "upper receivers" with "lower receivers" that had been altered. No one at the complex, an ATF records check revealed, had applied for a permit to own homemade machine guns.

Converting an AR-15 to automatic fire is not a simple job; it takes special equipment. The convertor must have a handful of "magic" or specialized parts, as well as milling machinery to prepare lower receivers for their installation. The ATF found no record that Koresh or anyone else at Mt. Carmel had purchased "magic parts," but milling machines they did have.

The ATF's investigative findings about Mt. Carmel had been recorded in a flawed and perhaps insufficient affidavit that the agency had used, a few days before, to seek and win permission to search the place. The affidavit had been written by Special Agent Davy Aguilera, who had headed the agency investigation of Koresh. In the affidavit, Aguilera had attempted to justify a search by listing *legal* gun parts and explosive ingredients that the residents of Mt. Carmel had ordered. If the affidavit provided any evidence that the suspects were converting semi-automatic weapons to fully automatic fire, that evidence showed only in a cryptic listing that read: "Four (4) M-16 parts set Kits 'A.' " Gun experts who've read the affidavit don't know to what the listing might refer, unless it's "A" as in "Item A" from a catalogue or mail-order ad—in which case it might refer to any number of benign parts.

The affidavit did not show intent, a requirement of the law. Most rural householders in the Waco area own both a shotgun and a hack-saw, but that does not make them guilty of any intent to own a sawed-off shotgun. Had Koresh and his crew paraded with converted AR-15s, or even declared an intention to sell or possess them, a search warrant would have been easily justified. But Aguilera made no such showing.

The affidavit that Special Agent Aguilera composed also attempted to cast suspicion over Mt. Carmel by alleging that an informant had "observed at the compound published magazines such as, the 'Shotgun News' and other related clandestine magazines," none of which were named. *Shotgun News* has for half a century been published thirty-six times a year in Hastings, Nebraska, and is mailed under a third-class postal permit. It is the blue book of the firearms trade, and most of its 145,000 subscribers—chiefly, gun, pawn, and sporting goods stores—would drop it in a minute, were it clandestine.

During a congressional investigation held after the raid, agency chief Stephen Higgins confessed to the weakness of the warrant, essentially pleading for sympathy. Referring to the residents of Mt. Carmel by a name that the government and press adopted, he said that "The Davidians, as you can see from the affidavit, legally were ordering various parts and components and bringing them onto the premises. What we were trying to establish was: Were they violating the law after they got them onto the premises?"

In an attempt to find grounds for alleging illegal activity, Aguilera had interviewed Marc Breault, a chubby, golden-skinned Mt. Carmel apostate. In his affidavit, Aguilera reported that Breault "participated in . . . firearm shooting exercises conducted by Howell. He stood guard armed with a loaded weapon." The affidavit did not mention that standing guard on one's property is not prohibited by law, nor did it point out that Breault is legally blind. He's a man who can see well enough to ride a bicycle, for example, or, after a fashion, to bowl; he can see the pins standing at the end of the alley, he says, but can't see which ones he's knocked down. Breault claimed that he had engaged in target practice with an air rifle, but he wasn't trained at Mt. Carmel, and former residents say, was never assigned to guard duty there.

Aguilera's affidavit concealed traces of bad faith in other particulars, too. It did not give a fair or full accounting of the relevant facts that he and the agency knew. It detailed ATF visits and interviews with a half-dozen other suppliers to Mt. Carmel, but did not mention the visit of July 30, 1992, when Aguilera and Special Agent Jimmy R. Skinner had stopped in to quiz Mt. Carmel's principal arms providers, licensed gun dealer Henry McMahon, age thirty.

Under the commercial name Hewitt Handguns, McMahon and his girlfriend and bookkeeper, Karen Kilpatrick, thirty-five, had for two years traveled to weekend gun shows across Texas, where they'd sold some four thousand weapons, most of them pistols. They'd also become friends of David Koresh. McMahon had sold a few handguns to Koresh's followers, and Kilpatrick had sent a 1969 Camaro for restoration by mechanics from Mt. Carmel. Though Kilpatrick appears to have taken some of Koresh's biblical claims to heart, when McMahon eyed him as a client, he took a more cold-hearted view.

Koresh bought guns as an investment, McMahon told the ATF. He wanted them because he believed that if federal gun-control proposals became law, prices for semi-automatic firearms purchased before the ban would double overnight. When Koresh bought guns, McMahon said, the preacher drove a hard bargain, demanding mint quality, even insisting upon boxed weapons. He was buying guns to resell, not to use.

"If I had a used gun with no box, then he would just hammer on the price," the dealer told the ATF in an interview recorded after the raid. "He would want a real discounted price. He was real sharp on his money."

Koresh was also a quick study, McMahon said. "When I first met him"—in September 1990, McMahon told the agency—". . . he didn't know about guns. He would buy cheap guns and shoot them and they would break. And he would say, I don't want this. I mean, he learned about these guns. He said, this is why it broke. See this cheap weld? . . . At the first he knew nothing about guns, at the end he knew more than I did. . . ."

As his savvy increased, Koresh began to see that money could be made—and also wasted—in the market for guns and paraphernalia. ". . . He wanted to know about how to make money at gun shows," McMahon recalled. "We took him to a gun show in Dallas or Fort Worth. He's finding out that he can find a little better deal at these gun shows. So he started easing off on buying as many guns from me."

Before long, Koresh and a disciple in his early thirties, Paul Fatta, were operating a booth at gun shows themselves, selling gasmasks, ammunition magazines, Meals Ready-to-Eat, or MREs—(the modern equivalent of K-rations), and miscellaneous other paramilitary gear. Under the name "David Koresh Survival Wear," they also manufactured and sold hunting vests, custom-cut for big men, sewn by Mt. Carmel's seamstresses. Some of their vests included an unusual adornment: dummy grenades, bradded onto their fabric.

If, after McMahon introduced him to gun shows, Koresh had quit buying from him, he didn't shun him in all things. Instead, he proposed a partnership, an arrangement that Aguilera and his partner stumbled across in their July 1992 check of Hewitt's records. The ATF's paperwork showed that McMahon had purchased more than one hundred AR-15 lower receivers, sixty-five of which weren't listed as having been sold, yet weren't on hand as inventory. McMahon explained that those weapons—AR-15 lower receivers are classified as firearms, whose first retail transfer must be registered—were being stored by Koresh because Hewitt Handguns didn't own a safe big enough to hold all of them.

McMahon also explained to the Special Agents the plan under which the receivers had been entered into his books. Koresh had discovered that by tapping various suppliers, he could assemble, or technically, "manufacture" AR-15s at a price that would undercut even gun show dealers. But Koresh couldn't buy lower receivers or sell AR-15s, because he wasn't a licensed dealer. McMahon couldn't buy the components because he didn't have the money: at the time, parts to build an AR were selling for about $400. Ready-to-use ARs were selling for about $600 at gun shows when Koresh proposed the scheme. Two years later, their price had shot to $1,400; just as he predicted, the assembly plan would have brought Koresh, as financial backer, a profit whose size depended largely on volume and time. His proposal to McMahon was that Mt. Carmel's residents would assemble the guns, splitting their proceeds with McMahon, if Hewitt would act as the sales agent. There was nothing obviously illegal about this plan, and once it was pacted, the two bought by mail order enough parts to assemble about one hundred ARs.

While the Special Agents were scrutinizing Hewitt's affairs in the McMahon/Kilpatrick living room, McMahon says that he went into a back room and telephoned Koresh, to tell him about the ATF enquiry. "If there's a problem, tell them to come out here. If they want to see my guns, they're more than welcome," Koresh had told him. With the preacher still on the line, the gun dealer says that he stepped back into his living room, offering a portable telephone to the Special Agents. But Aguilera waved him away. Aguilera would not visit Mt. Carmel until February 28, when he watched the raid from one of the helicopters above.

By the time that Aguilera and Skinner paid McMahon their visit, Hewitt had sold a half-dozen of the guns that Koresh had assembled. When Special Agent Skinner returned about a month later, McMahon presented him with signed forms, showing that the missing lower receivers had all been sold to Vernon Howell. But Skinner sounded a sour note about the assembly scheme: manufacturers of more than fifty firearms, he explained, must pay an 11 percent federal excise tax on their products—and keep records proving that they do. The specter of yet more paperwork discouraged McMahon and Kilpatrick, and they backed out of their agreement with Koresh. He was stuck with the lower receivers.

Chapter 3

ENTER THE PRESS

". . . The press and different magazines and all the other medias
and so forth, everybody's into sensationalism and anything to
have a unique or oddball story."
—Steve Schneider

Special Agent Sharon Wheeler had already planned a news conference
for "Showtime's" close. Part of her job was getting the media to attend.
Days earlier, she'd telephoned several television stations to find out who
would be available for a February 28 conference. It was a fairly sure bet
that the press would attend, because, besides the tiresome and obscure
material in the warrant about upper and lower receivers, Wheeler had
on hand every PR agent's dream: an independent report, not only con-
firming her agency's line of information, but adding accusations that the
ATF could not probe on its own. It was the sort of report that, in the
tobacco industry, for example, flacks spend fortunes to inspire.

The report was by Mark England and Darlene McCormick, two
journalists at the local daily, the *Waco Tribune-Herald*. It was a fresh
study, from a seven-part series whose first installment had been published only the day before, February 27. In some 2,000 words, the
opening article of the series spelled out the charges that the ATF would
make against David Koresh—and also some that were outside of the
agency's scope. In the second installment, 3,000 words long—being

distributed as Special Agent Wheeler was readying herself on the 28th—England and McCormick fleshed out their tale.

The first sentence of the series stated: "If you are a Branch Davidian, Christ lives on a threadbare piece of land about 10 miles east of Waco called Mt. Carmel. He has dimples, claims a ninth-grade education, married his legal wife when she was 14, enjoys a beer now and then, plays a mean guitar, reportedly packs a 9mm Glock and keeps an arsenal of military assault rifles, and willingly admits that he is a sinner without equal."

The two reports contained some provincialisms that readers elsewhere might have taken as signs of bias. Their references to beer were significant, for example, only because Waco is a stronghold of the Southern Baptist denomination, whose doctrine is Prohibitionist. Catholics might not frown at clerics who tipple, and Pentecostals might praise a preacher who "plays a mean guitar," but in Waco, the seat of Southern Baptist Baylor University—a school that doesn't hold dances because dancing is sin—David Koresh was thumbing his nose at local standards of decency.

As if he anticipated what the newspaper would say, Special Agent Aguilera had done as much as he could to corroborate the charges that the two journalists would raise. The ATF investigator and his colleagues had interviewed six former Mt. Carmel residents, most of whom knew far more about unrelated rumors of adultery and statutory rape than they did about guns. Though the ATF had no authority to investigate these complaints, Aguilera had passed on the allegations in his affidavit.

For its series, the *Tribune* had interviewed three of Aguilera's Mt. Carmel sources, most important among them, Marc Breault, Aguilera's informant. Breault had been a twenty-two-year-old student of religion in 1986, when he was drawn into the circle that adored Vernon Howell. The young grad student moved from California to Texas to join the bulk of Howell's some fifty-odd followers, who, at the time, were living in an encampment of school buses and 8-foot by 16-foot plywood boxes near Palestine, Texas, some one hundred miles east of Waco. Because Breault was good-natured and theologically fast, he soon won the endearment of the tribe. "He seemed to be patient and easygoing, and he took time to listen to people," co-religionist Sheila Martin recalls.

Breault was a memorable figure at Palestine, veterans of the encampment say, because he experienced dreams and visions that, he believed, were revelations from God. When Breault had a vision, he wrote it down and circulated it for study and analysis. In one of the visitations that he recorded, "The light became brighter and brighter until my mind could comprehend the Bible from cover to cover as if it were a one page summary of an article. When I say this, I mean that this is what it is to God . . . I realized that through God's Word—that is, through beholding God's word, I was becoming like the Word of God —like the Most High, in that I was beginning to perceive in the way that God perceives." Though the *Tribune* did not expose Breault's visionary side, today he confesses that "I . . . toyed with the idea of being a prophet." Sheila Martin says that rather than banishing Breault, Howell encouraged the blind man's ambitions, explaining to his followers that "if Marc was a prophet, God would show him the way."

Early in his relationship with the group, Marc Breault had noted that although Vernon Howell was married to a member of the flock, he also had conjugal relations with, and children by, several other women in the Palestine camp, including at least one who had not reached the legal age of consent. Howell's acolyte at first paid little mind. "As far as I was concerned, biblically speaking, what Vernon was doing was okay," he explained. "The Bible does not actually condemn polygamy outright. In fact, there are certain passages in the Old Testament that say it's okay." Nor did Howell's brazen disregard of laws against statutory rape disturb Breault. ". . . What we believed was that if the girl was living with her father . . . then Vernon would actually have to get parental consent . . . ," he would say. This, too, Breault had argued, was biblical. "Everything we did was based on the Bible and prophecy," he insisted.

Breault had completed his master's thesis from Palestine, and along with the others, had migrated to Waco in 1988. There he played keyboard instruments in the sect's musical group, whose lead guitarist and chief vocalist was, of course, Vernon Howell. Breault also built a reputation as a spinner of the speculative theology that Howell concocted best, and before long he was named an evangelizer for the group, making recruitment trips to Hawaii and the West Coast.

But as time went on, the Master of Religious Studies began to doubt his unlettered teacher—especially after Howell began to style himself as "the exclusive expositor of scripture," Breault explained. "Everyone else was wrong, and only he had the right and the ability to interpret the Bible." The acolyte's eyebrows were further raised, and his skepticism further deepened, he said, in the spring of 1989, when his leader bedded a thirteen-year-old who, Breault believed, could not have comprehended the theological importance of her act. The former pupil became downright obstinate—and bolted the group—after the teacher laid claim to his newly wedded bride, who, to Breault's great relief, was safely in Australia at the time.

Upon reuniting with his wife Down Under, Breault began campaigning to oust Koresh from his throne. Fully donning the prophet's role—this time insincerely, he now says—Breault approached members of the sect with a divine message whose upshot was that David Koresh was wrong, and perhaps, a fraud. In 1990, Breault and his apostate flock hired a detective to inform American authorities about the goings-on at Mt. Carmel. The emissary met in Waco with local and federal lawmen, but nothing came of the trip. No one seemed interested in Breault's tale until the *Tribune-Herald* called in mid-1992.

The "Sinful Messiah" articles accurately recorded the accusations that the paper's sources made, and by simplifying the tales they told, boosted their bias in several ways. The England-McCormick series leveled its charges outside of the context in which they arose. The series did not reproduce Breault's invocation of Old Testament beliefs about polygamy, nor did it explain to the *Tribune*'s readers why Koresh's followers regarded Breault as a rival prophet, tramping sour grapes. The two reporters also failed to distinguish between semi-automatic and automatic "assault weapons," legal and illegal guns. Though the newspaper presented ample evidence that Koresh was guilty of statutory rape, it did not explore the multiple layers of Bible-based logic that persuaded an incomparably conservative sect—and sources like Breault—to accept lawless behavior. Legal, scriptural, and Constitutional paradoxes lay beneath the leaves of the story like thorns on a rosebush, while sensational and salacious fruit was within easy reach—and the *Tribune*, as the press usually does, picked it unscathed.

As if to compound the problem, on the afternoon of February 27, Mark England declined to meet with Koresh to discuss the first installment. England probably turned down the meeting because the plan for Showtime, like the warrant that authorized it and the newspaper series that would justify it, was already in motion, despite one great flaw. In the case of the raid, the flaw was that England, like every alert journalist in Waco, had already surmised that it was only a sunrise away.

Lots of people knew, even though no one who was not directly involved was supposed to know. Some had known for weeks. England's co-writer Darlene McCormick had that fall told federal authorities that the *Tribune-Herald* was preparing a report, and her disclosure had led to several negotiations between ATF and Tribune executives. The talks produced no agreement, but during the week before the raid, the ATF had learned that the series was ready for publication. The ATF brass, for its part, had told members of the *Tribune*'s negotiating team that the agency was also preparing to make its move.

Even submanagement journalists guessed that the raid was coming. A cameraman from the local television station, which had no proprietary connection to the newspaper, has testified that he learned about the plan from an employee of an ambulance firm that the ATF had contracted. A reporter at the *Tribune-Herald* who was not a by-line writer of the "Sinful Messiah" series had returned from a routine trip to the courthouse with a tip about the action, from a source who, he said, was also outside of the ATF. The first installment of the series was accompanied by an editorial scolding local lawmen—but not mentioning the feds—for having turned a blind eye to goings-on at Mt. Carmel, perhaps because its composers knew that federal action was at hand.

Late on February 27, when helicopters landed at the command post airstrip and ATF forces gathered around, it didn't take a rocket scientist to figure out that something was brewing. A few of Waco's newsmen caught wind, and were elated. Television reporter John McLemore, for example, went out that night to celebrate the big event that he'd already been told to cover at sunup.

Chapter 4

THE BIBLE HOUSE

"To me the real world is the, the Word."
—Steven Schneider

Ten Waco reporters and camera handlers, in six vehicles, were already circling Mt. Carmel as Special Agent Sharon Wheeler made arrangements for the press conference that, she thought, would tell the world about the raid. Television photographer Jim Peeler, who was not familiar with the city's rural environs, drove one of the vehicles. Becoming lost, he pulled his white Chevy Blazer to the side of a heavily wooded road, hoping to get his bearings by consulting a map. In his car was a police scanner, its digital dial set to the frequency used by the Texas Alcoholic Beverage Control Board. Its face, in bright digital letters, read: "TABC."

A yellow Buick whose door carried the legend "U.S. MAIL" pulled up behind Peeler. The driver, David Jones, approached the cameraman, offering help. Jones was a thirty-eight-year-old, blondish white who spoke in what one of his friends called "a slow country accent." But Peeler was reluctant to speak to him until he noticed the sign on the door of the Buick. "Are you really a postman?" the cameraman asked. His logic couldn't have been more transparent: Postmen are sane, cultists are "crazy"; therefore if Jones was a postman, he could not at the same time be a member of the Mt. Carmel cult.

44

Jones assured Peeler that the car was no ruse—he was a mail carrier—and Peeler then explained his problem: he had to find "Rodenville," a nickname by which the Mt. Carmel complex had earlier been known. Jones pointed out the place, less than a mile away, and though he had always been a man of few words, he continued to talk with the photographer, whose jacket displayed the television station's logo. During their chat, an unmarked white Suburban carrying six ATF snipers in combat gear drove past, and Peeler—who says that he never told Jones about any raid plans—stepped away from the road for a minute, trying to get an uncluttered view of the sky; both men had heard the sound of helicopters. Before their speculations ended, Jones surmised that a police action was in the offing. He wished Peeler luck, returned to his Buick, and drove toward Mt. Carmel.

David Jones lived there. He'd grown up there, he'd been there for years before Vernon Howell had ever heard of the place. David Jones's grandparents had lived at what was called "the Old Mt. Carmel," several miles away. On the morning of February 28, David Jones's three children—Mark, twelve, Kevin, ten, and Heather, nine—his father, Perry, and two of his sisters were also living at Mt. Carmel; one of them was married to Koresh. David Jones's estranged wife, Kathy Kendrick, had also grown up there. She was the daughter of Woodrow "Bob" and Janet Kendrick, whom Perry Jones had brought to Mt. Carmel during the sixties. Through good times and bad, four generations of Jones's family had been partisans of the movement that made Mt. Carmel its home.

Nothing had been able to undo the ties that bound people like David Jones and Kathy Kendrick to the place. When Jones and his wife separated, she moved into town, but let him keep their kids at Mt. Carmel, she says, because "he was a good father, had a good job, and had medical insurance on them, and I knew that Mt. Carmel was a good place for them to grow up." Kathy's parents were still among its faithful, and Kathy wasn't completely out of touch. She had last spoken to Koresh just the afternoon before. "When are you going to come home?" the preacher had asked her; Kathy says his words had made her feel that deep in her heart, despite her departures and misgivings, Mt. Carmel would always be home.

45

David Jones had not always lived at Mt. Carmel, either. Three months earlier, he'd been with his children and his mother, Mary Belle—also one of its flock—at a mobile home he owned, about two miles away; he was en route from there to Mt. Carmel when he encountered Peeler. His mother still lived in the trailer, which was but an extension of Mt. Carmel: since Mt. Carmel's buildings were uninsulated and poorly heated, Koresh had asked Mary Belle to take in three elderly residents, to make the winter easier for them. To make room for the trio, Jones had moved back to Mt. Carmel with his kids.

More pointedly, he had been absent during most of the seventies, because, as he put it, "I grew up hating religion. I hated it with a passion, and I left home when I was seventeen, and I never wanted anything to do with religion again." Jones had joined the Air Force, taken drugs, traveled and lived outside the Mt. Carmel community for nearly a decade. "It was like most kids," his mother says. "When they grow up, they have to decide, did they want this religion or not?"

Kathy hadn't kept the faith in her adolescence, either. At fifteen she had briefly run away from home, and at sixteen, had left Mt. Carmel with her parents' consent. "Any of the kids who grew up at Mt. Carmel, who got to where they didn't like their parents and wanted to leave— you could leave," she recalls. "They'd find you a place to go, and they'd know where you were and how you were doing. Their attitude was, 'We'll let you see that the grass isn't greener on the other side.' "

At nineteen, when she married Jones, Kathy says, "We'd both pretty well had about enough of any religion, yet we still didn't find ourselves attracted to anyone who didn't grow up with the same beliefs." In 1978, Jones and Kathy had celebrated their wedding at Mt. Carmel's former administrative building, rather than at its chapel, because the community's leader of that era, Ben Roden, disapproved of Jones's smoking habit—and Jones wouldn't promise to quit. A year later, Kathy and David came back to Waco and moved into one of the houses that stood on Mt. Carmel's grounds, though it would be years before they'd resume the faith.

Their return was not consummated until 1985, after Vernon Howell had taken charge. David Jones was the reluctant party, so skeptical that for years he refused to attend services. But he did listen to recorded sermons from time to time. "He came back gradually. It was a learning process," recalls his mother, citing an Old Testament adage (Prov 22:6) that says, "Train up a child in the way he should go: and when he is old, he will not depart from it."

Mt. Carmel was David Jones's boyhood haunt, practically his home-town, a place to which he'd returned after wandering afar. It was his marriage venue, the locus of his heritage and of everything that was dear to him—and all of this, he'd just learned, was about to come under attack.

The building toward which Jones headed after his encounter with the cameraman was a rambling, rumpled, L-shaped structure, haphaz-ardly slapped together during the past three years. Its wood-paneled exterior was painted beige, but its interior was of raw fiberboard, sheet-rock, and plywood. The more than one hundred people who lived at Mt. Carmel spoke of their home more with amusement than with pride, as if of an old shoe. Its newcomers didn't even call it "Mt. Carmel." To them, it was "the anthill" and "the camp."

The long building's back pointed in the direction that its residents called north—though it was actually northwest—and the leg of its L pointed toward what they called "east"—as if Mt. Carmel set the di-rections of the compass. The building had a double front door, whose core was plastic foam, enveloped in steel, painted white, and stamped to look like wood. From the perspective of a visitor standing on its front porch, just inside the doorway, to the left, or "north," ran a 60-foot-long first-floor hallway that passed by a dozen ordinary-sized rooms, where men slept in bunks; males and females did not bed together at Mt. Carmel. The women and children slept in nearly identical rooms, off a hallway upstairs.

The sleeping rooms had no closets, and only a few had doors; they were mere enclosures of a space that had formerly been used as a gymnasium. Most tenants covered the entrances to their quarters with sheets or blankets, hung from nails. Only a few had chests of drawers, and clothing was slung on rods and hooks that occupants rigged as best they could. Because there were no suitable storage areas, many of them kept surplus belongings in the trunks of their cars, on the parking lot outside. Those who didn't have cars boxed their gear and stuck it in the long hallways.

At the "north" end of the second-floor hallway, a rectangular room had been added, larger than the others, and forming a higher, or third story. It was chiefly occupied by the women who had no children, and was sometimes called "the women's dormitory."

A section of the first floor, as one walked down the hallway, going "north" from the front door, had been turned into a kitchen, behind which—like a rectangular box added onto the face of the L—sat a cafeteria. On its south side was a food storage area, including a walk-in cooler. The cooler sat in a boxlike, single-story concrete building that had housed printing presses in an earlier day. Above it, square bedrooms had been built three stories high, forming what everybody called "the tower." On February 28, David Koresh was making his quarters in the topmost of the tower rooms.

Mt. Carmel's front doors opened into a foyer, from which, going "east," was a hallway that led past, on the left, what the residents called "the telephone room," and on the right, an enclosure they had named "the computer room." Beyond, a large chapel opened, with pews on each side of its aisle. A stage stood at the far end of the room, and behind it, like the serif of an L, a large building—the newest part of Mt. Carmel, completed in 1992—called "the gymnasium," though it had quickly become a miscellaneous storage area. The area above the stage was two stories tall. Its second floor contained two bedrooms that straddled a gabled roof. A hallway ran from just over the front door, inside the attic of the chapel, between the two stage-area bedrooms, and out "eastward," over the roof of the gymnasium, providing second-story access to the whole structure. It was an odd arrangement, but as Koresh liked to say, "There's no floor plan on this building, it just evolved."

Mt. Carmel was a Spartan place. Only the kitchen had running water. There was no basement, air conditioning, or central heating. The men had rigged a bathroom and shower beneath a tree outdoors, but women and children used chamber pots and took sponge baths. Waste water was carried in buckets to an old septic tank on the grounds.

When winters came, the residents plugged electric space heaters into the outlets in their walls, or ran cords from outlets that were screwed into the plain, ceramic bulb sockets in their ceilings. In summertime, they just sweltered. "It's like camping indoors," resident Steve Schneider remarked.

Its inhabitants believed that there was a reason why Mt. Carmel, though always under construction, was in a primitive state. The group had never organized itself as a true commune. Members did not pool their bank accounts, possessions were not held in common and, indeed, were so zealously guarded that some occupants put name tags on washcloths and initials on clothespins. But nobody paid rent or board. "I want to keep the building kind of rough in shape and not really finished and that way people that come here, they're coming for one reason, because they're coming to know something. . . . Let it be a stumbling block," Koresh had said.

As odd and unfinished as it was architecturally, as an intellectual edifice Mt. Carmel was solidly and luxuriously built, the faithful believed. Its cornerstone, they said, had been laid centuries before, and for more than a one hundred fifty years, beam by beam, precept by precept, they and their predecessors had been completing, expanding, and remodeling it, every working day. Though it still wasn't finished, it already contained a whole world inside, the only world that David Jones and most of the others understood.

That world was a common faith. That faith, and it alone, held Mt. Carmel's polyglot residents together. Included among the building's residents at the time that Jones met Peeler, for example, were British and Australian subjects, Caribbean islanders, Hawaiian and mainland Americans, one millionaire, several paupers, people of Asian, African, Native American, and European descent, former barflies and former teetotalers, an Argentine-Israeli Jew, and a set of adult twins. Though they had little else in common, Mt. Carmel's residents all were the intellectual heirs of the eight-million-member Seventh-Day Adventist (SDA) Church—perhaps renegade, but heirs nonetheless; of the seventy-two adults inside, all but seven had bathed in Adventism before they came. They had been raised in the church, or like David Jones, in one of its spinoff sects, or they had attended its primary or secondary schools, even its universities. Adventism was the homeland from which almost everyone at Mt. Carmel had come. And everyone at Mt. Carmel spoke of Adventism in terms that, though biblical, were reminiscent of the way in which the generation of the 1960s spoke of their parents and nation.

Chapter 5

THE THIRD ANGEL'S MESSAGE

". . . Adventists know nothing more about the Bible than they did in Ellen G. White's day. And even less, because now they're denying . . . the very foundational doctrines."
—Vernon Howell

The Seventh-Day Adventist Church had abandoned the intellectual edifice that the residents of Mt. Carmel were remodeling, the religious community's generations claimed. It was a story that all of them knew, much as the rest of us know the story of Original Sin, and it played no less a role in their lives than the tale of Adam's fall plays in the lives of other Bible believers.

The laying of the Adventist foundation—Mt. Carmel's foundation— had begun between midnight and noon on October 23, 1844, at the onset of what historians of American religion call the Great Disappointment. For nearly ten years, William Miller of New York and Vermont, a former captain in the War of 1812, who became a Baptist preacher, had been preaching a message based on an Old Testament verse, Daniel 8:14. The scripture reports from a prophetic dream: "And he said unto me, Unto two thousand and three hundred days; then shall the sanctuary be cleansed." William Miller believed that Daniel 8:14 referred to the Second Coming of Christ. By researching ancient history, and by converting biblical days to modern calendar years, he had arrived at a "key" to the prophecy, a date for the long-awaited Advent: October 22, 1844.

In an itinerant ministry, Miller emblazoned the October 22 date, and appropriate repentance, into the minds of Northeastern audiences, winning a large following in the years between 1839 and 1843. Scholars today estimate that, at its peak, Miller's movement commanded the talents of some five hundred traveling lecturers and two hundred men of the cloth. In forays into existing congregations, Millerite disciples sometimes won over whole flocks, but more often, split them into the nineteenth-century equivalents of non-denominational groupings. Their unifying tenet was Adventism, or the belief in "the soon coming of Christ." The Millerite warning, though foolhardy in its prediction, had a lasting effect on the dynamics of American religion, because it turned a school of Christians, searching to decipher the New Testament, back toward clues in the record of the Jewish past.

Among the Massachusetts families drawn into Millerism was that of a stern-faced teenager beset by ill health and periodic visions, Ellen Gould Harmon, later to be known across the English-speaking world by the name she took upon marriage, Ellen G. White—or more simply, "Sister White." By the end of the nineteenth century, Ellen White had published more words than any woman in history. The index of her works fills four volumes, and includes more than 20 pages—some 3,000 entries—on the subject of angels alone. As if Sister White's pronouncements had the authority of those of the prophet Isaiah, today Adventists cite her words by the initials of the work in which they appeared, followed by the page numbers on which they were printed in official first editions.*

In her masterwork, *The Great Controversy* (1888), White looks back with unmitigated nostalgia to the days of Millerism: "Of all the great religious movements since the days of the apostles, none have been more free from human imperfection and the wiles of Satan than was that of the autumn of 1844." "At the call . . . angels were sent from heaven. . . . Farmers left their crops standing in the fields, mechanics laid down their tools, and with tears and rejoining went out to give the

---

* For a list of these citations, see A Note on Published Sources, pp. 301–4.

warning." (GC, 401, 402) ". . . None who experienced this hope and trust can forget those precious hours of waiting. For some weeks preceding the time, worldly business was for the most part laid aside. . . . Sincere believers carefully examined every thought and emotion of their hearts as if upon their deathbeds and in a few hours to close their eyes to earthly scenes" (GC 373) ". . . parents were turned to their children, and the hearts of children to their parents. The barriers of pride and reserve were swept away." (GC 369)

In anticipation of the 1844 return of Christ, many Millerites had donned white robes and gathered on hillsides to hail His appearance in the skies. When He did not come, they were of course dismayed: life was going to continue, despite their distaste for it. Early on the morning of October 23, a handful of Millerites who had together kept the vigil, including Hiram Edson, a farmer, went into a barn to pray to God. They wanted Him to explain why the world was still on its course. God gave them no immediate answer, but after breakfast, Edson was walking across a corn field when "heaven seemed to open to my view, and I saw distinctly and clearly, that instead of our High Priest coming out of the Most Holy of the heavenly Sanctuary to come to this earth . . . he for the first time entered on that day the second apartment of the sanctuary; and that he had a work to perform in the Most Holy before coming to this earth." In a word, Edson's vision told him that a great event had indeed taken place, but had been misunderstood on earth. Jesus *had* initiated what Adventists refer to as "the investigative Judgment of the dead"—but the courtroom where he was to do this work, Edson's vision showed, was in heaven, not on earth. Both his vision and a prompt consultation with the Holy Writ convinced Edson that Jesus wouldn't tarry in His labor. The End—or the Judgment of the Living—was, as the Millerites had taught, shortly at hand.

Ellen White not only embraced the Edson proviso to Millerism, but during the evangelical tours that she would soon initiate to proclaim her own visions, she met the carrier of another doctrine on the fringes of Christianity, Boston-area sea captain Joseph Bates. Citing the Fourth Commandment—"Remember the sabbath day, to keep it holy" (Exo 20:8)—and the words of Jesus, "For verily I say unto you, Till heaven and earth pass, one jot or one tittle shall in no wise pass from the law. . . ." (Matt 5:18)—Bates argued that the period from sundown Friday until sundown on Saturday should be the Christian day of religious observance, as it had for millennia among Jews.

Not long after her meeting with Bates in 1846, Sister Ellen, then nineteen, had a vision in which "The temple of God was open in heaven, and I was shown the ark of God covered with the mercy seat. Two angels stood one at either end of the ark, with their wings spread over the mercy seat, and their faces turned toward it. . . . Jesus raised the cover of the ark, and I beheld the tables of stone on which the ten commandments were written. I was amazed as I saw the fourth commandment in the very center of the precepts"—an interesting mathematical postulate—"with a soft halo of light encircling it." (LS 95, 96) (The observation that the Fourth Commandment was in the "middle" of a list of ten, distributed onto more than one tablet, can be resolved in only one way: by deducing that the Commandments were inscribed upon seven tables, and not upon two, as is usually depicted in biblical illustration; Commandments One through Four occupied one tablet each, while Five through Ten were distributed among three tablets.)

After her vision, White steadfastly crusaded among the Millerite remnants for Sabbath-keeping. Other Christians, she said, had been diverted by "the representative of Satan—the bishop of Rome" into the pagan observance of Sunday. Though the change to Saturday worship may seem either purely formal or purely capricious to the casual beholder of Christianity, in theological terms—especially in communities like Mt. Carmel—it had a weighty impact: like the Advent doctrine, it turned Christians back to the Old Testament in their search to illuminate the Holy Writ.

During her long career—she lived to be eighty-eight—White experienced some three hundred visions, and as she expounded them to assorted congregations, she developed an intensely loyal and doctrinaire following. In 1863, her followers—today's press would call them cultists—organized themselves as the General Conference of Seventh-Day Adventists, or SDA, whose membership in the United States now numbers some three million.

Besides Sabbatarianism, Sister White and the SDA revived another Old Testament doctrine, dietary restriction. White insisted that Christians observe an Orthodox Jewish diet, eschewing pork and other foods proscribed by the Book as unclean. She also went a step further, into what can only be called a radical interpretation of the scriptures. Relying upon, among other things, an account in which the young Daniel turns up his nose at a royal menu (Dan 1:8-15; CD 154, 155), White encouraged her flock to shun all meat and alcoholic beverages—for starters.

A century before the health reformers whose influence is everywhere felt today, she assailed caffeinated beverages as enemies of God and man. Sugar, she said, "clouds the brain and brings peevishness into the disposition." (CD 327) White flour, mixtures of milk and sugar, and the custom of taking beverages with meals also drew her scorn. In towns where Adventism is predominant, such as Keene, Texas, for example, even today there are no fast-food joints or Dairy Queens, because SDA regulars spurn hamburgers, soft drinks, coffee, and ice cream.

Her dietary preoccupations, a fascination with hydrotherapy, and the evangelical usefulness of both also led White and her sect to establish several hospitals as the century drew to its end. The enthusiasts and experimenters who gathered around these wellness centers, in turn, established a legacy of their own. California's Loma Linda University grew out of an SDA medical school, and millions of Americans who've never heard of the church greet one of its byproducts every morning: corn flakes are the invention of SDA pioneer John Harvey Kellogg—who concocted Granola as well.

White also inculcated in her followers an aloofness from, and distrust of, government, and that is why Adventists have never been partisan to the Moral Majority, the Christian Coalition, the Southern Christian Leadership Conference, or other biblico-political movements, left or right. ". . . Today in the religious world there are multitudes who, as they believe, are working for the establishment of the kingdom of Christ as an earthly and temporal dominion," she wrote. "They desire to make our Lord the ruler of the kingdoms of this world. . . . They expect Him to rule through legal enactments, enforced by human authority. . . . Yet the Savior attempted no civil reforms. He attacked no national abuses, nor condemned the national enemies." (DA, 509)

Ellen White expected persecution, not deliverance or toleration, from the government. "By substituting human law for God's law," she told her followers, "Satan will seek to control the world. . . . The warfare against God's law . . . will be continued until the end of time. Every man will be tested. . . . All will be called to choose between the law of God and the laws of men." (DA 763) During an 1847 trance at Topsham, Maine, she foresaw that "In the time of trouble we all fled from the cities and villages, but were pursued by the wicked, who entered the houses of the saints with a sword. They raised the sword to kill us, but it broke, and fell as powerless as a straw." (EW 34) Years later, Koresh's followers believed that Ellen White's prophecy found its fulfillment in the raid on Mt. Carmel.

Although Sister White looked back to the Jewish past, her doctrine of the "present truth" was radically modernizing. With references to a New Testament admonition (II Peter 1:12), by 1850 she was referring to herself as the messenger of such truth. To explain the concept—and her unique status—she developed a history of Christianity in which God's message to man came not with finality during the ministry of Jesus (as most Christians believed) but was revealed by evolutionary means, step by step, from Adam's era into the future, one truth at a time.

If the notion is startling, even from a secular view, it is highly rational as well. It proceeds from the observation that, for example, before Columbus crossed the Atlantic, the world was not actually flat—but it was *true* that the world was flat. It was true because human beings discover truth through gradual means. In *The Great Controversy*, White attempts to demonstrate that absolute truth, or God's Truth, has always been beyond the grasp of the mortal mind; that's why huge sections of the Bible make no sense, she says. God's plan to enlighten mankind, according to White, is one of progressive revelation.

A struggle between God and Satan replaces survival of the fittest as the motive force of evolution in White's scheme. But unlike the Darwinian model, Sister White's evolutionism wasn't entirely evolutionary: in some respects, it was devolutionary instead. Not only did members of the species live longer in the past, she believed, but they had been larger in stature, too. (PP 45) This belief wasn't unique to White. Devolution was obvious in the Bible's vital statistics: Adam had lived 930 years, Abraham 175, Joseph, 110, David, 70. Genesis reports that in the days before the Great Flood, ". . . the Lord said, My spirit shall not always strive with man . . . yet his days shall be an hundred and twenty years. There were giants in the earth in those days. . . ." (Gen 6:3,4) As history advanced, White theorized, Satan's schemes increasingly gained hold on humanity, debilitating the race. Though a finding that human intelligence had also diminished would have been consistent with White's devolutionism, the American prophetess did not speak of any such decline. Its upshot would have been that each new prophet brings a progressively more demented message, or else attracts a progressively more demented audience! Instead of picturing herself as a voice of decline, Sister White, drawing from Revelation 14, spoke of herself as the messenger of "the Third Angel," naming Miller as the mouthpiece of the First and Second Angels.

An important corollary to the "present truth" doctrine was that "Only those who have a personal connection with the Source of wisdom"— i.e., men and women whom God addresses audibly, in visions and in dreams—"are able to understand or explain the scriptures." (GC 456) Though many contemporary Adventists deny as much, in writing about a "prophetic chain" that extended from "eternity in the future" (Ed 178), White seemed to predict that other seers would appear upon her demise.

Chapter 6

THE BULGARIAN AND
THE GODDESS

". . . One who allows prejudice to bar him from a candid investigation of anything new, coming in the name of the Lord, is
unwittingly an infidel."
—Victor Houteff

"We are trying to introduce the idea of the femininity of the Holy
Spirit."
—Lois Roden

The SDA's General Conference has not found any worthy successors to
White in the years since her death in 1915. Instead, successors have
found themselves, or, as is more often the case, they've been certified
by groups of Adventists less numerous, and less prudent or inhibited,
than the leaders of the General Conference. One of the first of these
was Victor Houteff, the theological grandfather of Perry and David
Jones; of Bob, Janet, and Kathy Kendrick; and of David Koresh.

Houteff was a short, 140-pound Bulgarian immigrant, a one-time
hotelkeeper and Maytag washer salesman who, in 1929, began to at-
tract the scorn of the Los Angeles SDA with novel notions about the
prophecies. Houteff published his opinions, including critiques of the
SDA leadership, in a series of tracts entitled *The Shepherd's Rod*, a
name which led his defenders to call themselves "the Rods." After

Houteff was several times ousted, as if from a bar, from SDA services in California, he decided to leave the state. Inspired by a prophetic passage (Ezek 47:8, 2 SR 296), at the age of fifty he moved with a few of "the Rods" to Texas. Seven miles northwest of Waco, in 1934, he established a community that he named Mt. Carmel, after the ancient site where the prophet Elijah tussled with devotees of Baal. The name wasn't merely honorific. It described the place where its residents thought they were and who they believed their leader to be.

"Carmel overlooked a wide expanse of country," Ellen White had written about the original Mt. Carmel, ". . . its heights . . . visible from many parts of the kingdom of Israel . . . Elijah chose this elevation as the most conspicuous place for the display of God's power and for the vindication of the honor of His name." (PK 143)

According to the Good Book (Mal 4:5), the Messiah couldn't arrive until Elijah returned from the dead to announce his coming. Jesus, aware of the tenet, had argued that John the Baptist was the resurrected Elijah. Houteff's name for his encampment indicated to many of his followers that he was another, or an "antitypical" Elijah, in Waco to announce the Second Coming. This expectation was further strengthened in 1942, when Houteff named his group the Davidian Seventh Day Adventist Association: the throne of the Old Testament's King David was to be occupied by the Messiah, according to Jewish belief, or by the Returned Jesus, in the Christian code. The hope of Houteff's followers was that sooner or later, after struggles to defend the faith, their leader would announce the return of Christ, whereupon the encampment would move to Jerusalem to welcome Him.

The Davidian designation of events as prefiguring, or "typical," and "antitypical," or fulfilling, antedated Ellen White, though she made use of the concept. At Mt. Carmel, Houteff's successors would turn such categorizations into an intellectual vice. According to views which accept typical and atypical happenings, historical events are not unique, but are variations on a pattern set in heaven, essentially for the education of the angels and mankind. History is like a spiral, over which human beings traverse until they learn what they must do to be saved from perdition. As one ascends the historical scale by going around the spiral, one passes over (albeit above) the points passed in prior runs. In any such spiral, there is only one point of origin, or "typical" event; but there's a new "antitypical" event, or point, at each round.

Houteff started his Waco colony with fewer than a dozen adherents, but within a decade, their number had multiplied tenfold. Residents of his community kept an Adventist diet, and took their meals in a communal cafeteria. Mt. Carmel educated its children in its own school, and even set up a bank that issued currency for use only at the encampment's general store. But Mt. Carmel was as raw as it was rural, too. An out-of-state visitor named E. T. White who stopped by in 1937 later wrote to the faithful that "One of the remarkable things to be observed at this place is the cheerful attitude of practically all, both young and old, toward the inconveniences which go with pioneering. . . . It should ever be kept in mind that the very name, 'Mt. Carmel,' indicates a place where we are being severely tested as to whether we will serve God or serve Baal."

Though they were not intrusive or troublesome, that Houteff and his tribe were radical Christians was apparent to their Waco neighbors, and to merchants, every year at Christmas time. Ellen White's followers celebrated Christmas, and Easter, too, but the Houteffians did not. Like the Puritans, they believed that Christmas marked an unscriptural, pagan holiday, rooted in Roman festivals for the sun. Houteff was especially acrid toward the custom of the Christmas tree.

He cited the Writ (Jere 10:2–5), ". . . Learn not the way of the heathen. . . . For the customs of the people are vain; for one cutteth a tree out of the forest, the work of the hands of the workman, with the axe. They deck it with silver and with gold; they fasten it with nails and with hammers, that it move not." And he likened the tree to ancestor worship: "By cutting down the tree, to the heathen it symbolized their dead chief," he explained, "and by propping it up, it symbolized life though one be dead. . . . Worshipping the dead prophets and killing the living ones, is a brutal effort to block the progress of Truth. . . ."

From Mt. Carmel, Houteff and his disciples proselytized Adventist ranks, at one point regularly mailing tracts to one hundred thousand stateside SDA members. Practically every word that Brother Houteff spoke in assemblies was transcribed, and his writings are in print today, cited like those of Ellen White.

The most important institution that Houteff established at Waco was the Mt. Carmel Training Center, a denominational college whose standard of admission was theological orthodoxy, not the student's academic preparation or ability to pay. The Training Center touted courses in "Christian English," "Revealed Psychophysics," and "Revealed Sociology," and its course on "Revealed History"—its catalogue promised—would provide "A survey of history from the divine point of view." Students began each day facing two flags, one Davidian, one American, and reciting that "As Christian students in America . . . we pledge our hearts, our minds, our hands, our all, first to the flag of God's eternal kingdom, and to the Theocracy for which it stands, one people made up of all nations, and bound by the cords of everlasting love, liberty, purity, justice, peace, happiness and life for all." After that, they pledged allegiance "to the flag of the United States, and to the republic. . . ."

By all accounts Mt. Carmel was a rather benevolent theocracy while Houteff was its king. Despite having married a seventeen-year-old member of the flock when he was fifty-two, Houteff kept himself above scandal, and kept the community in solvent financial condition. Houteff once commented that "My credit is unlimited . . . although I am not bonded and have no personal bank account! Furthermore, I pay my secretary as much as I pay myself and some of my workmen I pay twice as much." (2 TG 35:24)

But as the founder's health began to decline in the early fifties, the specter of succession split the Davidians into competing cabals. Houteff's wife claimed his mantle, but David Jones's father, Perry, cast his lot with a an oilfield worker named Ben Roden, whose faction called itself "The Branch," not only because it was an offshoot, but also because in its biblical use, "The Branch" has a prophetic significance, usually pointing toward the restoration of the Davidic throne or the coming of the Messiah.

Perry Jones's choice proved to be the prudent one—or lucky one. While hospitalized in 1955, the Bulgarian Elijah wrestled with the meaning of a pair of prophecies that, he had concluded, had heretofore been fulfilled only in type, not yet in antitype. The prophecies were those of Daniel 12 and Revelation 11, regarding the purification of the church by persecution—and the number "forty and two months." He

61

seemed to be recovering and was in hardy spirits on the night that his wife, the former Florence Hermanson, asked him when he would reveal the "present truth" of those predictions. "Tomorrow you will have the answer," he said. But Houteff died before sundown. Florence and his other close associates were astounded when they were told of his passing: What, had the antitypical Elijah not known that his death was imminent? If he knew, as he must have known, had he lied to them? To resolve this paradox, they concluded that "Tomorrow you will have the answer" meant that the forty-two-month period had begun on that "tomorrow." They also concluded that Victor Houteff, like the original Elijah, would be resurrected from the dead to herald the Second Coming.

Under Houteff's reign, Mt. Carmel's daily labors produced so much surplus that the Elijah once urged far-flung followers to save their money rather than sending it to him. A part of the financial success was due to the value of their real estate. Urban sprawl was catching up with the place, and even before Houteff died, the Davidians were selling parcels to developers. Looking for a new headquarters, in 1957 they began building homes on a rise in the prairie northeast of town, a site that they named "New Mt. Carmel"—the spot now familiar to television viewers around the globe.

Early in 1959, Florence Houteff, having declared herself the seer of the age and marking the prophecy of forty-two months from the moment of her husband's death, announced that on April 22 the faithful would be slaughtered, then resurrected and carried to heaven on clouds. Hundreds of Davidians gathered at New Mt. Carmel, and many pitched tents to await their last mortal days. "When the appointed (or anointed) hours came that afternoon," a journalist who was on hand wrote, "somewhere between 3 P.M. and dark, it was a bit pitiful to view the massive, collective disappointment. Of the thousands there, more or less, only one of them was relieved. Me." In the month following what can only be called the Lesser Disappointment, most of Florence's followers began to filter away. Some regrouped into an organization whose members still publish and cite Victor Houteff's works, just as before his death. But most followed Ben Roden and Perry Jones into the Branch.

Ben Roden's chief message, from the Fifth Angel—Victor Houteff having spoken for the Fourth—was of a back-to-the-Old-Testament kind, faithful to his heritage, if not to a seeming prohibition in a Writ from Houteff (2 TG 37). Roden instituted among his flock the celebration of the holy days that Jesus kept: Passover, Pentecost, the Atonement, and the fall Feast of Tabernacles. He even taught members of the Branch to perform ancient New Moon rites.

In 1958, Roden and a handful of followers went to Israel and won admittance to a vegetarian *moshav*, or communal village, near Safad, in the Golan Heights vicinity, just north of the Sea of Galilee. But when Florence Houteff's believers gathered at Mt. Carmel to await fire from the skies, Roden came back to proselytize. According to Clive Doyle, the best historian among Mt. Carmel's survivors, Roden's message that spring was "trade up your tents for a house in Israel"—an oblique reference to the government subsidies that the moshavers received. After the Lesser Disappointment, while dispatching others across the seas to Israel, Roden stayed in Texas, building his base. His wife, Lois, took charge of the some thirty families who settled in Israel. In 1964, she too returned to Waco.

The Rodenite flock was growing at several spots on the globe, and Mt. Carmel was becoming what Houteff had only wished it had been, a way station on the route to Israel. Clive Doyle and his mother, Edna, for example, had belonged to an SDA congregation in Australia when the moribund Houteff's message reached them. In the troubled months that followed his death, they had declared their allegiance to Roden and the Branch. As the sixties opened, young Clive, then in his teens, looked forward to the day when Roden would call him to take up residence in Israel, and in 1966 the call came, or so it seemed. "Ben Roden asked several of us to come to Waco, and we assumed it was merely for an orientation of some kind, before going on to Israel. So we bought plane tickets from Australia to the United States to Israel. When the immigration agents asked us how long we wanted visas for, we told them, 'Well, maybe for two weeks,' because we didn't plan to be in Texas very long."

But when Doyle arrived in Waco, he learned that he was needed to run the printshop at New Mt. Carmel, which Roden had acquired from the disillusioned followers of Florence. Though Roden didn't publish on a Houteffian scale, Doyle kept busy, and stayed on for two years, under a tourist permit, then, in violation of his visa, for two years more—until his marriage in 1970 to Deborah Slawson, an American member of the Branch whose parents were also members. Doyle's marriage to an American set a precedent for successive generations of foreigners at Mt. Carmel.

Ben Roden died in 1978. Even before he had expired, it was evident that Lois, a thin woman then in her early sixties, would be his successor—and that as the Sixth Angel's representative, she would deliver a revelation more controversial than perhaps any in Adventist history, a message so radical that, in honor of it, she'd rename her organization the Living Waters Branch. The Christian Trinity—God the Father, God the Son, and God the Holy Ghost or Holy Spirit—Lois had declared in 1977, was a family, in whose ranks the Holy Spirit was the female member.

Edna Doyle, who was still living in Australia at the time, recalls her reaction to the "New Light" of Roden's teaching. "It just seemed like common sense to me, and to tell the truth, I'd thought about it before, without ever giving it much investigation. I mean, God is to judge us, and that means He has to understand us. But what man understands a woman? None! And what woman understands a man? None of them do! I don't mean to say anything against men or women, either, but that's just the way things are."

Sister Roden, as she was called, of course gave her deduction a biblical basis. "We understand the Godhead by the things that are made!" she preached, alluding to Romans 1:20. "Since according to the Holy Bible, 'God said, Let us make man in our image, after our likeness [a reference to Gen 1:26, 27]' then we understand this in the light of the things that are made here on earth. Husband and wife bring forth children. It is not the children and the father, but the mother and the father who bring forth the children. God, the Father, and Jesus did not make man, male and FEMALE in THEIR image. Neither God nor Jesus look like a woman. Do They? "Sister Roden further added that in the scripture from Genesis, the Hebrew term used for God is Elohim—a plural form. Then she pointed out that in various Hebrew and

Greek manuscripts of the Bible, feminine word endings are used in reference to God.

Lois Roden's startling message merely added a biblical twist, and an Adventist cast, to the feminist movement that was popular across the United States at the time. "Satan's war against the women reflects his enmity against the Holy Spirit . . . ," she wrote. "All of her daughters from Eve to this day have been held captive and their image corrupted by Satan through putting the responsibility for the original sin upon Eve to conceal the fact that it was he alone who was the instigator. . . ."

Roden and her followers excoriated civil society for having subjugated women, and the Adventist Church for having denied women the pulpit. The papacy, which is generally the villain in Adventist circles no matter what the crime, came in for special criticism. The Catholic Church, Sister Roden said, had allowed the worship of Mary, Mother of Jesus, to usurp adoration of the Holy Spirit, in league with Satan's plan to keep the Spirit's femininity unknown. Though Sister Roden's doctrine warmed the hearts of many of the SDA's women believers, its male clergy branded her teachings as heresy. In 1980, she and Perry Jones were ousted from an SDA General Conference meeting in Dallas for trying to bring the message to the church leadership. Like Houteff, Sister Roden was expelled from her homeland.

Lois Roden was at the peak of her career in 1981 when, on an afternoon almost no one remembers, a bearded, stuttering Vernon Howell found his way into Mt. Carmel and the Living Waters Branch. "I was just a bonehead coming to see what was going on," he'd later say. But at Mt. Carmel, the bonehead would become a messiah.

Chapter 7

THE FLATFOOT

"I knew they were coming before they knew they were coming."
—David Koresh

When David Jones parked his yellow Buick and burst through Mt. Carmel's front doors on February 28, he saw that something irregular was happening. Twice a day, at the third and ninth hour from sunrise, according to an Old Testament prescription, Mt. Carmel's residents gathered in a chapel for brief religious observances, usually including communion. David Koresh normally lectured at these sessions, and it was about time for the morning service to begin. But when Jones opened the front door, he found Koresh in the foyer, seated in a chair. Alongside him were a half-dozen residents, including Steve Schneider and Sherri Jewell, both forty-three.

Schneider, a blond man with an athletic build and a Midwestern accent, had become one of Koresh's closest friends. He had a degree in comparative religion, having studied Hinduism, Buddhism, as well as many exotic and strange beliefs. Both Schneider and Jewell—a secondary teacher by trade, a petite woman whose mother was Japanese—were converts, part of a group of young people recruited to Howell's movement from an Adventist church in Hawaii in 1986. Though they knew little of Rodenism and not a great deal about Houteff, with Vernon's tutelage both had become teachers of doctrine, close associates of their leader. But they were in the foyer to observe a guest whose presence was foreboding. David Jones knew the guest by the name Robert Gonzalez.

What David Jones had to say, he didn't want to say in the presence of Gonzalez, because Gonzalez was a cop. Everybody knew that, though nobody was sure what kind of cop Gonzalez was. It was obvious that he was spying on the group, Koresh had said. "You know, his . . . eyes wander too much . . . he was counting people," the leader had warned after one of the suspect's visits. The preacher had told every-body to be on guard. But at the same time, for about a month, Koresh had also been inviting Gonzalez to stop by, even to move into the building. After all, Koresh had said, hadn't Paul persuaded a centurion to set him free? Gonzalez's "cover gave me the best advantage to be able to teach these young men," the preacher later told the FBI.

On January 10, 1993, Robert Gonzalez had moved into a house on EE Ranch Road, directly across from Mt. Carmel, at the end of its 200-yard driveway. Seven other men had moved in with him. Their coming had set off gossip at Mt. Carmel, because the home's owner had told them, months before, that he didn't plan to rent the place.

David Jones and a handful of Mt. Carmel's men had immediately gone over to welcome their new neighbors. But on that and subsequent visits, they'd been received with less than hospitality—even when Mt. Carmel's callers had brought beer. The eight new neighbors "never would let the guys come in . . . they'd just sit outside, stand outside in the cold," Koresh complained.

The new neighbors said that they had come from West Texas to enroll at TSTC, Texas State Technical College, in Waco. But they were all in their thirties and forties, older than most TSTC students. When a couple of Mt. Carmel guys who'd attended the school—David Jones was one of them—asked questions about teachers and adminis-trators at the campus, the new neighbors had been at a loss for words.

They were oddly prosperous, too. They drove new cars. Koresh said that he'd checked into registrations for three of the vehicles, and they showed no ownership liens. All were registered to the same address in Houston—a long way from West Texas.

On top of that, the eight guys claimed that only four of them lived at the house on EE Road. But the men at Mt. Carmel weren't fools: they kept watch with binoculars and night vision goggles, and they knew.

On January 28, a couple of the men from the EE house had come over to look at a horse walker that stood near the pond on the great expanse of land between Mt. Carmel's front door and EE Road. Several of the guys who lived at Mt. Carmel had gone out to chat with them. When one of the EE residents said that he'd been a ranch foreman in West Texas, gun dealer Henry McMahon, who was visiting that day, had asked him how many cattle an acre of dry West Texas land would support. The fellow hadn't been able to answer.

On February 19, Gonzalez had brought a pistol to show to Koresh, and the preacher saw in it a couple of things that deepened his suspicions. As Koresh told the story, in the argot of gun fanciers, ". . . He brought over this Eagle series, you know, .38, actually .45, you know, .38 upper on a basically a .45 calibre lower. . . . It had a special slide on it, it had a special compensator and everything. Anyway, you know, the guy's, the guy's telling me . . . that he really doesn't know that much about guns, and, and the very first thing he does is he brings over this weapon that, you know, no novice has."

Believing that Gonzalez might be an agent of the Immigration Service, Koresh had warned the foreigners at Mt. Carmel, most of whom had overstayed their visas, to stay inside—out of view of the lenses that he'd seen in the windows at the house on EE Road.

Mt. Carmel's residents worried about the identity of the men at the EE not only because their behavior was suspicious, but also because ominous signs had clouded Mt. Carmel's skies for eighteen months. Child welfare investigators had visited the place three or four times, following complaints from former resident Marc Breault. A sheriff's department official had told them that he had received reports from Breault, and in February 1992, a child custody lawsuit brought by Sherri Jewell's husband, David Jewell, had gone to trial in Michigan. The suit was for custody of the couple's daughter, twelve-year-old Kiri, who was living with her mother in California, near a home where Koresh and his followers stayed when in California for business or family reasons. During his testimony, Breault had told the court that

Koresh planned to rape the child, and the judge had ordered Sherri to keep her daughter out of the preacher's reach. When the trial concluded, though Sherri maintained joint custody of her daughter, she left her daughter with her ex-husband.

In March 1992, neighbors had watched men dressed in SWAT team uniforms practicing forced entries at a rural house nearby. A few months later, they spotted lawmen setting up a surveillance camera—an ATF "pole camera"—to watch Mt. Carmel. They told its residents about both moves. A delegation from the encampment had gone to the Waco sheriff's office to inquire about these signs. A deputy told them that they were under no suspicion, but it was obvious to them that they were.

About the same time that the pole camera was spotted, a couple of Koresh's followers had seen two mysterious men in white medical smocks, standing on the property of an adjoining ranch, fiddling with beepers on their belts. When two men from Mt. Carmel approached them, the pair turned, ran back to their car, and sped off.

During the summer of 1992, helicopters had flown low over Mt. Carmel, apparently taking photographs; the 'copters had returned again in late fall. In the weeks preceding February 28, they'd seemed to always be in the sky. Residents of Mt. Carmel had noted low-level overflights on December 16, January 6 and 14, and on February 3, 18, and 25. On January 27, a long-haired, unkempt young man—an ATF agent—came to Mt. Carmel in the guise of a UPS delivery assistant. He had shown up asking to use the bathroom at Mt. Carmel, and had aroused the suspicions of David Jones. Jones had given him a roll of toilet paper and sent him to the men's outhouse, then he'd talked over his suspicions with Koresh, who called the sheriff's office to ask why it was sending people to spy on him.

Any doubts that they'd entertained had cleared about ten days earlier, when Robert Gonzalez visited Mt. Carmel for target practice on the makeshift rifle range in back of the house. Gonzalez brought an AR-15 to the get-together, which had been his idea in the first place. Koresh and a couple of others joined, bringing their own pistols and AR-15s. They'd passed around weapons, everybody taking a couple of shots with the other guys' guns. As Koresh told it, the AR-15 that

Gonzalez brought was a stand-out, and by implication, its owner was, too.

". . . There's one thing that . . . you can never fake," he said. "Experience. You can never act like you don't know how to drive a car when you do."

Gonzalez acted as if his weapon were a new toy. "He's talking about he just bought this, you know, AR-15 and all that, and anyway, it's a one and seven twist, which is a mil spec twist, you know," Koresh said. "It's for the stabilization of tracers, the higher grains. . . . And the thing is—the thing had a trigger job on it. . . .

". . . The pull on it, it was probably, probably about—at the, at the max, a pound and a half, maybe two pounds at the max. You know, a good four pounds is . . . considered good for ARs . . . I took it . . . and I was plunking these little stones off, you know, just right off the ironsights. And he says . . . 'well, what do you think about it, you know, Dave?' . . . And I says . . . you know, in your line of work . . . this is a sniper rifle, you know."

On the morning of February 28, when David Jones noticed Gonzalez in the lobby with Schneider and Jewell, he scooted by without saying a word. He went into the short hallway that led to the chapel, where he saw that his father was sitting in a pew, near a group of women who were waiting for the morning service to begin. The postman stood in the hallway and beckoned his father to the telephone room, which was empty.

Perry Jones thought that the news should be passed to Koresh as quickly as possible, but Gonzalez's presence made the situation delicate. After thinking a few seconds, Perry stepped to the spot where the hallway met the foyer. He told Koresh that a telephone call had come for him, then he ducked back into the telephone room.

Koresh was too busy to notice. Gonzalez had brought over the second installment of the "Sinful Messiah" series in the *Waco Tribune-Herald,* and given it to Sherri Jewell. She'd glanced at it, snorted her disapproval, then passed the newspaper to Koresh. Since its report dealt mostly with the matter of his "wives," Koresh was disabusing Gonzalez, citing scriptures. Perry Jones stepped out again. This time he told Koresh that the telephone call was from England, the source of many of Mt. Carmel's faithful. Koresh got up and came to the telephone room. "Don't worry about it," he said dismissively when Perry gave him the news. "I'm going to talk to Robert right now. We've been giving him studies and I'm pretty sure that he's going to realize, you know, to hold this thing off." Koresh returned to his session with Gonzalez.

Koresh was "very nervous and shaking real bad," Gonzalez would testify, under a different name, nearly a year after the event. Robert Gonzalez *was* a cop, just as Koresh suspected. "Gonzalez" was an alias, the name that the former high school football coach, Special Agent Robert Rodriguez, forty-two, had taken while gathering information about Mt. Carmel. He had dropped into Mt. Carmel that morning to make sure that nothing out of the ordinary was underfoot. It was his job to confirm that it was safe for Showtime to begin.

Parts of Rodriguez's testimony about what he saw and heard that morning indicate that, inexplicably, Koresh knew more about the raid than either Jim Peeler or David Jones. "He turned and told me the ATF and the National Guard were coming," Rodriguez swore under oath. Yet photographer Peeler had believed that the raid was to be launched by the TABC. Though Koresh might have doubted that the liquor agency had any reason to raid Mt. Carmel, if he knew that the ATF and National Guard were coming instead, then perhaps he was a prophet. As if to capitalize on the opportunity to claim prophetic powers, at the end of the day Koresh claimed that he'd learned about the raid from an early morning vision, not from David Jones.

Koresh soon gave up his attempt to teach the Bible study. "I went to the window," Koresh explained, "and I says, Robert, I says, it's up to you now. . . . And I turned around and he just—his eyes were real big and everything. . . . And he goes, 'what do you mean?' I says, Robert, you know what I mean. . . . We know they're coming."

Rodriguez was nervous. "I said to myself, 'He knows.' I felt I was in danger. I just knew he had been tipped off," he later testified. "I told myself, 'Relax. Don't give yourself away.'" Rodriguez was especially anxious because, to make sure that he wasn't inside Mt. Carmel when the raid began, his commanders had told him to return to the undercover house by 9:15 A.M. It was already past nine.

Koresh crossed the doorway to look out of another window, then turned and eyed Rodriguez again. The preacher later said of the government agent, "Just his eyes looked down. . . . He was confused, same as Pilate. Pilate was confused. Pilate wanted to let Christ go."

Koresh said that he summed up his feelings about Rodriguez with a Mt. Carmel byword: ". . . You've got to do what you've got to do. . . ."

What Rodriguez had to do, he told Koresh, was return to the house on EE Road for breakfast. Koresh, according to the report Rodriguez gave, extended his hand to his visitor and said, "Good luck, Robert." Steve Schneider opened the front door for his exit and Rodriguez went out in a sweat: "I said to myself, 'They were going to shoot me in the back."

Rodriguez walked toward the parking lot, less than 25 yards from the front door. As he got near, for some reason, the pickup's burglar alarm went off. It sounded like a siren, Sherri Jewell would remember. Perry Jones, who was in the foyer looking out a window, noticed that when the alarm started to squeal, a vehicle belonging to one of the other guys at the undercover house came speeding home from a half-mile away.

Rodriguez blazed down Mt. Carmel's driveway, flashing his headlights as he neared its end. Parking outside the undercover house, he ran to the telephone, gave a report to a superior who was posted there, then dialed the command post. "Chuck, they know. They know," he blurted to the raid's commander, Charles Sarabyn.

The ATF's report on the affair says that Sarabyn, instead of ordering the raid aborted, "asked Rodriguez a series of questions from a prepared list provided by the tactical planners: Did you see any weapons? Was there a call to arms? Did you see them make any preparations?" Rodriguez responded in the negative to each question. Then Sarabyn asked what the people in the compound were doing when Rodriguez left. Rodriguez answered that "they were praying."

After the call, Rodriguez scolded his comrades for sticking the lenses of their surveillance cameras too near to open windows: the devices were obvious to passersby, he said. Then he ran back to his pickup and barreled toward the command center, hoping to stop the assault by collaring his superiors. "I was upset," Rodriguez would later say,

". . . because I knew what was going to happen." Perry Jones was still watching at the window when Robert Rodriguez pulled out; he remarked that the agent hadn't been home long enough to have eaten breakfast. When Rodriguez reached the command post, a few minutes later, it was too late: everybody had left. The raid was under way.

In the months that followed the raid, when congresspeople and cabinet officers were asking why the ATF had gone ahead with the raid despite Rodriguez's telephone report, agency executives at first denied that he had warned them of anything. Then, in a round of recriminations that haven't stopped yet, they gave reasons of a tactical kind. They didn't admit that they didn't trust their infiltrator, though it seems obvious that such was the case. Rodriguez had an earlier record of transfers and dissatisfaction, and while working undercover at Mt. Carmel, he hadn't spotted a single prohibited weapon or any explosive devices inside the compound, nothing to build the search warrant's text.

The Special Agent had known so little about the Holy Writ—and maybe about books in general, most of which have tables of contents— that when he was assigned to the case, he'd had to call his priest to ask where the Book of Revelation might be found. Koresh, of course, had educated him a bit, and during his studies at Mt. Carmel, the Special Agent had been touched, or influenced. Koresh thought that he had him thoroughly convinced. He at least had him confused. Upon his return from each of his visits to Mt. Carmel, Rodriguez says, he reported to his colleagues and superiors. "They would talk to me, bring me back. . . . They'd remind me that the interpretations David Koresh had were just interpretations," he said in a rare interview. "I would come out," he said under oath, "and I would tell them, 'You won't believe what I heard this time.' And they would say, 'Remember who he is. 'Remember what you're here for.' And I would tell them, 'I know that.' Actually, they didn't want to listen to it." At EE Road, it seems as though fellow agents took him for a dupe.

Nobody at the ATF wanted "to listen to it." Had anyone paid close attention to what Koresh had been preaching, or even to the history of Mt. Carmel, the agency would have known not to launch a raid.

Chapter 8

POOR GEORGE

"... My father told me one month before he died, that I was the Man Whose Name is the Branch and that it was my responsibility to rebuild the temple in Jerusalem just like Solomon was to do so at the death of his father."
—George Roden

When Vernon Howell first came to Mt. Carmel, he was not a ready pick for leadership. He had memorized the Bible, perhaps, and had developed some theology of his own, but he did not show the aggressiveness that distinguishes those people who rise in group hierarchies. He would have to change the group before it could follow him. His ascension would require the Living Waters Branch to reorganize, and to adopt a new and developing theology, to which only Howell had the keys. As things turned out, it also required the faithful, and at least one doubter, David Jones, to pass through a virtual birth of fire, a paramilitary campaign in which—foreshadowing 1993—Howell and his followers would raid the property, displacing the one who claimed to rule as messiah there. In the wake of the gunfight, Howell and his closest associates, like the survivors of the 1993 inferno, would face a jury on attempted murder charges. The young preacher and his comrades-in-arms won that fight, their first battle for Mt. Carmel, and that was among the reasons why they didn't flinch when Koresh pegged Robert Rodriguez as a cop.

If Vernon Howell had been living in a fog during his first months at Mt. Carmel in 1981, his potential had not escaped the eye of one of its denizens, George Roden, Lois's barrel-chested, bearded forty-three-year-old son. George had a future in mind for himself, and he instinctively feared that Howell would spoil it. Roden believed, on scriptural grounds, that when his mother died (she was not yet dead, or even ailing), he should take over leadership of the Branch.

Almost nobody bought George's message, for a basketful of reasons. He was not a decorous leader, and most people referred to him, almost derisively, as "Poor George." The hulking would-be heir was sorely afflicted. ". . . You'd be standing there talking to him, and he'd all of a sudden twitch and spit in your face," David Koresh recalled. "Not that he meant it. He just couldn't control it. He would be sitting there and all of a sudden slam his hand down on the table and he'd—the soup would go everywhere. And your, your plate would fly off, you know. He couldn't control it."

Not even Lois supported her son's bid. Looking for a relief preacher, two years after Howell came into the Living Waters Branch, she began letting him spell her at the pulpit. Howell came in and out of Mt. Carmel, leaving, he claimed, to take construction jobs in the cities, coming back when he was flush. But during weeks when he stayed at Mt. Carmel, followers saw him visit Lois's quarters at night. He told people that his visits were for private discussions of the theological issues that he would bring to his sermons.

Vernon would later confess that for several months in 1983 he'd also bedded Lois, in an attempt, inspired by a vision, to fulfill the scriptures (Isa 8:3), "And I went unto the prophetess; and she conceived, and bare a son. . . ." That Lois was years past menopause was no obstacle, Howell insisted: the Bible says (Gen 17:21) that thanks to God's intervention, at the age of ninety, Sarah, the mother of Israel, had borne Abraham a son.

Some detractors who did not distinguish between the imperatives of custom and those of Holy Writ—which celebrates several spring/

autumn marriages—had been appalled by the forty-year difference in Lois and Vernon's ages. Others were aghast at their unwed status. George Roden, never to be outdone, claimed that his mother had been raped. Frustrated and politically jealous, he began issuing tracts in which he predicted Howell's demise.

"There are three men who represent Lucifer today," he'd written in a bulletin to the Branch. "That is because Lucifer has three sets of vocal cords. First voice—public relations, Second voice—printed word, Third voice—music. Perry Jones, Clive Doyle, and Vernon Howell in that order. . . . But they cannot win for they are defeated foes, Jesus and the Antitypical Immanuel George Roden have conquered and their doom is certain," he prophesied. Roden also assailed Howell for practicing cunnilingus, which, according to Roden, was a diabolical act.

In the spring of 1984, as tension rose, Howell and his followers left Mt. Carmel for the Palestine, Texas, encampment. David Jones was at the time living in his house trailer in Waco, steadfast in his refusal to return to the fold. But he was not indifferent to the event. His parents and in-laws, all in their fifties, were now living among the school buses, tents, and plywood shacks of the raw camp. He thought that they deserved better. "Mt. Carmel was his parents' home. That's all they ever had," Jones's ex-wife Kathy explains. Jones blamed George Roden—not Vernon Howell—for his parents' loss, because as far as he could see, it was obvious that Roden was nuts. Besides, Howell was now a part of David Jones's family.

Shortly before the exodus to Palestine, Howell had become Jones's brother-in-law by marrying Jones's sister, Rachel, who was only fourteen at the time. The marriage was made with the approval of her parents, it was legal, and in the biblically intensive circles of the Branch, nobody had to point out that Rachel was older than the Blessed Virgin Mary when she wed old man Joseph.

Howell's marriage and exodus vexed Lois Roden, who was still formally the leader of the Branch. For months she traveled back and forth from Palestine to Mt. Carmel, hoping to salvage the organization. But the dispute was still unresolved when she died in November 1986. By this time, George Roden was practically alone at Mt. Carmel; most people had left in fear of him.

Desperate to justify his claims to leadership, George looked for a way to demonstrate that God was on his side. He dug up the casket of Anna Hughes, a one-armed believer who had been buried at New Mt. Carmel nearly two decades earlier. The "Antitypical Immanuel" then issued a challenge: Whoever could raise Anna from the dead, Roden proposed, would be revealed as the rightful leader of the Branch. "Not today, George," Howell told him when Roden threw down the gauntlet.

Seeing an opportunity to dislodge Roden, Howell consulted with Douglas Wayne Martin, a lawyer who had joined the Palestine camp. Martin pointed out that it's illegal to disinter people in Texas without a permit; "corpse abuse," he called it. Howell then went to Waco, to pay a visit to David Jones. He explained to the doubter that if George could be ousted, Jones's parents could return. The two went together to the McClennan County sheriff's office, to demand that Roden be arrested. Jones told the sheriff's department that he was concerned on behalf of the memory of a brother who was buried there: If Roden could dig up one corpse, he might dig up others, he argued. But as Howell and Jones told the story, the department's deputies weren't impressed. On the advice of then-prosecutor Denise Wilkerson, they demanded a photo of the crime.

Sam Jones, a younger brother of David Jones, was one of the stragglers living at Mt. Carmel. He had even helped George Roden—in whom he didn't believe—dig up the casket of Anna Hughes, or so his brother thought. Howell wanted to persuade Sam to take the pictures he needed, but Howell could not set foot on the property—Roden had already fired on a busload of visitors from Palestine—and Sam couldn't be reached by telephone. David Jones was the solution. He persuaded his brother Sam to take photos of the casket. Howell provided an Instamatic for doing the job.

The photographer took a half-dozen shots, and when his pictures were ready, David Jones and Vernon Howell went back to the sheriff's office to present the evidence. But the photographs didn't satisfy the lawmen. Sure enough, they showed a casket, draped in an Israeli flag. But the deputies wanted a picture of a body, or bones. And getting a new photo didn't promise to be easy.

A few days after he'd taken the pictures, Sam Jones had gotten into a wrangle with Poor George, and had moved away. His departure meant that if Howell wanted new photos, he'd have to sneak onto the property, a perilous prospect because Roden had taken to toting an Uzi semi-automatic. "Be careful, boys, there's some rough customers out there," a deputy named Elijah had warned Jones and Howell on their last visit to the sheriff's office.

For a month, Howell planned a paramilitary action, either to obtain the photo, or to oust Roden, or both. He enlisted David Jones and seven disciples from Palestine, and went to a Kmart and a hardware store to equip them for a raid. Because it was cold, Howell bought insulated deer hunter's coveralls for his army. He also bought an assortment of shotguns and small-caliber rifles, flashlights, and face paint. Just after midnight on November 2, 1987, the nine of them jumped out of a van on EE Ranch Road and crawled into the brushland around Mt. Carmel, sending one of the group, Mark Wendell, forward with a camera. When he came to the chapel building where Roden had kept the casket, Wendell found that it was gone. As he was returning to his comrades-in-hiding, Roden's dogs began howling and George emerged with his Uzi. The raiders decided to hunker down for the night.

The following day, they eased onto the property and began peeking into buildings, looking for Anna's casket. After they'd entered one or two of the structures, a "gentile," or non-religious woman who was living on the property—Koresh claimed that she was wearing short shorts and was bare-breasted at the time—spotted the group and immediately denounced them to Roden. The invaders promptly faced his Uzi again. Vernon's little army was trading shots with the Antitypical Immanuel when the sheriff's department came over the hill. Wendell, who must have seen them first, ran into the brush behind Mt. Carmel and wasn't discovered. But David Jones, Vernon Howell, and the others were nabbed. One of the arresting officers was a deputy named Bill Thorn, whom Jones greeted. "David, what are you doing here?" Thorn had asked, like Peeler, unable to place a postman in a shoot-out scene.

Howell best told the story of what happened after they got to jail. The group spent the first night in a holding cell. The following afternoon, deputies escorted them to a hallway, then slammed the bars behind them. "So, there's guys in there, boy, and I'm talking about they, they are like tough-looking guys," Howell said. ". . . They're like, all like, you know, side by side down this hallway, this run. And they're going, 'Yeah, yeah, come on'—some black guys, 'Come on down here, we all, we all done cleared out a room just for you guys.' . . . And they treated us with such respect! And they treated us with such decency! And they were kind of standing back from us, you know?

"Well, we didn't know—we thought . . . we was going to get in there and get a lot of trouble, right? But these guys were just so nice. What had happened was . . . they had played on the news that eight PLO terrorists had assaulted Mt. Carmel Center."

The confusion, Howell liked to explain, came about because one of his Christian commandos was the young Hawaiian who would later become his gun show partner, Paul Fatta. Somebody (newsman or jailbird) had mistaken his name for Al-Fattah. Either that, or—heaven forbid!—their jailbirds had believed a *Waco Tribune* report in which Roden described the assault as a "jihad" and Howell's army as a branch of the then much-feared Palestine Liberation Organization.

Roden had been slightly injured, a bullet to the thumb. Howell and his captured commandos were charged with attempted murder, a felony. Howell and Fatta each paid $5,000 to a bondsman, and David Jones, fearful of losing his postal job, paid up, too. But when he reported for work, he learned that until the felony charge was cleared, he was suspended, and a petition people along his route circulated in his behalf couldn't change that. For the next six months, while five of his comrades remained in jail, David Jones became a roofer, a framer, a handyman. "He did anything he could do to pay our bills," ex-wife Kathy says.

Then came the trial, which dragged on for ten days in April 1988. Again, it was Howell who told the best stories about the affair. ". . . The district attorney would . . . hire these professional analysts to analyze certain things. . . . One guy was a professional in regards to paramilitary weapons and tactics. . . . So . . . they presented the jury some baling wire," he began. "And what happened was that Shabazz"—El Hadi Shabazz, the lead prosecutor—"stands in front of the jury and says . . . 'Now what was this used for do you think? What was this intended for?' . . . And the guy goes on to explain that in certain paramilitary

79

groups such a wire is used for strangling . . . So the guy gets up . . . walks down in front of the jury, grabs the wire and puts it around Shabazz's neck, and—you know, this is, this is extreme, right? And so the jury . . . their eyes are getting real big, right?

"And so anyway," the story continued, "they also had some, a red piece of shirt, several pieces of red checkered shirt there. And Shabazz is saying, 'Now what might this possibly be used for?' And he says, 'Well . . . such things or items can be used as, as signalling devices, things to signal a, a movement or a, a preconceived intention, you know.' And so the jury is like well, wow, you know, all these neat paraphernalias here.

"And so what happened at that time is that Paul Fatta is there on the, on the stand, and Shabazz is asking him. He says, 'Well, Mr. Fatta, is it not true that, that you were using these things for signalling devices? Isn't that the way you communicated to everybody in regards to the way you'd move on the property, and, you know, you would flank Mr. Roden and, and, and kill him?' And he goes, 'No, sir, that is not true.' He goes, 'Well, just what is the truth about this then?' And Paul goes, 'Well, do you really want to know?' . . . And Shabazz goes, 'Oh, yes, I would like to know.' And he goes—Paul goes—'Toilet paper.' And Shabazz looks at him kind of funny. He goes, 'Would you explain that?' And Paul says, 'We were down at the barn, we'd been out all night. Some of the guys needed to relieve themselves and all we found down there was an old shirt. So we tore the shirt up and we gave it to different guys in case they had to relieve themselves for toilet paper.' "

The defense countered the charge that the raiders had carried garrots with the testimony of Stan Sylvia, fifty, a New Englander who was the shortest and most muscular of the group of accused murderers. Sylvia demonstrated for the jury that the coveralls Howell had bought for him were four to five inches too long for his legs. Dressing in the garment for the jury, Sylvia "pulled up the bottoms of the pants . . . tucked them over and wrapped the wire around and around them to make them short so they wouldn't fall down below his shoes."

The government did not call George Roden as a witness. Defense attorney Gary Coker called him instead. On the stand, the cunnilingus foe admitted that he *had* tried to resurrect one-armed Anna, and that he sometimes closed prayers at Mt. Carmel with the words, "In the name of George B. Roden, amen."

That was enough for the jury. It acquitted the seven commandos and balked at any verdict regarding Howell. The case went down as a victory for the defendants, attorney Coker told the *Waco Tribune*, because "our witnesses are nice people with no criminal record who don't believe they're Jesus Christ."

Not only did the criminal trial turn against Roden and the state, but other events did, too. Nobody had paid taxes on the Mt. Carmel property for nineteen years, the assessments had accumulated a value of $62,000, and in mid-1987, the county had taken steps to exercise its lien. Poor George had over the past five years filed some fifty *pro se* civil suits, demanding a tax exemption on the Mt. Carmel acreage, and in one of them, filed shortly before the raid, he'd asked, "Who does the Texas Supreme Court think they are, 'God'?" Roden's brief answered the question by saying that "If you think your [sic] God then God would have taken the poor into account but you son of bitches have your goddamn click [sic] to take care of. . . . You can't afford to allow the poor to get any benefit or you might loose [sic] your ass in the process. . . . Maybe God will make it up to you in the end and send you herpes and AIDS the seven last plagues and shove them up you goddamn bastards asses."

While George was assailing the judiciary, he was living at Mt. Carmel in violation of a 1979 restraining order that had never been rescinded—or forgotten. On March 23, 1988, about two weeks before the trial began, a federal judge sentenced him to six months in jail for contempt of court. That same day, a Waco state solon imposed the 1979 injunction ordering Roden not to return to Mt. Carmel. Poor George said that his persecution was obviously part of a Communist conspiracy, directed by the comrade Pope.

Taking advantage of Roden's myriad troubles, Howell's supporters rushed to pay the taxes owed upon the property, and to secure an order authorizing their return. When they moved back to Mt. Carmel in April 1988, they found Anna Hughes resting in her coffin in a mechanic's shed, and the roofs of their former quarters caving in from neglect. "Hogs wouldn't even go in my home," Bob Kendrick told the

Waco Tribune. "But I'm glad to be back. I lived there 21 years. It's home."

Soon after his release, George Roden ceased to trouble Howell's followers entirely. He moved to Odessa, Texas, where in 1989 the Antitypical Immanuel hacked an ostensible follower to death because, Roden reportedly said, "I am a Jew and he said that he was a Nazi, and I felt threatened." George Roden remains in a hospital for the insane, reportedly giving interviews to reporters in exchange for black Stetson hats.

That first persecution, David Koresh had often told David Jones, showed that behind everything, God had a plan. True Christianity had been purified by the thinning of its ranks—Poor George was out the picture, anyway—and the government's plot to imprison the raiders had been undone. Robert Gonzalez, Koresh now said, was only the mysterious face of a divine new plan to advance the message of the present truth.

Chapter 9

THE SEMI-LITERATE MESSIAH

"David didn't read anything but the Bible and Camaro magazines."
—follower Wally Kennett

Vernon Howell's rise to the throne of the Living Waters Branch was, in theological terms, a pretty unremarkable ascent at first. During his initial years in the pulpit, 1983–85, he laid out no startling new doctrines, brought no epochal messages, and little was revealed to him. But the way in which he began to reshape the group's ministry, both at Palestine and after retaking Mt. Carmel, was nothing short of revolutionary. Vernon Howell put oxygen—or maybe ammonia—into the nose of an asphyxiating sect.

Howell did not suspend the formality that is commonly associated with the religious profession; he defied it, he burlesqued it, he chased it out of the sanctuary. He came to the pulpit in jeans and jogging shoes, sometimes unshaven, sometimes with motor oil on his hands. He did not deliver his sermons in a stentorian style, but as a conversationalist. His approach to homiletics was so casual as to be downscale. Vernon Howell was capable of preaching:

"That nasty old sin, how can you get rid of the stuff? It's like a booger on your fingers, right? You're trying, you know, and you're picking, and it gets on your other finger? Even when you're going 50 miles an

83

hour down the road and you're trying to flick it off! I know what I'm talking about, you see."

His explanation of the purpose of religion, and all of the scriptures, was equally direct. What's the purpose of faith? According to Howell: "We want out of here. . . . We want to go from here to a place of freedom where we're no longer in bondage to the flesh, our stupidity, our good looks. We want to get away from the guy in the mirror, don't we?"

Howell was anything but self-righteous. When a hearer expressed doubts about the Bible, he countered with a contemporary lecture whose opening line was, "Let's pretend that the Bible is just a game that the Jews made up, okay?"

When Texas Rangers in 1993 sifted through the ashes of what had been Mt. Carmel's cafeteria, they unearthed a large sign whose inscription they couldn't believe. The sign read: "This is not a restaurant. If you don't like the food, f.u." The Rangers thought that they knew what "f.u." meant, and they couldn't imagine that a preacher of any kind would resort to such slang. It was pure Vernon Howell: fully aware of his congregants' language, he didn't shrink from it himself.

He also brought a touch of the salesman's art to his pulpit. He touted the Bible's densest, most dubious sections by equating them with journalism. ". . . The prophets are the press, too," he said. "They're giving you a hot scoop on the future. . . . I mean, the press today tells you what's happened, but the prophesies tell you what's going to happen." When he talked about the divine revenge that is described or predicted in many prophecies, he'd toss in commonplace parenthetical observations like, "The Lord is beating some butt, right?"

Even as David Koresh, developing the doctrine that would be his trademark, an explanation of the Seven Seals of the Book of Revelation, the young preacher eschewed pretense. In explaining his plan, he sometimes spoke the language of childhood, of television. "When you're watching football one day and all of a sudden a commercial comes up for some new thriller movie," he'd say, "it doesn't show you the whole movie. It shows you a couple of fast, action-packed pictures, right? . . . So, by the previews we say, 'Man, I, I'd like to see that movie, what that movie is really all about.' So also it is with the opening of the Seals. The man on the white horse is part of a more in-depth truth."

Howell also dispensed with the trappings of denominationalism—starting with the church name. Howell did not name or rename his movement, as White, Houteff, and the two Rodens had done. The press would later call the residents at Mt. Carmel Branch Davidians, because on property deeds, the ownership group was known as the Branch Davidian Seventh-Day Adventist Association. But the Branch was Ben Roden's group, which Howell and his aides took lightly. ". . . None of us here have ever called ourselves twigs or branches or roots or anything else," disciple Steve Schneider quipped. Rather than taking a denominational name, Koresh's followers called themselves students of the Bible, or later, students of the Seven Seals.

During Lois Roden's years, the Living Waters Branch had done a steady trade in audiotapes, sold by mail order. Howell suspended even this. "He didn't want to do a business in selling tapes. He didn't want us to become like a church," Clive Doyle explains. He also laid down a derivative law: those who wanted to partake of biblical "truth" would have to come to Mt. Carmel to get it. The fiat at once reduced his potential following and increased the commitment of those whom his message held. It also freed Howell from the dangers of fixing "present truth" in stone, allowing his doctrine to evolve as he willed.

While Ben and Lois Roden had been Mt. Carmel's prophets-in-residence, they cited Houteff and Ellen White's writings alongside the Bible. But unlike Houteff and White, the Rodens had not published their tracts in bound volumes whose pages were amenable to notational systems. Had they done so, or had Howell resurrected the tradition, his messages would have been hobbled by chains of footnotes. He'd have had to invoke four authorities for any new doctrine that he preached.

Instead, the semi-literate Texan downplayed all latter-day texts. Perhaps at his urging, Lois Roden had prophesied that the Seventh Angel's message would not come in print, but instead, in song. Vernon Howell retired the musty old hymns that the Living Waters group had sung, and replaced them with a repertoire of folk-rock ditties that he composed himself.

As Howell gained confidence in his ability to exercise the leadership that had fallen to him, he also began forming the theological doctrines that were to make him, for better or worse, a unique figure in the Adventist tradition. Like his predecessors, he leaned in the direction of the prophecies, and in a way bolder than any of them, he began envisioning the messianic antitype into which he would fit. Though the press and public would miss the point, there was nothing new on the road he was traveling—a road on which pilgrims had been marching long before Ellen White.

Chapter 10

MERLIN THE MESSIAH

"The alimentary canal of the alchemico-organic macrocosm is in the form of discular vacua, in which are the amalgamated mercurial disci which float or move in spirals through the interstices of the metallic plates which comprise the outer rind and pediment of the alchemico-organic kosmos."
—Cyrus Teed ·

Bible prophecies have their origins a long way from Waco and Dallas, in the ancient troubles of Palestine. In introducing his encyclopedic work on Christian Messianism, *The Pursuit of the Millennium* (1957), historian Norman Cohn points out:

> It is natural enough that the earliest of these prophecies should have been produced by the Jews. What so sharply distinguished the Jews from the other peoples of the ancient world was their attitude towards history and in particular towards their own role in history. Save to some extent for the Persians, the Jews were alone in combining an uncompromising monotheism with an unshakable conviction that they were themselves the Chosen People of the one God. . . . Precisely because they were so utterly certain of being the Chosen People, Jews tended to react to

peril, oppression and hardship by phantasies of the total triumph and boundless prosperity which Yahweh, out of his omnipotence, would bestow upon his Elect in the fulness of time.

Seen in this light, the prophecies are, in simplest form, "get-even" predictions. The ancient Jews believed that there was but one God, both omnipotent and just; when they suffered what could only be called injustice—an invasion, an uprooting, a religious persecution—to save faith and face, their spokesmen predicted that God would even the score, by and by. As human civilization neared its end—the point where there would be "time no longer"—a messiah would punish the wrongdoers, reward the righteous, and restore the previous, more idyllic state of affairs.

But the Jewish disposition to believe in would-be messiahs was largely exhausted by the start of the Christian era. "Simon bar-Cochba, who led the last great struggle for national independence in A.D. 31," Cohn points out, "was still greeted as Messiah. But the bloody suppression of that rising and the annihilation of political nationality put an end both to the apocalyptic faith and the militancy of the Jews. . . . It was no longer the Jews but the Christians who cherished and elaborated prophecies in the tradition of 'Daniel's dream' and who continued to be inspired by them."

Christianity inherited messianic hopes—and messiahs, one after another in a seemingly unending series, almost without interruption into the present. In general, these Christian would-be messiahs did not deny the divinity of the Saviour from Nazareth, only that He had fulfilled all of the tasks of the messianic mission. They drew for themselves a theological position more Christian than Jewish, but somewhere between the two. For them, Jesus was the Messiah, but not the last or complete Saviour.

In his landmark work, Cohn traces the history of Christian messianic movements from A.D. 156 forward, with closest attention to the some two dozen religious rebellions recorded between 1190 and 1535. As a rule, these movements begin, Cohn thinks, during times "of general uncertainty and excitement," and draw their ranks "not from the poor and oppressed as such, but amongst the poor and oppressed whose traditional way of life has broken down and who have lost faith in their traditional values."

Though today's common wisdom presumes that all such would-be messiahs were insane, and historical accounts do not completely dispute that view, most of our knowledge comes from the enemies of these rebels. Their own declarations were either unrecorded, or records of them were destroyed by Inquisitions of various kinds.

The scraps that are available to us indicate that if these bygone Saviours were insane, they were nevertheless consistent, and the same is true of their followers, not all of whom, presumably, could have shared similarly clouded or afflicted minds.

The *Encyclopaedia Britannica*'s report on the earliest Christian Messianic movement, that of the Montanists, says: ". . . Certain fasts were prescribed and the time of fasting was lengthened; it was forbidden to flee from martyrdom, second marriages were prohibited and marriage itself was at least discouraged." Not only were some outlines of doctrine similar to those that would be attributed to David Koresh, but so was the movement's end: "Its destruction as a sect was tragic, for, when they were proscribed by a decree of Justinian, the Phrygian Montanists shut themselves in their churches and burned them down."

Vernon Howell's musical ministry was nearly prefigured—Cohn's history indicates—by that of a fifteenth-century Messiah named Hans Bohn. ". . . We are told," Cohn writes, "that from earliest youth he had been regarded as half-witted, that until he began to preach he had never been able to form a coherent sentence." But Bohn, like Koresh, had a way with music. He was "a popular entertainer, drumming and piping in hostelries and in the marketplace—whence the nickname, by which he is still known, of Drummer (or Piper) of Niklashausen." When the authorities ordered his arrest, essentially for sedition, the Drummer organized a revolt. Within weeks, he was burned at the stake.

Vernon Howell probably did not know anything about any of the heretics who preceded him, except for Thomas Muntzer, whom Ellen White scored for having taken Lutheranism beyond the bounds of reason, and the Waldensians, to whom White devoted a chapter of *The*

Great Controversy—and whose relationship to Catholicism, Koresh would have said, was like his movement's relationship to the SDA. Because Ellen White did not mention him, the Texas messiah was probably unaware of his nearest predecessor in ideology and time, the nineteenth-century American Cyrus R. Teed—a man who called himself Koresh. Teed was one of the mysterious figures who, long after his death, rated a passing mention in the esoterica of Umberto Eco's novel *Foucault's Pendulum.*

Cyrus Teed was a stout man, with large eyes, a broad chin, and a prominent nose, who was born in upstate New York in 1839, and served in the Union Army during the Civil War. Upon discharge in 1863, he enrolled in the Eclectic Medical College of the City of New York, and after graduating, according to his biographer, R. L. Rainard, he made himself a student of alchemy. That ancient pursuit, Rainard cautions, sought not only to turn lead into gold, but also to transform human beings into divine souls.

One evening in 1869, Teed claimed, his experiments to turn base metal into gold were successful. "The transmutation," Rainard writes, "simply proved that the alchemist had found the 'Philosopher's stone,' the lapis, or the elixir of life. Communion with the deity"—who, Teed discovered, was a woman—"and the solution to human suffering which might accompany the experience, hinged upon possession of the Stone." That same night, Teed laid aside any concern for lucre and summoned up his goddess in prayer. If he had the secret to riches, he never revealed it or took advantage of it again.

Teed's goddess gave him a vision, which he described in the pseudo-scientific jargon that distinguished him among holy men. "Suddenly," he wrote, "I experienced a relaxation at the occiput or back part of the brain, and a peculiar buzzing tension at the forehead or sinciput. Succeeding this was a soft tension about the organs of the brain called the lyra, crura, pinealis, and conarium."

The goddess told Teed that he'd reached his seventh and final incarnation. His arrival, she said, came with a duty or mission. The mission was the same as that given to the biblical Cyrus—whose Hebrew name is Koresh—a Persian conqueror, known to historians as Cyrus II, who began to rule over Babylon in 539 B.C.

According to the Bible (II Chron 36, Ezra 1), Cyrus invited the Israelites to return from the exile that Babylonian conquest had forced upon them. To show that he meant business, Cyrus provided a grant for the rebuilding of Yahweh's Jerusalem Temple, and stocked it with items sacked from the previous seat of worship. Though he is merely a cameo figure in the Bible, Cyrus has long since attracted the attention of speculators because, despite being a pagan or gentile, God chose him to begin the Messiah's work. Cyrus Teed proclaimed that he had come to complete the agenda of his namesake.

One of the intellectual chores that fell to Teed, as to other Christian American seers, was to assess the fate of Millerism, which remained alive through the SDA movement. William Miller, he believed, had made several mistakes in calculation, not all of them caught by Edson and Ellen White. "According to Teed," Rainard writes, "based on the prophesies of Daniel in B.C. 457, calculating a day as a year, seventy weeks as 490 years, adding thirty-three years for the life of Jesus and computed on lunar time, the year 1839"—not 1844—"marked the beginning of the last phase preceding the harvest and cataclysm. It marked the year when the Messiah, the Messenger of the Covenant, resumed his physical form. It also marked the year of Teed's birth."

To deal with the objections of leery Christians, Teed and an associate, Dr. J. Augustus Weimar, developed a set of eighty-nine proofs of the alchemist's unusual standing. One of the first of them is the finding, well known to more orthodox Bible scholars, that "Christ" is essentially an honorific, not a name: in modern terms, calling Jesus "Christ" is something like calling Aretha Franklin "the Queen of Soul." In the Hebrew, the word "anointed" means Messiah, equivalent to the Greek word *Christos*. Both terms designate a status, not an individual.

Since Christ is a title, not a name, Cyrus Teed, in regarding himself as the Messiah, was not seeking to defrock Jesus, but to share his mantle; indeed, Teed claimed to be the seventh earthly Messiah, Jesus having been number six. Like the Drummer, Cyrus Teed saw himself not as *the* Christ, but instead, as another or latter-day Christ.

One of the differences between himself and Jesus, Teed pointed out,

91

was that Jesus had been born by supernatural conception, and had never sinned. By contrast, Teed styled himself as the "man of sin" referred to in II Thessalonians 2:3, 4. The scripture describes a false messiah, whom Teed rehabilitated by retranslating the Greek from which it came. According to Teed, Jesus was the perfect Messiah, Cyrus Teed, the sin-blotched saviour. David Koresh, who was far more sinful than Teed, would probably have lifted the rehabilitating retranslation, had he known of it. Instead, circumstances required him to achieve the same effect by other scriptural means.

Teed's picture of human civilization included a biblical belief in its end by fire, embellished by the pseudo-science which was his specialty. The final conflagration, Rainard notes, "was an alchemical fire which altered the structure of the materials it consumed. It changed . . . 288,000 virginial common men and women into 144,000 noble Sons of God."

Like David Koresh, Cyrus Teed's reputation was assailed because of his unorthodox relationships with women. He was several times sued for having alienated the affections of men's wives, and in their suits, the jilted husbands usually alleged that the prophet had slept with their wives. None of the suits came to successful conclusions, however, in part because Teed was able to persuade all inquirers that his sect practiced the celibacy that it preached. In 1894, partly to avoid courtroom entanglements, Teed moved his following, which numbered about two hundred, from its bases in Chicago and San Francisco.

The group established a utopian community about twenty-five miles south of Fort Myers, Florida, where the founder died of natural causes in 1908. When he didn't rise from the grave, his following dwindled. Speculation, of course, continued: in 1921, a hurricane struck his tomb, carrying his body either to the heavenly throne or the bottomless sea. In 1941, the disappointed remnant of his flock turned their settlement over to the state of Florida, which has preserved it as the Koreshan State Historical Site. Reprints of the master's works continued to be made until the early 1970s, but there are today no traces of a living Koreshan movement.

Chapter 11

GOD'S FLYING MACHINES

"Chariots of the Gods ain't fiction."
—David Koresh

Bereft of the kind of historical savvy that would have led him to the theology of the Florida Messiah, "bonehead" Vernon Howell had to wing his way to saviourdom, or, as his followers insist, had to follow the lead which God gave him. It didn't come overnight. But it began to come almost as soon as he set foot in the Holy Land.

An inkling came after a late 1983 trip to Israel that Howell made with, among others, Lois Roden. "He always worried about eating," recalls Robyn Bunds, who would bear one of his children. "He was afraid he was being a pig." Sometimes he'd fast for days, then binge. On the trip to Israel, he experienced great difficulty in restraining his appetite, and he returned speaking of himself as the "ravenous bird" of Isaiah 46:11, "the man that executeth my counsel from a far country." Howell may not have known, but Bible scholars regard Isaiah's mention of the bird as a reference to Cyrus II.

In early 1985, the young preacher returned to Israel, he said, to see if Mt. Zion really were big enough to serve as the staging ground for the 144,000 true believers who, according to Revelation 7, would receive a Christ-like angel, usually thought to be Jesus, during the End Time days. Mt. Zion was just a molehill, Howell concluded, but while he stood there, surveying the site, he learned that when the last days came, an earthquake would enlarge it—and he learned much, much more.

Howell rarely talked about this, his most important vision, and many of his followers did not know of it. No one was supposed to be told until they were grounded in the teachings of the First Seal. But during the fifty-one-day 1993 siege at Mt. Carmel, Howell did tell bits and pieces of the story to FBI negotiators to whom he spoke by telephone. In a conversation with one Bureauman, he explained that "Well, in 1985 I was in Israel. And there was, there was these Russian cosmonauts that . . . gave the report that they saw seven angelic beings flying towards earth with the wings of a size of a jumbo jet. Okay, so what happened was in 1985 when I was in Israel, I met up with those people. Seriously."

The agent pressed for clarification:

FBI   . . . And you met these seven angelic beings?
KORESH   Exactly.
FBI   Where?
KORESH   In Israel.
FBI   Yeah, but where in Israel?
KORESH   On Mt. Zion over in Israel.

After blurting that, the preacher advanced an explanation. "You know," he said, "angels don't really have wings. It's really . . . it's a, it's a spaceship. . . . It's a vehicle, I mean, and it travels by light, the refraction of light."

What Koresh was talking about, as he'd explain to the thoroughly befuddled G-Man, was the Merkabah, a sort of celestial flying saucer. It was a concept acceptable only to Bible scholars, the Living Waters Branch and its heirs, and to a few very Orthodox rabbis. The notion was rooted in Howell's understanding of Ellen White, who believed that "innumerable worlds" were inhabited.

After an 1846 vision, Sister White had written that "Wings were given me, and an angel attended me from the city to a place that was bright and glorious. The grass of the place was living green, and the birds there warbled a sweet song. The inhabitants of the place were of all sizes; they were noble, majestic, and lovely. They bore the express image of Jesus, and their countenances beamed with holy joy, expressive of the freedom and happiness of the place." (EW 39–40) In the same vision, White visited "a world which had seven moons," where she met "good old Enoch, who had been translated." But Enoch told her that he was only visiting the planet; angels and other deities resided in the heavens, not the "innumerable worlds." Enoch did not tell White how it was that he managed to skip about the universe as he did: that was for her successors to figure out.

White's successors, living in a more modern and comfortable age, provided for the angels a motorized means of transport. They found twentieth-century uses for it, too. Houteff began the work in his pamphlet, *The White House Recruiter.* "One may be incredulous . . . at the thought of Heaven's having flying saucers," he had written in 1951. "But why? If God has given man knowledge to develop aerial mechanisms, no one can reasonably suppose that Heaven does not have incomparably superior ones. . . . And if the flying saucers are indeed the Lord's, then what else are they come for but to deliver every one whose name is found written in the Book (Dan 12:1), and to slay those who oppress them (Isa 66:16)?"

Ben Roden cited a biblical basis for Houteff's contraption in *Heaven's Flying Saucer, God's Traveling Throne,* a little tract published in purple and green type and illustrated by an artist's conception of the prophetic vision described in Isaiah 6:1–4. But neither Roden nor Houteff had been the first to draw the conclusion that God's vehicles were flying machines: rabbinical students had preceded them by centuries.

When she turned her attention to Isaiah's "traveling throne," Lois Roden investigated much of the Jewish literature on the subject. In a tract called *Chariots of Fire,* whose cover illustrated a Haifa-built, modern Israeli tank called the Merkava, she pointed out that according to Psalms 68:17, "The chariots of God are twenty thousand," and also cited, from the *Jewish Encyclopedia,* the Hebrew tradition of the "vision of the Merkabah."

". . . Those under this strange hallucination," the *Encyclopedia* says, who imagine themselves entering the Heavenly Chariot and floating through the air, are called "Yorede Merkabah." . . . In this chariot they are supposed to ascend to the heavens, where in the dazzling light surrounding them they behold the innermost secrets of all persons and things, otherwise impenetrable and invisible. . . . Particularly significant is the warrior-nature of the angels surrounding the Throne-Chariot . . . they ride upon fiery horses. . . .and are armed with weapons of fire. . . . In order to be allowed to pass these terrible beings the Merkabah-rider must provide himself with amulets or seals containing mysterious names. . . .

What Koresh was trying to tell the puzzled G-Man was that what the Soviet astronauts had supposedly seen were not angels, but Merkabah, which had come to earth to take Vernon Howell, aka "Mr. Retardo," into the heavens with them, just as, according to Jewish tradition, they'd been doing since before the time of Christ.

"I was taken up past Orion . . . ," Koresh told the G-Man. "I went up and found that God was actually [the creator of] an ancient civilization that was before the world." While visiting the City of God—to which Ellen White refers a dozen times—Vernon met the Big Guy himself, afterwards to report that "He's flesh" and "there's not a blemish" upon His body. "The City of God," Vernon told his advanced students, "travels on this laser . . . and that's where the Merkabah travels."

When Koresh made reference to the constellation of Orion, as in explaining his Merkabah vision, the choice was not arbitrary, nor was it likely the result of any astronomical studies of his own. It was pure Ellen White. The New Testament (Rev 3:12, 21:2) says that in the last days, God will send down from the heavens a new Jerusalem, to replace the battered and abused city that we have known. How will He send it? Sister White gave the answer in an 1848 vision. "The atmosphere parted," she wrote, "and rolled back; then we could look up through the open space in Orion, whence came the voice of God. The Holy City will come down through that open space." (EW 41)

But there are several problems with the story Howell told, not least of which is that the cosmonauts of whom he spoke did not see their "giant figures in the form of humans . . . with wings and mistlike halos" until July 1985, several months after Vernon and Rachel had returned to Texas and given birth to their first child, Cyrus. Beyond that, it's unlikely that Howell knew of their experience until January 1986, when a brief account was published in *Parade* magazine.

Howell's followers insist that he came back from the Holy Land radically changed. "God planted in his brain," says disciple Catherine Matteson, "a perfect picture of the Bible." Though the trip soon also cured it, its initial effect was to aggravate Howell's stuttering problem, says Clive Doyle. "The way he saw the Bible was like a video, and at first he couldn't speak it as fast as he could see it." "He was really intense," says a former concubine whom interviewers have named "Diana Ishikawa." "When he spoke there was kind of a spirit in the room. It was kind of like having a religious conversion experience all over."

But despite his command of the Writ, Vernon Howell never became a charismatic leader, in the usual sense of the word, anyway. He didn't have the persona. People who met him for the first time were almost always disappointed. Alisa Shaw, a young New England apostate, told an interviewer that when she first set eyes on Koresh in early 1993, "He was smaller than I expected and he didn't seem as overwhelming as I expected. . . . He was just wearing jeans and a t-shirt and a leather jacket. He hadn't shaved and he just seemed a regular guy . . . I never would have expected him to be this person that I had a few Bible teachings from over the phone." Sincerity, scripturalism, and enthusiasm were his saving graces. ". . . Ministers and other people couldn't help me with my questions in understanding the Bible," government witness Marjorie Thomas later testified, but ". . . David answered my questions without me asking. . . . He also managed to, from the Old and New Testament, put the passages together." "He would always start out with, do you have any questions? He loved being asked questions," apostate Shaw recalled.

One of the places Howell sought to demonstrate his newfound powers was the General Conference meeting of the SDA, celebrated every five years. During the summer of 1985, it was held in the Superdome in New Orleans. Howell's message to the group came from Isaiah 23:15–18: "And it shall come to pass in that day, that Tyre shall be forgotten seventy years . . . after the end of seventy years shall Tyre sing as an harlot. Take an harp, go about the city, thou harlot that hast been forgotten; make sweet melody, sing many songs, that thou mayest be remembered."

His interpretation of the passage was that the Davidian throne was to be vacant for seventy years from the date of Ellen White's death, in 1915, to be restored in 1985 by his coronation. He and a handful of followers buttoned General Conference leaders inside the 'Drum and pressed literature upon them, but were unable to win a plenary hearing for their ideas. Frustrated, Vernon recalled that his message was supposed to have come by music, anyway—and he drove back to Waco, a day's distance, loaded his amplifiers and guitar, and came back to the Conference as it was closing. For a few hours, he serenaded departing delegates from the parking lot.

"One of the events at this conference was a parade of nations," detractor Marc Breault writes. "Seventh Day Adventists from all nations marched in the New Orleans in a rather spectacular parade. Vernon interpreted this as meaning that the church, instead of listening to himself, the true prophet, paraded to the world acting the part of the harlot. The church had fulfilled the prophecy."

By reference to another scripture about seventy years, Psalms 90:10, Howell not only buttressed his argument that he was the rightful successor to Ellen White, but also made a prediction about his future. His message, he said, would take ten years to disseminate. Two lessons were obvious from that. The first was that, in picturing the Adventist movement as "forgotten seventy years," he seemed to be dethroning Houteff and the Rodens. The second was that, since Vernon Howell was bringing the Seventh and last Angel's message, the End Time would open in 1995. The world as we know it would, in a decade, be no more.

In addition to a mastery of the Bible and spoken English, Howell claimed that in Israel he'd been given a complete knowledge of physics and astronomy, confidant Steve Schneider always said. Indeed, according to at least some of Howell's followers, in Israel God had given Howell an inside track on . . . everything! Because of what he'd learned in heaven, Howell's faithful began to regard him not as sinless, but as having perfect knowledge. After all, in the King James Version of the Writ (Isa 45:13), God, speaking of Cyrus, says ". . . I will direct all his ways." Stan Sylvia, one of the veterans of the '87 assault on George Roden, today regrets having argued with Howell, shortly after the trip, over the proper method of putting tarpaper on the decking of a roof. Howell argued for laying the paper vertically, Sylvia for rolling it out in a horizontal direction, as roofers usually do. "If David wanted to do it that way, I shouldn't have argued. He had a reason," Sylvia says now.

Howell's mastery of the Bible, however, needed no spacemen or supernatural beings to stamp it as authoritative. The Bible was second nature to him. Howell's relationship to the Holy Writ was like that of a current affairs junkie to a collection of old newsweeklies. He knew every character in them, and constantly relived their exploits. He spoke of obscure Old Testament kings, of Saul, Hezekiah, Ahaz, Rehboam, Sihon, Amraphel, even of Zippor and Og, in the same way that newsroom editors, for example, speak of Spiro Agnew, or Margaret Mitchell, or Billy Carter—acquaintances from the global village, undying and familiar. As the *Reader's Guide to Periodical Literature* would be to a news junkie, the Seven Seals of Revelation became to Howell. The Seals were his index, his key to the whole.

Howell combined his news junkie's grasp of seemingly passing personalities and trivial detail with a mechanic's eye for harmony, or co-ordination. He made the Bible a smooth-running machine, much in the same way that a garageman tunes an auto motor. The auto mechanic, when tuning a motor, sets the timing of the spark and then, adjusting here and there—oxygen and gasoline mix, the idle rate, choke settings— twists and turns until the engine runs efficiently. Howell took as his starting point the Book of Revelation, and then, tweaking meanings here and there, brought the whole Bible into what his followers, anyway, regarded as an impeccable harmony. As it does not matter to the mechanic when the parts of his engine were manufactured—a 1981 Yamaha carburetor can be adapted to work with a brand-new Volkswagen distributor, for example—so it did not matter to Howell that different books of the Bible had been written in different epochs, for very different readerships. The mechanic's job is to wring a smooth performance from the cacophony of moving parts. Vernon Howell's ambition was to devise order from the dynamic chaos of the Bible. Like most believers, he saw in the Bible a unifying subtext. For him it was the Good Book, not the Good Books; the Holy Writ, not the Holy Writs; the Word of God, not a happenstance collection of the Words of God.

One of the things that he'd been told in Israel, Howell informed his followers, was that he was the antitypical Cyrus, sent to do the Messiah's work. He took as his fundamental text chapters 40–66 of the prophetic Book of Isaiah, called by some scholars the "Second Isaiah." These chapters are believed by some academics to have been written in the eighth century B.C.—long before Cyrus II—and by others to date to the period between 535 and 515 B.C.—the time when, at the invitation of Cyrus, the Jews were returning from exile. The advocates of both the prophetic and historical schools agree that the "Second Isaiah" sets forth a proposal for King Cyrus, predicting that he will, among other things, judge those who had treated Israel harshly. But historians say that he didn't do anything like that; Cyrus was bland with the conquered Babylonians, too. Rabbis therefore view Isaiah 40–66 as a list of feats that the Messiah has yet to perform, while Christian ministers have argued that Jesus did—or someday will—fulfill these prophecies. Isaiah 40–66 stands at the center of the divide that parts Christians and Jews.

Vernon Howell's interpretations of the "Second Isaiah" were not radically different from those of Cyrus Teed. Like Teed, Howell claimed that in fulfillment of Isaiah 45:1–3, God had given him the name and mission of Cyrus. He predicted, as Teed had, that he would "not fail nor be discouraged, till he have set judgement in the earth" (Isa 42:4), that he would "raise up the tribes of Jacob, and . . . restore the preserved of Israel" (Isa 49:6), and that nations and kingdoms that refused to recognize his sovereignty "shall be utterly wasted" (Isa 60:12).

All of this wasn't going to happen, of course, without setbacks. Isaiah 53 warned that the Messiah would, before his triumph, be "despised and rejected of men" and "wounded for our transgressions . . . bruised for our iniquities . . . brought as a lamb to the slaughter . . . and taken from prison and from judgment." The latter, Teed's followers had said, had been fulfilled when their leader was bludgeoned, but released, by a Florida sheriff. Howell's followers pointed to the dismissal of the charges filed against him in the 1987 Roden assault. Isaiah, in predicting these contretemps, also provided Vernon Howell with two credentials that Christians had never claimed for the historical Jesus, and to which Teed never paid much mind. The Writ said (Isa 53:10), "he shall see his seed." Jewish commentators had always interpreted that phrase as Vernon Howell did, as meaning that the Messiah would father offspring. Christians had spiritualized it, saying that the church was Jesus' "seed."

The Writ also said (Isa 66:15–16), "For, behold, the Lord will come with fire, and with his chariots like a whirlwind, to render his anger with fury, and his rebuke with flames of fire. For by fire and by his sword will the Lord plead with all flesh: and the slain of the Lord shall be many."

The implication was that the Messiah was to be both a lover and a fighter.

To advance his novel claims, Howell and his closest associates developed an urgent sales message. It was especially suited to the ears of SDAers, accustomed as they were to believing that God had commissioned prophets in the years since Jesus died. ". . . We might believe the message of Noah, right?" he'd say. "But in the days of Noah, no one believed it. They perished because of unbelief.

"Now we may believe the message of Moses," Howell would continue, "but the message of Moses is over. Those in his day didn't believe it. But you see, now we may believe the message of Christ, 2,000 years ago, but of course, when it was being given, nobody believed it. . . . Everybody believes in Jesus today, just like everyone believed in Moses in Christ's day." Then he'd usually add a remark for the guilt-driven, like, "When you have a dead prophet, you have a dead voice. . . . You have someone that's not even here to get on your back and tell you you'd better shape up."

Having shown his listener that only an elite recognizes and obeys a holy man during his lifetime, Howell would throw out his invitation to join the vanguard: "Now, today, we've got one final revelation"— naturally, Howell's own. His appeal gave life to stale religion by styling Christianity not as the study of the deeds of dead white men, but as a present-day challenge: it gave the believer a chance to improve upon old-time religion.

Chapter 12

THE SEVEN SEALS

"You can't believe in what you don't understand."
—David Koresh

Howell's "one final revelation" was his interpretation of the Seven
Seals of Revelation, by which he proved, to his followers' satisfaction,
that he was another, or third, Christ, a mortal embodying the spirit of
God. His explanation of the Seals is the key to explaining both his hold
on his followers, and why they behaved as they did when government
troops assaulted them. So critical are the Seals to any account of Mt.
Carmel's last days, and so densely poetic is Revelation's text, that it
deserves careful scrutiny.

"Revelation is the book in the New Testament," warns a popular
Protestant reference, "that modern Western readers find the most foreign. Ancient Jewish and Christian apocalyptic literature is highly symbolic; often the symbolism is bizarre."

The book opens by saying (1:1), "The Revelation of Jesus Christ,
which God gave unto him, to shew unto his servants things which must
shortly come to pass; and he sent and signified it by his angel unto his
servant John."

Most Christians assume that the "John" who authored the book is
the same John who was an apostle of Jesus, and Koresh's followers

adopted this faith. But Bible historians disagree. "No internal evidence suggests any connection between the author and an apostle of the same name," the reference books say, and indeed, the tendency is to regard Revelation as a coded, historical commentary, probably written by a Jewish convert, on affairs of the Roman Empire between A.D. 70 and the end of the first century. Catholic theologians have in modern centuries regarded the book as commentary; only among Protestants is it taken as prophetic.

In Protestantism's fundamentalist wing, however, Revelation is perhaps the most powerful book in the Bible. For example, Southern Baptist ayatollah W. A. Criswell, the Godfather of today's Christian Right, argues that "No other book in the Bible has such circumference and height and depth. . . . It describes the great consummation of the age, and we are in that plan and that program and that unfolding now. . . . It is a part of our life and ultimately a part of our destiny. . . . It is not something far off; the time is at hand." "In the Revelation all the books of the Bible meet and end," Ellen White had declared. (AA 585) "All the books of the Bible begin and end in Revelation," echoed Howell.

Revelation's author says (1:9) that he was on the island of Patmos, in the Aegean Sea, as an exile or religious prisoner one "Lord's Day" when he was taken up to heaven in a vision. The significant text leading to the Seals reads:

> Rev 4:2 And immediately I was in the spirit; and, behold, a throne was set in heaven, and one sat on the throne.
>
> 5:1 And I saw in the right hand of him that sat on the throne a book written within and on the backside, sealed with seven seals.
>
> 5:2 And I saw a strong angel proclaiming with a loud voice, Who is worthy to open the book, and to loose the seals thereof?
>
> 5:3 And no man in heaven, nor in earth, neither under the earth, was able to open the book, neither to look thereon.
>
> 5:4 And I wept much, because no man was found worthy to open and to read the book, neither to look thereon.

103

5:5 And one of the elders saith unto me, Weep not: behold, the Lion of the tribe of Judah, the Root of David, hath prevailed to open the book, and to loose the seals thereof.

5:6 And I beheld, and, lo, in the midst of the throne . . . stood a Lamb as it had been slain, having seven horns and seven eyes. . . .

5:7 And he came and took the book out of the right hand of him that sat upon the throne.

* * *

6:1 And I saw when the Lamb opened one of the seals, and I heard, as it were the noise of thunder, one of the four beasts saying, Come and see.

6:2 And I saw, and behold a white horse: and he that sat on him had a bow; and a crown was given unto him: and he went forth conquering, and to conquer.

6:3 And when he had opened the second seal, I heard the second beast say, Come and see.

6:4 And there went out another horse that was red: and power was given to him that sat thereon to take peace from the earth, and that they should kill one another; and there was given unto him a great sword.

The text goes on to describe the opening of five more Seals, the sounding of seven thunders, war with the saints, the fiery lake, the number 666, and almost everything else that popular culture and serious students of the Bible associate with the End Time, the Apocalypse, the Second Coming, the Millennium.

David Koresh was far from the first believer to wrestle with the meaning of Revelation's Seals. Among his predecessors was the father of calculus and physics, Sir Isaac Newton. The great scientist, however, concurred with the Bible scholars of his day in regarding the first Four Seals as relating "only to the civil affairs of the heathen Roman empire," though he took the last three as prophetic statements.

Cyrus Teed danced with the Seals, but wouldn't take them home. He once declared that "I have come to open the Seven Seals," and after his death, his followers published works in their newspaper, *The Flaming*

Sword, in which the alchemist made a stab at interpreting Revelation. Working, as seers usually do, from the preconceptions of his native culture, Teed said that the First Seal's white horse stands for chastity, white being the color of "purity." He also implied that he was the rider described in the Seal, and said that his doctrine was the bow. But Teed backed away from making the Seals the linchpin of his doctrine, and never advanced beyond a brief analysis of the first of them.

It's no wonder. So inscrutable are the Seals that in 1937, believers asked even American psychic Edgar Cayce to unravel them. The backwoods oracle laid out a table of symbology in which "him that sat upon the throne" is the "Overself, Superconscious Mind," the book is the body, the Seals are "the endocrine system in normal closed state," and the Lamb "consciousness, perfected through experience in matter." Teed would have savored Cayce's scientific bent. According to Cayce's followers, the white horse of the First Seal represents not chastity but the gonads, and the red horse of the Second Seal the adrenal gland. "John perceives the energies of the gonads as this center is opened by the forces of regeneration within his own body," Cayce explained. "The intelligence of the gonads bids him 'Come and see.' "

Howell's Adventist predecessors had tried to explain the Seals, too. Like almost all other Christian commentators, they saw the sealed book as the Lamb's Book of Life, a historically comprehensive record of human behavior. "In the book of God's providence, the volume of life, we are each given a page. That page contains every particular of our history," Sister White had written. (DA 313) "The angels of God are walking up and down the streets . . . marking the deeds of men." (7 BC 987)

"The book sealed with seven seals, in the right hand of God the Great Judge, must contain the names of those whose sins are to be blotted out," Houteff opined. (2 SR 192) Beyond upholding White, he extended her foray into the Seals. "Plain it is," Houteff said, "that the Throne of Judgement, the white horse, the rider, and his crown, figuratively identify Adam, God's created king, and his kingdom. And if the only thing which he was commanded to conquer was the earth, by replenishing it and subduing it, then what else in the field of symbolism can the 'bow,' the instrument to conquer with, logically represent but Eve?" (15 T 39)

105

Vernon Howell regarded his predecessor's interpretations as simplistic. The Seven Seals were for him nothing to be passed off in a couple of pages or phrases of routine commentary, both for theological and strategic reasons. He and his more adept followers approached the Seals with great wariness and caution—like men carrying traps.

Ordinarily, newcomers were given only the doctrine of the First Seal, complex enough in itself. If they understood and accepted that much of the doctrine, they were urged to continue in a course of study involving the rest of the Seals, though the content of the latter ones was never entirely clear: The first Four Seals had been opened not only in teaching but in life, the doctrine held. But the events predicted in Seals Six and Seven, Mt. Carmel's surviving believers say—an earthquake, stars falling from the skies, the return of the Lamb—have not yet been fulfilled.

Koresh's first move in explaining the Seals was ordinarily to point to Revelation's opening phrase, "The Revelation of Jesus Christ." For centuries, commentators have interpreted those words as synonymous with "A Revelation *by* or *from* Jesus Christ," saying that it was through Jesus' power that John was shown Revelation's contents. Koresh battled for the literal meaning of the words: as Jesus had revealed the Truth of God the Father, he said, somebody else—the Lamb—was to reveal the Truth *of* God the Son. He read Revelation as a message concerning Christ, one whose delivery would require a "Christ's Christ," much as God the Father had required a Jesus two thousand years ago.

Howell and his evangelizers soon discovered that most Christians, and even most priests and ministers, were unable to locate the Seven Seals in the Bible. Those who did know where to find the text usually regarded it as inscrutable. The clergy's puzzlement gave Koresh and crew an opening: "If it's a mystery to you, that means that you're an imposter, you're not the servant of God," Steve Schneider would say. "Clearly the book says that this is a Revelation of Christ, given to Him to show to His servants."

If the Seals were given to the servants of God, and you didn't understand them, the message implied, you weren't really a servant. But one could want to serve God, without really being able, Koresh and his lieutenants would say. One became able, became a servant of God, by learning the Seals. "Learning a lesson is the whole key to redemption. True religion is education," Howell proclaimed. And then he'd launch into a critique of established churches, saying, "God is a spirit, he is a truth, and he is a light, and he's got a Word and he's got something to say and we're to know what it is. . . . Instead of having a big, old, nice, fancy, expensive building, we're supposed to have heads full of knowledge."

If the minister or believer whom Howell and his evangelizers addressed was already familiar with the Seals, and tried to explain them, as Houteff and others had done, the Mt. Carmel missionaries countered with a new tack. According to the text, only the Lamb of God can decode the Seals; anyone else who tried was either ignorant—or an imposter. And since the Seals were seen at Mt. Carmel as a key to the rest of the Bible, not only was the Lamb the only figure capable of interpreting them, he was also the only trustworthy interpreter of the entire Bible. Koresh and his lieutenants were laying an exclusive claim to Christianity.

Having disarmed, deflated, or dazed the hearer, Howell and his crew would launch into their second lesson to acolytes, contempt for the traditional rendering of Revelation's book as the Lamb's Book of Life. The very notion was juvenile, Howell said. "I mean, this is not like Santa Claus checking his list," he quipped. Instead, the book in the Lamb's hand was the Bible, whose meanings had been "sealed" in mystery since it was written.

In a 1994 treatise, SDA theological school graduate Livingstone Fagan, a diminutive, intense Afro-Brit, and the best living exponent of Koresh's teachings, says quite plainly: ". . . The sealed book in heaven, with all its symbolic codes written in a language heaven understands, is in fact the scriptures here on earth. . . . Naturally, someone was to emerge in the earth to open the book and reveal its meanings."

That messenger, to which a dozen scriptures alluded, aides like Steven Schneider would say, was not to be a figure like Jesus. "All of these places talk about a man in the last days that's a sinner. He can do one thing, open up the words of the book, open up the Seven Seals. Can't do any miracles, doesn't raise the dead, heal the sick, isn't a psychic, but . . . if people have questions about life and death, eternal life, no matter what the question is, he will show it in context from the book."

According to Fagan, it was Johann Gutenberg who put an end to the

Age of Miracles. "Miracles were performed," Fagan says, "in the time when most people couldn't read, and didn't have access to the Law. Miracles were a way to reach them. But today, we have the Bible, and almost everybody can read."

Miracles couldn't prove Christhood, Howell and his followers said. In support of the contention, they pointed, first of all, to the traditional definition of Christ in John 1:1: "In the beginning was the Word, and the Word was with God, and the Word was God." This scripture, which commentators have termed "the locus classicus of the Christine doctrine," is probably the densest sentence in the New Testament. But it says nothing about miracles. Instead, it indicates that the figure we know as Jesus was the Word of God—not because he was Jesus, who did not exist "In the beginning," but because he was Christ, Howell would explain. Christ was the incarnation of the Word of God, in Howell's doctrine, as in that of all other Christians: the difference was just that Howell, like Teed, believed in the possibility of more than one Christ.

The voice of God had spoken to Moses (Exod 3) from a burning bush, Mt. Carmel's theologians pointed out. Wasn't that bush also Christ, also the Word? In their review of the Bible, Howell and his researchers found two seemingly human instances of Christ, in addition to the lower forms of life. The first of them was the mysterious character mentioned twice in the Old Testament as Melchizedek, and nine times in the New Testament's Book of Hebrews as Melchisedec. An ancient and revered priest, Hebrews (7:3) said that he was "without father, without mother, without descent, having neither beginning of days, nor end of life, but made like unto the Son of God. . . ." Howell and his followers read this passage to mean that Melchizedek was of divine parentage, the child of God the Father and the feminine Holy Spirit.

Jesus of Nazareth had been next in the divine birth order. As the Son of God the Father, he had no paternal lineage, in worldly terms, anyway. The third Christ that the earth had known was Vernon Howell, who had both a very worldly father and mother. The picture that this genealogy drew was one of devolving lineage, each Christ in his turn more mortal, more human. That scheme fit squarely into Ellen White's devolutionary account of human history, and it possessed the honesty to confess that the present-day prophet was of inferior clay.

108

Howell's evangelizers could expound other doctrines, but the preacher usually reserved the opening of the Seals for himself. He'd start by pointing his hearer to the text, to the man on the white horse, carrying a bow, wearing a crown. And then he'd call up the text of Psalms 45, which both he and Bible historians regarded as prophetic: "Ancient rabbinical and early church writers consistently recognized here an announcement of the messianic king," a common Protestant commentary notes.

During the fifty-one-day siege at Mt. Carmel, Koresh produced a written guide to the First Seal. But his tract is more nearly presumptive than explicative; most readers can make neither heads nor tails of it. The clearest explanation of the Seals, and a fair facsimile of the interrogatory style in which Koresh delivered the lecture himself, comes from an unpublished manuscript by disciple Livingstone Fagan. It opens by citing Psalms 45, the key to Koresh's understanding of the First Seal.

". . . Our introduction to . . . Psalms 45 . . . begins . . . with the first seal," Fagan writes. "Consider verse 1, very carefully:

'My heart is inditing a good matter: I speak of the things which I have made touching the king: my tongue is the pen of a ready writer.'

"Here the questions arise," Fagan says, "whose heart is this, inditing a good matter, and what is the matter being indited? Whoever this person is, the matter he's inditing has something to do with a king. . . . 'My tongue is the pen of a ready writer.' What does that mean? Could it be he has written the matter concerning the King? Perhaps in a book, what book? . . . Maybe the one inditing the good matter . . . might just be God! It could be He sits on a throne with a book in His right hand."

Koresh, in presenting the Seals in this style, was careful not to preach. It was a shrewd psychological move. He presented mere propositions to his hearers, interpretations that they could accept or reject, depending upon not their morality, but their intellect and preparation. The believer had to decide, for example, whether the king mentioned in the scripture was, or was not, Jesus Christ, another Christ, or a non-Christ; it was all a great exegetic problem, which only the deeply enlightened could accomplish.

Fagan continues, again from Psalms 45:

> In Verse 4, the maker has more to say concerning this king:
>
> "And in thy majesty ride prosperously because of truth and meekness and righteousness; and thy right hand shall teach terrible things."
>
> Wait a moment! . . . Ride a what? A motorbike! Maybe it's a horse. Maybe it's a white horse, a red one, a black one and a pale one. What do you think? . . . Why does his right hand teach him terrible things? What's in his right hand? Could it be a book! Maybe it's those arrows he shoots in the heart of his enemies in verse 5. But how can he shoot arrows without a bow? Must be the one he has in Rev. 6:2. Note verse 5.
>
> "Thine arrows are sharp in the heart of the king's enemies; whereby the people fall under thee."
>
> What has [sic] these arrows got to do with Psalms 127:3–5?
>
> "Lo, children are an heritage of the Lord: and among the fruit of the womb is his reward.
>
> "As arrows are in the hand of a mighty man, so are the children of the youth.
>
> "Happy is the man that hath his quiver full of them; they shall not be ashamed, but they shall speak with the enemies in the gate."

". . . The King is to be married, and his children reign as princes throughout the earth," Fagan concludes.

The implications of Howell's interpretation of the First Seal were breathtaking, though his modification of the doctrine he inherited was relatively minor. Howell adopted Houteff's scheme, in which the bow was Eve, and he deduced that the arrows would be children. His chief alteration of the doctrine was to dismount Houteff's Adam, taking the reins himself. He stays mounted through various changes of horses, as all Seven Seals open. As Koresh explained it, the "great sword" carried by the rider of the red horse in the Second Seal is, in the context of contemporary life, a rifle. Given this line of interpretation, Koresh was authorized to "take peace from the earth" by the Second Seal, and by the Fourth Seal, to "kill with the sword."

Chapter 13

WINNING IN THE BEDROOM

"... In Christ, though we might keep the laws of God, the laws of men may condemn us."
—Vernon Howell

According to his reading of the Bible, Revelation and the "Second Isaiah" provided Vernon Howell with an imperative for fathering many children, by various females, including virgins. And this command, as Howell would have called it, was given him without the caveat of an age of consent. The writers of the Bible regarded females of child-bearing age as appropriate mothers: God, not legislatures, established the age of consent, by natural or developmental means. Like most devout Christians, Vernon Howell and his followers believed that the laws set forth by God are of greater consequence than those made by earthly powers.

Like Adam, too, the Waco Messiah believed that his conquest of the world would come through replenishing it. "... Man's power comes through his mind and his ability to enforce his mind by the numbers of his procreation . . . if you don't win in the bedroom, son, you're not going to win on the battlefield," the new Messiah said. Howell, who had been "winning" in the bedroom since he was eighteen, continued his streak at Mt. Carmel. Before he died, he would father seventeen children, two by underage mothers who were not his wives, and others by adult women who were already wed.

"Winning in the bedroom" was the most radical, and costliest doctrine ever preached at Mt. Carmel. It caused grief among people who would outlive Koresh—Stan Sylvia, for example. Sylvia, despite a reputation for challenging Howell, had been a loyal follower at Palestine and Mt. Carmel. But Sylvia's devotion tried him as few men have been tried since Job's day.

His wife, his daughter, and his best friend, Floyd Houtman, all died in the April 19 blaze; he learned of their deaths from television. At the time, Stan was living with other followers in California, in what some people took to be an exile. At Mt. Carmel, Lorraine Sylvia had borne to Stan a son, Joshua, then seven—who left Mt. Carmel during the siege—and had also given birth to another child, Hollywood, two years old when she died in the blaze. Hollywood's father, the scuttlebutt had said, was David Koresh. The story tested Stan's loyalty, and he refused to accept it, either in theology or as fact. In the months that followed the Mt. Carmel fire, a videotape and DNA tests would confirm Koresh's paternity. Sylvia isolated himself from other survivors, they suspected, to "leave the message." But in the end, he didn't. In 1995, after regaining custody of Joshua, he returned to the fold, though he still won't talk much about Hollywood. "I'm not interested in who was screwing who," he snaps. "I'm interested in who killed who, and the FBI killed my wife and children. If you're interested in who screwed who, turn on the soap operas."

Koresh's sexual practices were not only a stumbling block to preserving the flock, they impeded its extension as well. Shannon Bright, a drummer with a Waco rock band, admitted to the *Tribune* that he might have been recruited by Koresh, had the issue of sex not stood in the way. "What David showed me made more sense than anything that anyone has ever shown me in my life," he said. ". . . Anything you wanted to ask David, you could, even why the leaves fall off the trees. He could take you to the Bible and show you why. . . . The way I see it, if he is who he says he is, he wasn't doing anything wrong. He was just telling the truth. If he's not, he's stupid if he thinks he's going to take my girlfriend and I'm not going to do anything about it." Rather than take that risk, Bright backed away from the group.

The doctrinal basis of the seed scattering that Koresh said was his duty was both far-reaching and complex. It started when he quit defining marriage as the civil courts of Waco, ten miles away, defined it. One of Howell's evolving definitions was drawn from Deuteronomy 22:28–29, "If a man find a damsel that is a virgin, which is not betrothed, and lay hold on her, and lie with her, and they be found; Then . . . she shall be his wife; because he hath humbled her, he may not put her away all his days." "Vernon went on to state," Marc Breault recalls, "that God's plan"—though it could be construed as condoning polygamy—"was much more responsible than the rampant single-mother policy of today. He believed that if society followed God's plan, men would be forced to take responsibility for their offspring regardless of their legitimacy."

By this Writ, Vernon Howell was married to his first love, and she to him. But Howell was also married, in this biblical sense, to Rachel Jones, and later, to other women. Because he believed in the doctrine, Vernon Howell, as an adult, even urged his father, whom he had tracked down in Houston during the mid-eighties, to reunite with Bonnie Haldeman. She wasn't interested in the prospect.

Spiritual wedding vows were exchanged, Howell taught, whenever attractions developed. "He said that if you so much as go up and kiss a girl, you're married," Clive Doyle recalls. By these terms, some people were married to hundreds, and almost everyone was married to a score of folks. Beyond sexual attraction lay the marriage of Christ and the church, according to which, in almost all Christian traditions, all believers, regardless of sex, are "brides of Christ." Because these doctrines yield multiple definitions of marriage, when questioned by reporters, G-Men, and child welfare investigators, Howell was able to deny that he was married to anybody but Rachel, his wife under the doctrine of civil law, and/or to claim marriage to others whose first sexual experience had been with him, and/or to invoke the Bride of Christ tenet, saying, "I'm married to the whole world." His inquisitors were thoroughly confused.

113

Beginning in 1989, Howell/Koresh taught that his followers—males, anyway—were to observe celibacy. It wasn't a new idea; the Catholic priesthood has sworn by it for years. The Writ says: "Whosoever is born of God doth not commit sin; for his seed remaineth in him. . . ." (I John 3:9). Even most Protestant examiners of the Writ conclude that celibacy, if not required of the pious, is nevertheless the ideal: ". . . The NT teaches the value of celibacy. John the Baptizer, Paul, and Jesus himself might be cited as examples of celibates," a popular Protestant commentary says.

"Mt. Carmel was like a monastery," Livingstone Fagan declares. The regime that prevailed after 1989 was an inverted Catholicism, in which the rank and file were expected to observe celibacy, but Koresh, the analog Pope, was expected to scatter his seed; females departed from celibacy only to serve his purpose. The number of female partners Howell might take was seemingly unlimited. After all, did not the scriptures authorize for the Messiah "threescore queens, and fourscore concubines, and virgins without number"? (Song of S 6:8)

Fagan pictures sexual abstinence as a test of the believer's aloofness from worldly values, including romantic love. "It is certainly a test to have God take your wife or husband away through death," he observes. "But does this thoroughly prove the ideal . . . of loving God above your spouse? . . . Is it not a more piercing test were God to take your spouse whom you deeply love, and while yet still alive, have him or her enter the bedchamber of another?"

He also argues that the celibacy of Koresh's followers had biological justifications. According to their belief, mankind's devolution had not been merely moral or spiritual, as Ellen White had tended to picture it, but had been physiological as well. ". . . Before the Fall, Adam was of God's DNA," Fagan writes. "Since that time there has been a gradual reshaping of that—mutations—as mankind has degenerated into sin. This has drawn us away both in mind and body from that of Adam and God. In our present form, we are mutants. . . . The 'cease ye from man' truth of Isa 2:22, a continuation of Isa 1:2,4, seen in the light of the Judgment of Rev. 4ff, was brought in to put an end to DNA degeneration. This is among the reasons for our temporary celibacy."

Other disciples invoke what might be called the doctrine of Edenic twins. The details are obscure, and involve an expansion of the Judeo-Christian myth of origin—the basic tale of the biblical religions. The expansion has to do with the fundamentals of human reproduction, and with where Adam and Eve's sons, Cain and Abel, got their wives.

"You see, in the Bible, God created Adam and Eve almost as what we'd say today were twins," Clive Doyle explains. "It says in the Bible [Gen 5:2] that 'he called *their* name Adam.' The two of them had only one name. It was Adam, the man, who gave Eve a name to herself [Gen 3:20], and began to look at her differently, kind of setting her apart." In those days, Doyle says, human beings were not born singly. "Why do you think a woman has two breasts?" he asks, posing a rhetorical question that's a favorite among Koresh's advanced followers. "The females of other animals, which have multiple births, have multiple teats, and women have two breasts because they were intended to bear twins," Doyle contends.

In the days of Adam, everybody was united with his or her twin in a marriage that was profound and conflict-free, because one's mate was a copy of oneself. Cain and Abel were wed to their twins, Doyle argues. "When Cain killed Abel, as the Bible says he did, "that's when modern marriage began. Cain took Abel's wife."

The upshot of this interpretation was that in the contemporary world, people are estranged in a most heart-rending way: each of us goes through life without our intended spouse, who is no longer born. In another world, in heaven, or after the Kingdom of Christ is established on earth—Mt. Carmel's faithful believe—everyone will be wed as God intended, to a twin of the opposite sex. Meanwhile, marital harmony is impossible, and since it's practically a form of adultery, the most sagacious and sacred course is to avoid it.

Key to all of the sexual doctrines taught at Mt. Carmel, indeed, to all of the doctrines taught there, was the idea that God does not have to present Himself in a way that man likes, wants, or understands. Nor does He have to order what men like, want, or understand. The believer's duty is to accept God and His commandments on God's terms, not ours.

By this logic, David Koresh did not have to forgo copulation, nor were his wife and his concubines expected to observe abstinence. They had to do what God willed. Jesus, when asked why He broke the Law, answered that "in this place is one greater than the temple" (Matt 12:6)—and that same view justified Koresh's actions at Mt. Carmel.

Though the argument is somewhat the religious equivalent of the proverbial "refuge of scoundrels," the residents of Mt. Carmel, like thousands of Old Testament Hebrews, believed that once a person is a bona fide mouthpiece for God, he may break the Law as God instructs. "The Book teaches us that Isaiah married two prostitutes, and if he came up to you, with these whores hanging on his arms, and said he had a message from God, would you listen to him?" Paul Fatta asked reporters from the *New York Times*. The lesson the residents of Mt. Carmel drew, Fatta says, was, "Do not judge a person by his actions, but by the message that he has."

Koresh's followers, even—or especially—his dozen concubines, accepted these doctrines, though they rarely understood them fully, and indeed, couldn't have. As Stan Sylvia puts it, "Ezekiel was told by God to mix dung in a cake, human dung. He complained, and God let him mix in cow dung instead. That story is in the Bible to tell us that there would always be error in the message, and it's been there ever since." At Mt. Carmel, even living with a doctrine that was mystifying and potentially erroneous was part of the game.

The Law, or the interpretation of it, had traditionally been stricter at the encampment than among ultra-Orthodox Jews and the followers of Ellen White. "The Beast says that it's alright to eat a Snickers candy bar. God says it's not," Koresh had preached in 1987.

But at Mt. Carmel the Law was under review, not merely in regards to sex. Koresh reintroduced beef and poultry to the fare at the encampment, explaining that when its inhabitants went to Mt. Zion as a sort of welcoming committee for the Messiah, the Hebrew faithful, in accord with ancient tradition, would bring them animal sacrifices. In homage to that same tradition, he said, his followers would have to eat the sacrifices. The change was not popular among Mt. Carmel's majority. At least one resident vomited the first time she ingested animal flesh, and others turned their heads whenever meat was served.

Koresh also lifted the ban on alcohol, citing a dozen scriptures that urged its use in moderation. Though most residents continued to es-

116

chew all brews, he and other members of the band fueled their practice sessions with beer. When Koresh began to puff on Marlboro Lights, however, Victorine Hollingsworth asked the Messiah to justify himself. He pointed to Psalm 18's description of God: "There went up a smoke out of his nostrils. . . ."

Not all believers accepted explanations like this. But they all tended to believe, as Jaime Castillo still does, that "David didn't like cigarettes. . . . We at Mt. Carmel believed that David had inspiration, but along with that responsibility, David was told by God . . . to do certain things that David himself didn't like or couldn't understand."

The scriptural explanation for Koresh's waywardness harkened back to the tradition of a double sacrifice among ancient Jews, a sacrifice of a lamb whose fleece was unblemished—whom Mt. Carmel's residents identified with Jesus—and of a blemished lamb, or scapegoat, bearer of the sins of the world. In this scheme, Koresh was to take on the sins of the world, so that, as one believer puts it, "when you criticized David for something he did, you were really only criticizing yourself." But, "at the end of the day, it's all very complex, and that's why David finally said, that it can't be understood until the Kingdom," Livingstone Fagan explains.

The Messiah that Koresh envisioned was to be both a lover and a fighter. ". . . Seventy-five percent of the Bible is nothing but about Israel being expert at war," he argued, with characteristic hyperbole. "The Bible is a whole book about nothing but killing."

Koresh, unlike the ministers of sweetness and light, didn't overlook the true cruelty and gore extolled in the Good Book. Indeed, he confronted his followers with it. During the siege of Mt. Carmel, a naive FBI agent asked believer Scott Sonobe, "Would you . . . violate any of the ten commandments?" "Even God does!" was Sonobe's reply. God's law, theologian Fagan says, is "case law," an evolutionary and progressive body of rules, subject to considerations of equity. Like civil law, it is a form of present-day—and situational—truth.

Koresh argued that the Ten Commandments were God's standard of behavior, before which all men, excepting Jesus, had failed, and were destined to fail. It would be cruel, he argued, for God to require an impossible obedience. "No man is to be saved because he's good,"

Koresh preached, "and no man is to be lost because he's bad. Because a person that may be naturally bad may be trying to be good, and a person who has evil thoughts may apparently be good." In Vernon Howell's plan of salvation, humanity gained or lost according to how much "light" or true doctrine it rejected. Those who had never heard of the Bible were entirely blameless before God, regardless of their deeds—and those who had partaken of the Seals were at greatest risk in the oncoming Judgment.

Howell's followers had been armed ever since the shoot-out with George Roden, and they remained vigilant against the return of his thuggish friends. The guns Koresh bought and kept were, however, not the only or even principal weapons in his arsenal. Nor, according to the way he read the Writ, should they have been. "And the remnant were slain with the sword of him that sat upon the horse, which sword proceeded out of his mouth . . . ," says Revelation 19:21, in a recapitulation of the Seals. Since a rider can carry neither a rifle nor a sword in his mouth, Koresh read the scripture as saying that his message was the sword. It was the Bible, the doctrine of the Seven Seals, that the rider would use to assault the world.

Even though by 1993, Mt. Carmel was a virtual armory, its guns were no match for smart missiles and Stealth bombers. On the plane of material life, the conquering Messiah was outgunned, and he knew it. He expected to lose any confrontation with the government, or, if he won, to secure his victory only by supernatural means. ". . . There is 20,000 chariots parked all around this world. . . ," he warned the FBI during the Waco siege. "I'm talking about the chariots that come from heaven, God's chariots . . . I'm talking about my army." When the Merkabah came over the horizon, Koresh would trounce history's best-armed police squad!

Howell/Koresh's picture of himself was mainly just words. It described what he, in flights of wild imagination, wanted to be. His material performance was far more modest, beginning with the question of his first love. For several years, he visited her now and then, to offer her a queenship in his verbal kingdom. But she always turned him down. In time he resigned himself to the reality that his kingdom would not be of this world.

118

"In the flesh, as a human being, he at first thought that God would give her back to him pretty quick," recalls Clive Doyle. "But as time went on, as he saw from the scriptures that he was going to be killed, he began to see that wouldn't be until he came back."

According to Revelation, in the End Time, 144,000 true believers are to be gathered by the Lamb, and after them "a multitude without number." His first love, Vernon came to believe, would certainly be among them. She would be his again, though "not in a personal sense," Doyle points out. Not only did Howell conclude that the young mother would be "his," but legions of other women he admired would join her ranks. One was rock star Madonna, promised to Howell, Doyle says, in a vision. "I think that David prayed over her, that she would not be his any time soon," the faithful disciple recalls. "Whenever a new person came into Mt. Carmel, they always brought a lot of headaches, and Vernon knew that with somebody like Madonna, he was going to have a lot of ironing out to do."

In the theology that Vernon Howell came to espouse after 1985, the Messiah was to be a lover and a fighter; but like Jesus, he would realize his full stature only across the divide of End Time.

Chapter 14

THE GOVERNMENT'S FLYING MACHINES

"Before a standing army can rule the people must be disarmed."
—Noah Webster, 1777

". . . We use the military all the time, as does the FBI, Secret Service and other federal agencies."
—ATF executive Daniel Hartnett

If David Koresh's Bible interpretations were the stuff of fantasy, they met their match in the bold, flying leap that the ATF took at justice on February 28. Both Koresh's procreative activities and the ATF raid required their actors to spring high and long from the texts that justified their pronouncements and deeds. For the ATF, the foundational document analogous to Holy Writ was the United States Constitution and its reams of derivative law, counterparts to the writings of White, Houteff, and the Rodens.

In a 1994 ground-breaking study of the historical background to the Constitution, published by Harvard University Press, Professor Joyce Lee Malcolm of Boston-area Bentley College—certainly no hotbed of redneck mischief—provides evidence that the American legal tradition for untrammeled gun ownership dates back to the Plymouth Colony. In 1623, Plymouth's elders promulgated a measure ordering that "every freeman or other inhabitant of this colony provide for himselfe and each under him able to beare arms a sufficient musket and other serviceable peece for war . . . with what speede may be." Most colonial enactments regarding firearms, Malcolm discovered, dealt with the need for arms, not their ill effects, in part because gun ownership was established as a right in England long before the American Revolution began.

American colonial and Revolutionary leaders, chaffed by the impositions of the British Army, generally took a reluctant view of standing armies. "Armies in time of peace are allowed on all hands to be an evil," James Madison noted. "I am for relying, for internal defence, on our militia solely, till actual invasion," wrote Thomas Jefferson. The preference of most of the American Founding Fathers was for a general, or universal militia, staffed by all able-bodied, free adult male citizens, unselected by authorities, and called to service only in times of emergency. The Fathers were of course aware that in real life, most citizens used their guns for private, not militia purposes. But like the English commentator William Blackstone, they argued that gun ownership was a part of a "natural right of resistance and self preservation."

Revolutionary-era preoccupation with the tyrannical potential of a standing army, and the liberating potential of universal gun ownership, made itself manifest in the Second Amendment, which reads: "A well regulated Militia being necessary to the security of a free State, the right of the people to keep and bear Arms, shall not be infringed."

The leading Constitutional argument for gun control renders the Bill of Rights as authorizing gun ownership by members of police forces, the army, and a "select militia," the National Guard—but not by the citizenry at large. But the framers of the Bill of Rights, Malcolm points out, rejected a proposal that the words "for the common defense" follow "to keep and bear Arms," precisely because they wanted to protect the private use of firearms. If control advocates are right, she says, then the Second Amendment granted gun ownership only to government entities, and not, as its language says, to "the people" as a whole. The Bill also grants freedom of speech and assembly to "the people," and Articles IV, IX, and X grant other rights to "the people"— not merely to those associated with military or police agencies.

"The Second Amendment was meant to accomplish two distinct

goals, each perceived as crucial to the maintenance of liberty," Malcolm states. "First, it was meant to guarantee the individual's right to have arms for self-defense and self-preservation. Such an individual right was the legacy of the English Bill of Rights. . . . These privately owned arms were meant to serve a larger purpose as well . . . when, as Blackstone phrased it, 'the sanctions of society and laws are found insufficient to restrain the violence of oppression,' these private weapons would afford the people the means to vindicate their liberties.

"If the government and people in their wisdom come to the conclusion that . . . such a right does more harm than good," Professor Malcolm cautions, "then amendment is the course that should be followed. . . . To ignore all evidence regarding the meaning and intent of one of those rights included in the Bill of Rights is to create the most dangerous precedent, one whose consequences could . . . endanger the fabric of liberty."

If the findings of Professors Malcolm and other Constitutional scholars are trustworthy, the laws that the ATF sought to enforce at Mt. Carmel on February 28 were unconstitutional. But in an atmosphere in which an American president would, only months afterwards, call for a new wave of gun controls, the ATF was determined to enforce the laws that are now on the books.

The ATF did not act alone. Instead, the agency called upon military forces for support, bringing into play the historically delicate issue of the use of standing armies. As with the gun-control question, legal and historical scholars find that today's superfice of law is a slippery slide of citizen rights.

The statute governing the deployment of American soldiers against the civilian population is the Posse Comitatus Act, adopted by Congress in 1878. In its present form, the law imposes fines and prison terms upon "Whoever . . . willfully uses any part of the Army or the Air Force . . . to execute the laws. . . ." In everyday terms, the act denies the American military the authority to conduct searches and seizures, or to arrest a citizen on criminal charges. DEA agents can riffle our desks, policemen can issue traffic tickets; soldiers can't.

The reasoning behind the law, a federal appeals court found in 1975, is that "It is the nature of their primary mission that military personnel must be trained to operate under circumstances where the protection of constitutional freedoms cannot receive the consideration needed. . . ." It is the duty of soldiers to intimidate, maim, and kill declared enemies of the nation. Since the police are given authority not over national enemies, but over their statutory peers, more restrained behavior is expected of them.

The Posse Comitatus Act was originally drafted to prevent federal troops from supervising elections in the Reconstruction South. Its first apparent violation in modern times came during the fifties and sixties, when National Guard troops were dispatched to guard integrated schools, to guard demonstrators, and to restore order in riotous streets. Military actions like those were justified, the courts said, because ". . . Congress intended to make unlawful the direct active participation of federal military troops in law enforcement activities; Congress did not intend to make unlawful the involvement of federal troops in a passive role in fulfilling law enforcement activities."

Along the way, the Coast Guard was exempted from the provisions of Posse Comitatus, and in 1981, Congress, in a sterling contribution to the nation's longest-running and most popular conflict, the Drug War, authorized the military to participate in interdiction efforts. When victory still didn't come, and in response to the designation of drug trafficking as a national security threat by Defense Secretary Richard Cheney, in 1989 Congress passed new legislation, authorizing military forces to train civilian drug warriors.

In the legal goulash created by such enactments and findings, all that remains clear is that the military may not take an "active" role in civilian law enforcement, except where drug interdiction is involved. Its "passive" role can be quite comprehensive. Military personnel can provide a civilian lawman with a rifle, teach him how to use it, supply him with ammunition, even load his weapon for him. But because of the wishes of the Founding Fathers and the authors of the Posse Comitatus Act, soldiers can't pull the trigger.

Just what the military can and can't do, and when, is of course, subject to interpretation. Governor Ann Richards, titular commander of the Texas National Guard, which, like the Army, was called up to assist the raid, took the position that only drug interdiction could justify the use of military resources. So did congressmen who quizzed the ATF's brass in a post-raid hearing.

The congressmen were, of course, themselves befuddled about the status of the law. "Is my understanding correct," Representative Peter Visclosky (D-Ind) asked the ATF executive whom he was supposed to be interrogating, "that the only nexus or connection to the operation which would allow United States military to participate with a civilian law enforcement agency on such an operation is the assertion that a drug crime has been committed and that there is a drug connection in terms of your operation?"

Dan Hartnett, the ATF's Associate Director for Law Enforcement, or ADLE—his subordinate, the Deputy Associate Director, is known as the DADLE—gave the agency's answer.

"No, that is not correct," the law enforcer said to the lawmaker. "We use the military all the time for law enforcement support. Many of the bureaus do . . . but it has to be with reimbursement.

"The issue is if they are going to provide us support in training . . . we reimburse them at their cost. . . . The military has a law enforcement support plan, which means that you have to reimburse them, unless there is a drug nexus, then they are not reimbursed."

According to ADLE Hartnett, the intent of the Fathers and the Posse Comitatus Congress was not to ban military involvement in civilian police affairs, but to set forth rules governing reimbursement.

In connection with the February 28 raid and the fifty-one-day siege that followed, both the ATF and the FBI called upon military units for various kinds of assistance and equipment, including training sessions conducted by Green Berets, tanks, CS gas, and fixed-wing aircraft. The most striking item, however, involved the loan, with pilots, of the three National Guard helicopters that flew over Mt. Carmel seconds before the onset of hostilities below.

In making the initial request for use of the helicopters, on December 14, 1992, the ATF's Houston office did not mention any "drug nexus." "For the past six months, this investigation targeted persons believed to be involved in the unlawful manufacturing of machineguns and explosive devices. These targets are of a cult/survivalist group," its letter requesting the flying machines said. Four days later, however—just to be safe—the agency's Austin office followed with a similar request, which added that "the individual is suspected of unlawfully being in possession of firearms and possibly narcotics."

After the February 28 raid on Mt. Carmel, when the use of the helicopters became a matter of controversy, deputy director Hartnett hastened to assure Governor Richards that the "drug nexus" was firmly established. In a March 27 letter, he told her, "There are eleven members of the compound that have prior drug involvement, some with arrests for possession and trafficking. Additionally, open court testimony in Michigan in February 1992 documented Koresh's possession of a methamphetamine lab within the compound." When the hubbub reached Congress, in June 1993 hearings before a House subcommittee, Hartnett was equally sanguine about the "drug nexus." "First of all, there was any number of people inside the compound who had trafficking convictions, possession convictions," he told the hearing. "We have information from people inside the compound, of course, who have actually seen the meth lab."

The basis of the ATF's claims went back to 1987–88, to George Roden and his dispute with Vernon Howell over control of the Mt. Carmel property. During his period of waning influence, Roden had rented the family homes on the grounds to non-believers, including two men, Donny Joe Harvey and Roy "Boy" Wells, one of them an ex-convict. Howell's followers alleged that the two were making drugs on the grounds. Upon retaking the property in 1988, they found there either a manual for manufacturing methamphetamines, or a complete lab; memories of the survivors are sketchy, and do not correspond. In an unpublished memoir, follower Catherine Matteson recalls that "When we went in to clean up we found proof that George had allowed people to have an amphetamine lab. . . . When we found this David called the sheriff's department. When they arrived he spread what we had found on the hoods of the cars. He showed them the powder and the other things that had turned up as we cleaned the building. The sheriff wet his finger and touched the powder, touching it to his tongue, and then picked up everything off the hood of the car. They left very hurriedly, never saying a word." Howell then temporarily posted sentries at Mt. Carmel's entrances, to guard against any return by Harvey and Wells.

No one familiar with Howell, before or after his rise as Messiah, associates him with drug use, though he admitted that he'd once smoked marijuana, even confessed that he'd inhaled. He distrusted medicines that came in injectable and even pill form: after he was wounded in the February 28 raid, he wouldn't take so much as an aspirin.

Hartnett's "information from people inside the compound . . . who have actually seen the meth lab" was information from those who had seen the lab—if that's what it was—that Howell turned over to the sheriff's office. The "open court testimony in Michigan in February 1992" that, according to Hartnett, "documented Koresh's possession of a methamphetamine lab" was testimony by Marc Breault about the 1988 incident. Breault today insists that he never tried to link Howell with the drug trade. "There were no drugs of any kind used during my time in the group. I have no reason to believe that drugs were used afterwards . . . ," he says. "Never at any time did I accuse Vernon of . . . drug dealing or usage." The ATF's allegation about the methamphetamine lab was fabricated from the shreds of a misconstrued and bygone incident.

The agency's other claim, that Mt. Carmel was populated with "any number" of drug runners, is equally a product of bad faith. In a supplemental report to the House Appropriations Subcommittee, intended to document the testimony its personnel gave during the June 3 hearings, the ATF listed the specifics behind the charges that it had lobbed. "In November 1988," the document said, "Margaret Lawson was arrested by the U.S. Customs Service in Los Angeles, California, for possession of 4,970 grams of cocaine and failure to declare monetary instruments in excess of $5,000."

Margaret Kiyoko Hayashi Lawson is a diminutive woman of Japanese ancestry, one of the Adventists of the Hawaiian group who came to live at Mt. Carmel during the late 1980s. She was born in 1917, and would have been seventy-one years old at the time of the alleged offense. Lawson says that she came to Mt. Carmel in April 1988 and never left the place, until it—and any records of her prior where-abouts—were razed in its apocalyptic conflagration. The Customs Service says that it would have turned any seizure of some ten pounds of cocaine over to the Los Angeles Police Department for handling, and the LAPD says that if it did process a Margaret Lawson for cocaine possession in November of 1988, she wasn't the same Margaret Lawson.

Additionally, the ATF alleged that resident Kathryn Schroeder had been arrested in 1990 in El Paso for possession of cocaine and marijuana, and that her husband, Michael Schroeder, had been arrested in 1982—six years before he joined the Mt. Carmel group—on similar charges in Miami. Follower Brad Branch, the ATF said, had been arrested for pot possession in 1983 in San Antonio—five years before he came to Mt. Carmel. And Raymond Friesen, it reported, in 1989 "was a passenger in a motor home that was seized at the Port of Entry (POE) at Pembina, North Dakota, by the U.S. Customs Service. Allegations of marijuana smuggling and pornography were made."

In sum, the ATF alleged that five residents at Mt. Carmel—Lawson, Branch, the two Schroeders, and Friesen—had been involved in police incidents in which drugs were suspected, and that four of the five suspects had been arrested for drug possession. But as with Margaret Lawson, the allegations against the others were mainly bunk. The U.S. Customs Service says that it has no record of any detention or arrest of Kathryn or Michael Schroeder, anytime, anyplace. Only Brad Branch had been clearly implicated.

The "eleven members of the compound who have prior drug involvement" cited in Hartnett's letter to Governor Richards were identified by equally specious means. The eleven included the four innocents defamed in the ATF's report to Congress, and four others, cited as former drug users. "In correspondence between former cult member Breault at the ATF, Breault alleges that Oliver Gyarfas, Kevin Whitecliff, Greg Sommers, and Peter Gent all had a history of drug use," the report said, though it admitted that "Breault did not elaborate on a timeframe of drug use." In addition to the four innocent people mentioned earlier, and the four cited by Breault, plus Branch, two other associates of the flock were named: "Convicted narcotics trafficker

Donny Joe Harvey and his associate, Roy Lee Wells, Jr.," the men whom Howell had evicted from Mt. Carmel for hoodiness.

Among the factors that the ATF did not take into account in compiling its misleading report to Congress is that higher arrest-and-usage levels characterize most National Guard and Army barracks, and that Governor Richards—who on the campaign trail styled herself as a recovering addict—was, by the ATF's reckoning, just as guilty of "drug involvement" as the former users named by Breault. But perhaps there was no need to be overly worried. As the Treasury Department pointed out in its investigation of the affair, "there is no formal standard by which the military defines a drug nexus."

Controversy over military involvement in the raid at Mt. Carmel might never have developed had the three helicopters dispatched by the National Guard been used as the ATF says that they were. The helicopters carried more than a dozen ATF troopers and brass, dressed in bulletproof vests, helmets, and other combat gear. These executives planned to supervise the raid from the air—the helicopters were to be what they termed a "command platform"—then take charge on the ground after the dangerous work was done. As a diversion, the arrival of the choppers at Mt. Carmel was timed to occur just seconds before the raiders piled out of cattle trailer rigs below, starting the land assault. "The helicopters arrived at an altitude of approximately 500 feet and a distance of approximately 300 to 500 meters off the backside of the compound . . . they were going to hover there until the raid teams secured the compound," ATF intelligence chief David Troy told the Congress.

But what actually happened, as the agency explained to the public in its 400-page report on the affair, was much different.

> The helicopters approached the rear of the Compound at approximately the same time the trucks pulled along the front, which failed to create the intended diversion. When they were approximately 350 meters from the rear of the Compound, the helicopters were fired upon, forcing them to pull back. . . . Two of the helicopters were forced to land in a field to inspect for damage. . . . The third helicopter, although also struck by gun-

fire, was able to remain airborne. It circled overhead to watch for additional attackers.

During the trial of eleven survivors of the Mt. Carmel events, held in San Antonio in early 1994, two warrant officers assigned to the National Guard helicopters provided details of what had happened to their plan. About 9:30 A.M., the helicopters left the airport near the command center at Texas State Technical College (TSTC), Warrant Officer Doyle Stone, Jr., testified. Believing that they were in danger of arriving too early at Mt. Carmel, the helicopters twice circled over the intersection of U. S. Highway 84 and Texas Highway 31, several miles from Mt. Carmel, he told the court. They then made one pass at their target, only to see that "the agents were already getting out of trucks" below. As the helicopters swooped over Mt. Carmel, somebody fired upon them from its rusting water tower. "Only his head popped out and you couldn't see it below," Stone recalled.

Warrant Officer Jerry Seagraves, whose helicopter carried eight agents and a "video man," testified that when the aircraft came within about 350 meters of Mt. Carmel, their occupants heard sounds like "popcorn" from the ground. Inside their craft, they heard banging noises "like a baseball hitting the side of a car." "We broke right, heard another bump, which was another round, and got out of there," he said. "At no time did I fly over that compound." A video from Seagraves's craft showed a single pass, at high altitude, turning rightward, as he described.

Almost none of the government's report squared with what two disinterested witnesses, John McLemore and Dan Mulloney, said during the same trial—nor with their videotape, introduced into evidence to document their claims. McLemore, a newsman, and Mulloney, a cameraman, both working for a local television station, had been driving along Farm-to-Market Road 2491 that morning, not far from its juncture with EE Ranch Road, about a half mile from Mt. Carmel. The two telenewsmen say that they saw the helicopters make first one, then another pass, not at the faraway intersection of Highways 84 and 31, but directly behind Mt. Carmel, at low altitude. The pair halted their Bronco a few yards from the juncture of 2491 and EE, removed their equipment, and captured the third pass of the aircraft on film: the footage shows a 'copter passing along Mt. Carmel's "north" side, within inches of the building's roof. As the pair finished recording the swoop on film, two cattle trailers loaded with agents passed by, speeding down 2491, then turning onto EE Ranch Road. McLemore and Mulloney tailed the raiders into Mt. Carmel.

McLemore and Mulloney's reports are consistent with the recollections of surviving inhabitants of Mt. Carmel, including those of government witnesses and apostates. Eyewitnesses who had been on the building's "north" and "west" sides tell most, because they had the best view. They claim that the helicopters strafed the complex.

Marjorie Thomas was an attractive, slender Afro-Brit, a practical nurse by trade, whose testimony was introduced by the prosecution during the trial of her co-religionists. On the morning of the 28th, she said, after his confrontation with undercover agent Rodriguez, David Koresh told Thomas and the other women who had gathered in the chapel to return to their quarters. Thomas went to her room in the third-floor loft, and shortly afterward, noticed that two of the other women who lived there were staring intently out of one of the windows, on the building's "north" side. She joined them at the window.

Government prosecutors had called Thomas to testify, but because of her physical condition—during the April 19 fire, she received third-degree burns over some 50 percent of her body—they introduced a videotaped deposition instead. In her statement, given over a period of two days, Thomas reported that "I saw three helicopters approaching. . . . There was one at front and two behind, and the one at the front had very bright lights. I could see a person hanging from the side of the helicopter, because it was that close. . . . As the helicopter drew nearer, I heard a sound. It was a bullet coming—which came through the window and shattered the blinds. We all dived to the floor." While looking out of the window, Thomas told the court, she had not seen any raiders on the ground below.

Victorine Hollingsworth, who is a stout British Afro-Caribbean in her late fifties, went from the chapel to her second-story room. When she heard the noise of the helicopters hovering overhead, she joined other women in the second-floor hallway. The women crouched or lay themselves over Mt. Carmel's children, hoping to protect them from harm. ". . . There was firing above . . . ," she said in a deposition given to Texas Rangers. Kathy Schroeder, the government's key witness, from her room on the front or "west" side of the first floor, didn't see the helicopters, and was not quizzed at trial about collateral observations. But today she declares that after the raid, she inspected "holes in our water containers which I believed could only come from above. I also saw some holes from above because of the angle of the sheetrock around the holes."

The recollections of Catherine Matteson, a survivor who was not brought to trial, place the helicopters in an approximate time frame. Matteson says that she had not attended the meeting with the other women, but had instead gone downstairs in search for a copy of the *Waco Tribune*'s "Sinful Messiah" installment. "I picked up the story and started for my room," she writes in her memoir.

> As I crossed the floor, I noticed as I looked out the two windows and saw two cattle car-trailers coming down the road toward the house. . . . In my room I threw the paper on my bed and started to lay down when I heard the sound of helicopters roar in my ears. They sounded as if they were in the room with me. My room was at the back of the building on the second floor. As I went to the window to my amazement there were three helicopters in formation and facing David's room and firing as they came. As the helicopters came near the building they were between the second and third floor level. . . . As they made a turn toward the front of the building I realized there existed a great possibility of my getting shot, so I hit the floor. When they reached the front of the building, all hell broke loose and everyone at the front of the building started shooting.

Others who were inside confirm that the helicopters opened fire in the area just beyond the cylindrical water tower, some 25 yards "east" of the cafeteria, spraying bullets from its "southern" end, from which the residential tower rose—where Koresh had his bedroom—to its northern end, where three white vinyl tanks sat. The blasts of fire punctured Mt. Carmel's water tanks, and, most of the survivors say, killed three residents, Peter Gent, Peter Hipsman, and Winston Blake.

Matteson's account of the tanks dovetails with the observations of government witness Schroeder. "When the shooting stopped, I went down the hall between the rooms," the septuagenarian Matteson recalls. "Every window was shot out. The glass was all over the rooms and the venetian blinds all hung on one side of the window. I went downstairs and Kathy was filling containers with water. She said, 'Grab anything to hold water. They have shot holes in our water tanks!' So we both worked filling anything that was a clean container until there was nothing we could use."

Another of the arguments made by Mt. Carmel's survivors points to drawings made by children who were sent out of Mt. Carmel after the firefight. Their drawings, sketched with crayons while the children were in the custody of Texas welfare authorities, show bullet holes in Mt. Carmel's roof and helicopters hovering overhead.

The autopsy findings regarding Peter Gent also provide the basis for a claim of aerial firing. Gent and the four others killed on Mt. Carmel's grounds on February 28 were buried by their peers during the siege, and their cadavers, unlike those recovered after the April 19 fire, were found with all limbs intact, and with what coroners called minimal decomposition. Dead men do not tell definitive stories, but they sometimes point toward truths that the living can confirm.

Gent was a twenty-four-year-old Australian whose twin sister, Nicole Little, also lived at Mt. Carmel, and whose father, Bruce, was an apostate member of the group, once again living Down Under. Peter, before he came to Mt. Carmel, had been the family's troubled child, dabbling in drugs, tobacco, drinking, and gang fights. He had cast off his worldly ways under the tutelage of Koresh and the Mt. Carmel work-study regime. For about two weeks before the assault, says survivor Clive Doyle, Gent had been working inside the property's old steel water tower, which had been in disuse for years. Gent had welded supports to its interior walls, erected scaffolding between them at several levels, and connected them with a ladder, under a plan to restore the tower to use, either as a water reservoir or storage bin. From perches on the scaffolding, he was chipping away the encrusted rust inside.

On the morning of February 28, Gent returned to the tower, perhaps armed, and alone: none of his comrades was on hand to witness his fate. At the tower's top was a hatch, which could be raised to peer outside. Gent did look out—or perhaps, shoot out—and was felled. During the San Antonio conspiracy trial of Doyle and eight others, an ATF ground trooper, Lowell Sprague, testified that Gent fired upon the pedestrian raiders, and that, in self-defense, he had dropped the Australian from his roost with a rifle shot. Other agents said that they'd seen Gent's AR-15 fall from the tower, apparently as he dropped inside. Like Sprague, two others claimed credit for dropping Gent.

The story as told by those who lived at Mt. Carmel was different, and more uniform. "And one young man. . . ," David Koresh told the FBI, "had climbed up on top of the water tower. . . . He heard helicopters and he climbed up and stuck his head through the tower. . . . See, he was working in that tower . . . getting it ready, to paint the inside of it to hold water. . . . He was in there and when he heard everything going on outside, he climbed out and looked out the top and they shot him in the head, the helicopter."

The autopsy performed on Gent's body at the Tarrant County examiner's office in Fort Worth (site of all the autopsies done in the case) showed a single bullet wound, "located over the upper chest 53 inches above the heel," and "coming to rest near the right pulmonary hilus 53 inches above the heel." The heel-to-wound measurements indicates a level trajectory for the bullet that took his life. The finding is ostensibly consistent with Gent's death by helicopter fire, but inconsistent with the claim that he was shot from the ground, some four stories below. On the other hand, human bodies are not like buildings. They move. Had Gent been leaning downwards, an ascending bullet might have traveled a level path through his chest.

Peter Hipsman was a twenty-seven-year-old native of upstate New York, known at Mt. Carmel as an entertainer of its children. When he wasn't working or around the building or worshipping, he strummed an acoustic guitar, sang badly, and put his limited talent to best use by imitating Donald Duck and making up ditties for the kids. When the helicopters made their fatal swoop, survivors say that he was either in the area of the two rooms above the chapel, or the fourth-story bedroom where David Koresh slept and Hipsman died. In either case, they say, it was the helicopters that felled him.

Hipsman's autopsy showed four wounds, two of them to the body. One of the bullets that struck him passed on a level keel, between the seventh ribs on his left and right sides—a finding inconsistent with a shot delivered from ground level, but in accord with fire from an airborne source. A second round entered his left arm, on the back side, and exited at a slightly lower position on his front side, again, in consistency with reports of aerial gunfire—provided, of course, that Hipsman was reclining or standing erect at the time that he received his wounds. The autopsy, oddly, also shows that Hipsman was wearing Steve Schneider's underwear.

The "holes from above" which Kathy Schroeder says that she witnessed were in the fourth-floor bedroom where Hipsman died. Those holes were also inspected by defense attorneys Dick DeGuerin and Jack Zimmermann, the latter a Marine Corps Reserve colonel and former combat artillery officer. DeGuerin and Zimmermann entered Mt. Carmel during the federal siege as representatives of two clients who are now dead, Koresh and his confidant Schneider; when their clients died, the attorneys' financial stake in the case died as well. Both men claim to have seen holes indicating an up-to-down trajectory in the bedroom's ceiling. Zimmermann told investigators from the Texas Rangers that "there were clearly exit holes in the ceiling. . . ." "Exit holes," he explained, "meaning that the rounds had to be initiated outside coming in, and there was no question about that. . . . There are only two ways that could happen. You can have a guy standing on the roof shooting in, and it would look just like that, or you can have someone shooting from a helicopter that would look just like that." In similar testimony at the 1994 San Antonio trial, he told the court that the nearly one dozen holes that he had scrutinized in the bedroom had "paper and building material hanging down, pouched in," in the pattern of descending fire.

Steve Schneider told the FBI during the siege that he had visited the wounded Hipsman after the gunfire stopped on February 28. Hipsman stated that his shoulder wound had come first, followed by the bullet that crossed his midsection. Hipsman was in "excruciating pain,"

Schneider said. Perhaps that explains his manner of death: Hipsman also suffered two head wounds, both, according to the coroner's office, fired at close range, one of them in an upward direction. Somebody inside of Mt. Carmel put Peter Hipsman out of his misery.

The Tarrant County autopsy report which probes Winston Blake's remains describes him as "a normally developed, obese black male," and surviving comrades have little to add to that. He was twenty-eight years old, six feet two inches tall, weighing some 190 pounds. His peers called him "Big Boy." Blake had come to Mt. Carmel from Great Britain several years earlier, along with his girlfriend, Beverly Elliot, who perished in the April 19 blaze. In England, he'd been a baker. His room, where fellow residents say his cadaver was found, was on the back, or "east" side of the complex, just down the hallway from the cafeteria. The view from its window was eclipsed by the plastic water tanks just outside, the "water containers" in which Kathy Schroeder says she discerned bullet holes with a descending trajectory. At the moment of his death, two eyewitnesses say, Blake was sitting on the edge of his bunk, eating a piece of French toast. He was not alone; two comrades, one of them a roommate, were in the enclosure with him.

Blake was clad in a black "Beefy-T" knit shirt, bearing the legend: "DAVID KORESH/GOD ROCKS." Because it was cold and Mt. Carmel unheated, he had also wrapped himself in a long-sleeve turtleneck sweater. On top of the turtleneck, he had added a black V-necked sweater, and outside of it, he'd strapped on a black ammunition vest which bore the label, "David Koresh Survival Wear," a part of the gun show inventory. He was also wearing three pair of trousers, the topmost, apparently, a pair of black jogging pants.

A single bullet entered Blake's head, just below the right ear, stopping at a shallow depth inside the skull. Projectile fragments from a .223-caliber, or AR-15 bullet, were recovered from the wound, but told nothing; both the raiders and the defenders utilized AR-15s. But coroners found traces of gunpowder on the surface of the skull and inside Blake's head, an indication that he was shot at close range. The coroner's report, if it is trustworthy, points to Winston Blake's death by friendly fire.

His black clothing and ammunition vest gave him an appearance similar to that of the agents outside, and a passing and panicked resident, spying him from behind, could easily have mistaken him for a raider. The weapons of his comrades inside the room, in the congestion and jostling that prevailed, could have gone off, especially since most of Mt. Carmel's defenders had only perfunctory training. The conspiracy buffs who've studied the case like to point out that a wound caused by a shot from afar can be faked as a near-range wound by firing a blank round into the opening. But if agents of the ATF or FBI tampered with the cadaver, they had to do so by stealth. Winston Blake's body was disinterred, not by federal agents, but by technicians from the Smithsonian Institution and the Fort Worth medical examiner's office. They turned it over, says examiner Rodney Crow, to a Waco funeral home. If there was foul play with Blake's corpse, the conspiracy that enveloped the February 28 raid extends far beyond the bureaucratic limits of federal police forces.

But no thesis can be discarded yet. Winston Blake's body was subject to a second autopsy, less than five months after his death, when it was returned to his family in the North of England. The physician who examined it for the Manchester Police Department came to a conclusion radically different from that reached in Texas. He found no powder burns on Blake's head, and paid special attention to the somewhat jagged shape traced into the victim's skull by the bullet that ultimately stopped within. "I formed the opinion," the British expert wrote in his findings, "that this injury had probably been caused by a destabilized high velocity rifle bullet of relatively low weight. This missile had probably been destabilized so as to cause it to yaw in flight prior to striking the victim. Such a destabilization could have been achieved if the bullet had previously passed through a light screening cover, such as the light-weight material reported to have been used in the construction of the building walls."

When examined on the other side of the Atlantic, Winston Blake's body told a tale, not of a bullet fired by someone close at hand, but of a shot that entered his room from outside.

Chapter 15

DOGS AND DOORS

"We just got off from—out of church and went up to my room, opened the window. All of a sudden these guys came—get out of that trailer and just start shooting. . . . My kids . . . were in . . . the bunk bed. And if you'd see it, it's all full of holes. . . . If they know there were kids and children, how come they just come out of the trailer and shoot?"

—Mt. Carmel resident Floracita Sonobe

During the siege of Mt. Carmel, several vehicles on its parking lot, and a station wagon belonging to the *Waco Tribune-Herald*, parked in front of the undercover house, were flattened by tanks. But two pickup trucks—those that ATF agents had abandoned on the property—survived unscathed.

All of the Mt. Carmel vehicles were taken to the TSTC campus, where they were garaged, then examined by FBI forensic experts. As a part of their job, these technicians stuck dowel rods into bullet holes, a procedure that reveals trajectories. The red-and-white expanded-cab pickup that Special Agent Dan Curtis drove to Mt. Carmel was struck by two bullets whose path, in courtroom testimony, he could not explain. One of the shots entered the pickup's windshield and exited its rear window in a straight pattern, as if it had come from a spot directly in front of the vehicle. The second telling shot entered the pickup's grille, passed through its radiator, and came to rest in the engine compartment, again, in a head-on trajectory.

Curtis had parked his pickup parallel to Mt. Carmel's front door. The compound and its residents were off to his right, 25 yards away. Directly in front of Curtis, at a distance of about 40 yards, was the other cattle trailer that carried raiders, pulled by a white pickup. The raiders from the white pickup's trailer, having arrived, according to plan, a few seconds earlier than the Curtis crew, were already emerging into view when Curtis halted his rig. He quickly bailed out of his pickup, and when questioned later in the courtroom by defense attorney Douglas Tinker, denied knowing anything about the two shots that struck it from the front. But the conclusion drawn by observers at the trial—and some jurors—was that the first shots fired during the ground assault at Mt. Carmel were accidental, and came from the ATF. The observation is important because the human ear is a notoriously poor instrument for pinpointing the origin of sounds, and as the adage indicates, the first shot fired in any war is an act of aggression; the rest are self-defense.

The number of raiders who disembarked at Mt. Carmel has never been authoritatively established, but between seventy-five and ninety people were involved. The man who led the group whose job was to enter the building's front door was Roland Ballesteros, a Houston Special Agent in his thirties. His task on February 28, he has testified, was "to clear the front porch area of any obstruction" for two comrades who would "breach the door with a ram, a tool."

Ballesteros arrived at Mt. Carmel in the Curtis trailer, and was the "third or fourth" agent to dismount from it. Those who exited before him, in the Special Agent's words, were assigned "to address any encounter with the dogs that supposedly were to pose a threat at the front door." A half-dozen dogs, mostly Alaskan Malamutes, lived at Mt. Carmel, the pets of its children. Those assigned to "address" them carried fire extinguishers, whose carbon dioxide foam can repel animals. They were also armed with pistols and shotguns, just in case the CO_2 blasts didn't achieve the desired effect. Five of the dogs were the first fatalities of the ground assault.

In the wake of the raid, Texas Rangers interviewed all those who, according to the information available to them, had participated in the Mt. Carmel debacle. Those interviews were recorded and transcribed. But only some twenty interviews with ATF agents, those who were selected as potential prosecution witnesses, have been made available to defense lawyers and the public. In one of those declassified interviews, held on March 10, 1993—while Mt. Carmel was still under siege—Special Agent Ballesteros told the Rangers that while he was running toward the gate of the chest-high picket fence that enclosed the building's front yard, "I heard gunfire, and I assumed it was our teams assigned to secure any animals." Other agents gave similar reports. John Carpenter, of the ATF's Fort Worth office, who dismounted from the first trailer, told the Rangers that "As soon as I got out or a little bit before, I heard gunfire coming from the front of the house. Um, at this time, I thought that agents were probably killing the dogs." On March 3, Special Agent Claire Rayburn of the ATF's Austin office, who also arrived in the first trailer, told the Rangers that "As the agents were unloading, I heard gunfire. At that point, I believed that they were just taking care of the dogs."

During their exercises at Fort Hood, the raiders had seven times rehearsed their entry. Their plan called for them to burst from the trailers in a run, neutralize the dogs, batter down the building's front door, and arrest Vernon Howell aka David Koresh. In federal practice, there are two kinds of search warrant authorizations, one for "no-knock" or surprise raids, and another in which agents are expected to announce their presence and duty. Though the search warrant issued for the February 28 action did not authorize a "no-knock" raid, in their sessions at Fort Hood, Ballesteros and his team had practiced only a forcible entry.

As Ballesteros raced to the front yard's gate, he testified in a pre-trial hearing, "I observed the front door open, and [a man] whom I recognized as Vernon Howell standing at the front door with a couple of other individuals behind him." Howell, he said, was unarmed, and had one hand placed on each side of the doorway. Without breaking his pace, Ballesteros said, "I instinctively yelled at him, 'Police! Search warrant! Lay down!' " He thereby gave notice to the occupants, as required by the search warrant's terms. At about the same time, a half-dozen other agents were also giving notice with similar shouts.

According to his testimony, Ballesteros made his run with his shotgun tilted toward Koresh, as he'd been taught to do: it's standard procedure in raids of this kind. Another agent had a gun trained on Koresh as well. Special Agent Joseph Patterson, who had dismounted from the cab of the Curtis pickup, spotted Koresh in the doorway and, he told the Rangers, "in a loud commanding voice, uh, I told the man, I stated, 'Police! Search warrant! Get down!' . . . The man turned and looked at me and kind of smiled." (Koresh would later tell the FBI that he was looking over Patterson's shoulder, toward the undercover house; three reporters from the *Waco Tribune* had just pulled up and were standing on its roadway.)

"Uh, and he kept his attention on me but he did not comply with my commands," Patterson said. ". . . There was nothing in his hands, uh, I could not see anything in his waistband. Therefore, in my mind, he was not a threat to the agents which were approaching the door. Uh, I withdrew my service weapon which was a Sig Sauer 9mm semi-automatic pistol . . . and pointed it at the man in an attempt to get him to comply with my demands."

Meanwhile, Special Agent Ballesteros was covering the last 20 yards that lay between him and Koresh. In one ear, the agent had a radio monitor, in the other, a sound-deafening plug. ". . . As I continued to approach him at the front door," Ballesteros said, "he yelled, countered back, and said, 'What's going on?' something to that effect. And again I yelled, 'Search warrant! Lay down!'. . . After I made that second command to him, I arrived closer to the front door and he stepped back and shut the door in front of me. I there landed on top of the porch and tried to open the door that just closed, and in doing so, I could hear and see bullets or something exiting the front door. I assumed, naturally, that they were bullet rounds. And after, I couldn't say, 20, 30, I don't know how many bullets exited, I finally sustained a bullet wound to my left hand." The agent threw himself to the ground beneath the porch, and remained there for the duration of the raid.

The first shots fired, according to Ballesteros and his comrades, may have been aimed at the dogs, but the first shots fired at human beings came from inside Mt. Carmel's front door. The residents, the ATF says, started the ground war.

A somewhat different story was told by the survivors inside. In a February 28 telephone interview with David French of the Cable News Network, David Koresh gave this account: ". . . They came up in the truck, and it had a goose-neck trailer behind it. . . . They came all locked-and-cocked, and . . . I opened the front door as they were running up. Of course, you know, their tactical expertise; they've got their guns aimed and everything. They were in complete combat uniform, and they started hollering, you know. All of them hollered, I didn't know what they were saying."

The preacher would later explain to the FBI that he didn't know what the raiders were shouting because, "you've been to a football game and you hear a roar but you don't hear what anybody's saying, right?"

"They started firing at me," Koresh told CNN, "and so what happened was is that I fell back in the door and the bullets started coming through the door. And so then what happened was that some of the young men and stuff started firing on them. And I was already hollering. I was saying, you know, 'Go away,' and I was hollering, 'Go away, there's women and children here, let's talk.' "

The differing accounts given by raiders and residents concur on one point: That the first shots at human beings were fired through Mt. Carmel's closed front door. It was a double door. Eyewitnesses from both sides of the combat agree, and contemporary photos indicate, that it was the left side of that double door, from an assailant's point of vision, that Koresh held open as the raid began. It was that left door, the only one of the two equipped with a knob, that Koresh slammed shut, and it was that left door through which Ballesteros received his wound.

But David Koresh told the FBI, and his survivors at Mt. Carmel still insist, that the first shots fired through the doors came not through that left-hand door, but through its twin on the right. Those shots were, their version says, fired by a semi-automatic or automatic weapon. ". . . The evidence, from the front door, will clearly show how many bullets and what happened," Steven Schneider warned the FBI. Photos taken during the siege show a half-dozen punctures in the metal skin of the left door, and more than a dozen on the right-hand twin, including a crescent-shaped series, probably the product of a burst from an automatic or semi-automatic weapon. When defense attorneys DeGuerin and Zimmermann inspected the building, they reported that the burst and most of the perforations on the right side of the door were from incoming rounds. "They were all punched in and they were various calibers," DeGuerin told the Texas Rangers. The claim is controversial because ATF agents deny firing any shots through the front doors; their standing orders, they say, are to fire only at clearly identifiable targets.

Mt. Carmel's front doors were in clear view of television cameras during the fifty-one days of the federal siege. Thousands watched on April 19 as an armored vehicle piloted by FBI agents rammed the doors, raised both into the air, then brought them slowly toward the ground. The armored vehicle then backed off, dragging the doors with it, away from the building. About three hours after Mt. Carmel's blaze was extinguished—enough time to dispose of damaging evidence—Texas Rangers took custody of the property from the FBI and ATF. The following day, the Rangers began combing the ruins for evidence. The front door that they found—the left door—was warped, apparently because a vehicle had passed over it. But its paint was still in place, and it showed no smoke damage. The right door wasn't found. In courtroom wrangles during the San Antonio conspiracy trial, Ranger and ATF agents were only able to surmise that somehow, the missing steel door had "melted" during the blaze. Yet other metal items inside—guns, cartridges, tricycles, cans of food, and kitchenware—and some items of glass survived the inferno that destroyed the scene of the crime.

Chapter 16

MYTHS AT THE DOOR

"Christ is a deceiver."
—David Koresh

A three-tiered myth has arisen from the events that happened inside
Mt. Carmel's front doors on February 28. The facts behind the myths
are known only to two men, Jaime Castillo, twenty-four, and Brad
Branch, thirty-four, who were standing at the front door when David
Koresh hailed the raiders. Branch has not given a full account of what
happened at that door. And some of Castillo's recollections contrast
with the facts of record.

The notes of an interview that Castillo granted to Texas Ranger
Gerardo de los Santos just hours after he emerged from the April 19
blaze indicate that David Koresh was wounded while standing at the
front door. "Castillo said that when they got to the front door, Howell
opened the door and yelled out, 'Wait a minute. There's women and
children in here,' " the de los Santos report says. "Then all of a sudden
shots were fired at the front door where he believes Howell was shot."
Other survivors, who were not present at the door, give similar reports,
based on what they were told after the event.

Part One of the Myth of the Door says that David Koresh received his
wounds—or at least one of them—from the blast of gunfire that came
through the front door.

143

Part Two of the myth says that a child was killed at the door. The tale was first told by Koresh while responding to questions asked during an interview on Dallas radio station KRLD on February 28, shortly after the attack. Station executive Charlie Seraphin was on the other end of the line:

SERAPHIN Who, who died?
KORESH Two-year-old baby, my girl.

David French of CNN apparently followed Seraphin's line, recording a second confirmation of the death.

FRENCH Is it true, David, that one of the children, a two-year-old, is dead?
KORESH Yeah, that's true.

On February 28, apparently before he made the claim about the child to KRLD, Koresh told a negotiator by telephone, "You brought a bunch of guys out here and you killed some of my children." A few days later, he told the FBI's negotiators that "You're going to have to take a look at some of the pictures of the little ones that ended up perishing."

Steve Schneider told the FBI that "a child was killed when they came to the door and started shooting." Kathy Schroeder, who would become a witness for the prosecution, taunted the FBI on March 6 with the child's death: "Are they going to get thrown in jail for the people they killed? What about the baby they killed?" But as the Rangers and FBI questioned adults who came out of Mt. Carmel during the siege, and as custody workers interrogated the children, they began to have doubts about the existence of the dead child or children, whom everyone inside Mt. Carmel refused to name.

Part Three of the myth tells the fate of Perry Jones, whom the survivors say was one of the four adults who was standing at the door when the fateful shots came. Jaime Castillo says that "When I approached the front door, David was in between our doorway exchanging words with what later turned out to be the ATF. Perry was right behind him, kind of peeking around David to see who was outside. By the time I got to the front door, I heard David say, 'Wait a minute! We got women and children in here! Let's talk!' Then I heard the first

MYTHS AT THE DOOR

gunshot outside, and a few seconds later I heard Perry yelling, 'David, I've been shot!' . . . I saw him holding his side by his ribs. Apparently, when he was leaving the front door [going] away from it, he got hit again on his leg by his thigh. The last time I saw him . . . I think Clive [Doyle] was trying to help him. . . ."

Almost all of Mt. Carmel's residents report that they heard Jones screaming, "I'm hit! I've been shot." One of them told the FBI that he'd been awakened by the shouts. After hollering and groaning in agony for more than an hour, the survivors say, Perry Jones died. But it apppears that none of these things actually happened, unless the evidence that places these claims in doubt has been falsified.

Kathryn Schroeder, in a formal statement upon which much of the government's conspiracy case against her peers was based, stated: "I was told that David Koresh and Peter Hipsman had both been hit in the tower at the same window." But neither she nor anyone else implicated or credited helicopters in the wounding of Koresh; he was in the foyer area, far from the tower, when the helicopters passed.

Koresh told a version of the tower/window story to defense attorneys DeGuerin and Zimmermann, and it jibed with remarks that the Waco Messiah made to the FBI. In one of his telephone chats with negotiators, he said, ". . . I went to see what was going on . . . I was just walking around seeing what was going on. And when, when I went up to one place . . . you know, I looked out the window. Some rounds came up and that's, that's when they hit me. . . ."

But several days later, Koresh gave a different version to the G-Men. "That agent that shot me," Koresh said, ". . . the only reason why he . . . shot me was because I was going to say something to him, and he wasn't fired upon." According to this account, Koresh was trying to offer peace to the agent—who could not have been within earshot if Koresh was standing on the tower's top floor. The accounts that Koresh gave seemed to discredit both stories: that he was shot at the door or in the residential tower.

As the siege wore on, the tale about the child who was killed at the door dropped out of conversation. In response to March queries from the FBI, Steve Schneider once claimed that he hadn't had time to ask about the details. In early April, the following exchange was recorded:

create

145

SCHNEIDER You people have always wanted to know who was killed and so I, you know, I, I've told you what I know.

NEGOTIATOR Was, was, was—we had some information that maybe one of David's kids was killed.

SCHNEIDER Well, maybe he was revi—maybe the person, if that's so, was revived.

As the lie gave way, on April 14—five days before the consuming fire—Koresh capitulated, after a fashion.

NEGOTIATOR There wasn't a child killed in there?

KORESH No. . . .

NEGOTIATOR . . . I heard that initially that you had lost a two-year-old that was in your arms.

KORESH No, no, no, no. That was never said. . . . Never was that said. That's not on tape or nothing. You'll never find it nowhere.

Perhaps Koresh was disowning the claim that he'd been holding the child in his arms—a detail that he had never supplied to any of the parties who were recording his every word. But today, even his followers concede Koresh was either misinformed—or lying.

In the months following the April 19 fire at Mt. Carmel, some investigators developed a new line of inquiry concerning the phantom child. It was that Koresh and Schneider had at first told the truth, then, for theological reasons or to conceal a sexual indiscretion, had repudiated it. In support of this thesis, the sleuths pointed to coroner's reports which seemed to show the remains of an unidentified child, estimated to be two and a half years old.

Medical examiner Rodney Crow brushes the theory aside. The problem in identifying the dead at Mt. Carmel, he says, is not that his office has more corpses than names, but the reverse. "We were short some corpses," he says. The questionable sets of remains, he points out, have not been identified by sex or race. "They are of small body parts, and could be parts of Bobby Howell"—one of Koresh's children—"because he was very fragmented." If the phantom child was killed on February 28, Crow adds, there's no need to look for its remains among those pulled out of the ashes. "Why wouldn't the infant have been buried," he asks, "with Perry Jones and the others?"

The myth concerning Perry Jones was either built on the tallest tale of them all or reflects unusual acts of bad faith or incompetence by the medical examiners. During the siege, Koresh sidekick Steven Schneider time and again bemoaned Perry's unnecessary suffering. On February 28, he told the FBI that "He got hit in the hand first. He started walking down the corridor. A bullet went right through three walls and nailed him down and down he went." Survivors of the attack uniformly said that Jones was wounded in the stomach, but his second wound they sometimes placed in a hand, an arm, or a leg.

Jones's body was buried beneath the dirt floor of Mt. Carmel's tornado shelter—one of three structures that government agencies and the press would call "the bunker." The corpse was laid to rest alongside those of the other residents who died indoors: Jaydean Wendell, a female; Winston Blake; and Peter Hipsman. Perry Jones was a white male, gray-haired and sixty-four. Coroners were unlikely to mistake him for any of the others. The autopsy on his corpse shows that he suffered a single bullet wound. The shot was fired at pointblank range— into the roof of his mouth. If the coroner's report can be believed, Perry Jones either killed himself or was put out of a faked misery by one of his peers.

Clive Doyle now wishes that he'd taken a second look. "I heard Perry screaming, and I went down the hallway a bit, and then I came back, to move him out the way," he says. "Somebody came by, I think it was Livingston Malcolm, and he tried to help me lift him. When Livingston or whoever it was got hold of his arms, Perry let out a shriek. He was quite hysterical, and making a lot of noise. We eventually managed to hoist him up, and we carried him to a bedroom, laid him down on a bunk.

"He kept on screaming. He was kind of freaking everybody out. He was begging me to go ask if he could end it all. So I went up to David, who said for him to hang in there, that they were trying to work things out with negotiations and that it would be just a little while before they worked it out."

Doyle says that he "grabbed two or three guys who were standing around," posted them with Jones, and went about other business. "I guess about half an hour later," he recalls, "somebody came and told me that Perry was dead. I don't know if he died, or if he killed himself, or

147

if he got one of the guys who were watching him to put him out of his suffering."

During the San Antonio trial, government witness Kathy Schroeder says that resident Neil Vaega, who did not survive the April 19 inferno, delivered the mercy shot to Jones. She was standing near Koresh when Vaega came to ask permission for the killing, she said. About half an hour later, according to Schroeder, Vaega returned to report that he had finished off both Jones and Peter Hipsman. But since Schroeder did not see Jones after the shooting incident at the door, she does not know if he was wounded while standing there.

Clive Doyle believes that Jones was wounded, but even he is not absolutely certain. When he carried Jones to the bedroom, Doyle says, "he was holding his hands on his stomach. A thousand times since, I've asked myself why I didn't move his hands, to look and see what his wounds were, and how bad they were. I thought I saw blood on his shirt."

Jaime Castillo also believes that Jones was wounded. "I don't know that Perry or anyone else put Perry to rest," he says, "but I do know that from what I saw and heard that he was bleeding pretty much because there were bloodstains near the area where Perry was. The whole situation with Perry at the front door is what caused me to react in trying to defend myself and those inside. I saw a sixty-three-year-old man get shot in his own house by what turned out to be the ATF. . . ."

The obvious solution to the controversy surrounding the presumed wounding and death of Perry Jones, an examination of the corpse, is no longer possible. Jones's body, like others recovered at Mt. Carmel, was from April until August of 1993 stored in a cooler at the medical examiner's offices in Fort Worth. During that time, the bodies decomposed beyond usefulness. Maybe the cooler was too crowded, maybe the condenser on its air-conditioning unit was malfunctioning, perhaps its warning light was not working as it should; but in any case, examiner Crow says, the cooler kept the bodies at temperatures in the low forties rather than the mid-thirties, as it was designed to do. By the time the bodies were frozen, in August 1993, Crow says, they were "like soup." As part of their routine work, the Fort Worth coroners make photographs of their corpses, and those photos, Crow points out, should show that Jones's stomach "was as smooth as a baby's." But the photos are not available for inspection by lawyers or the press.

Reports from the Tarrant County medical examiner's office can be accepted at face value only by the credulous. In a brief to challenge the appointment of the examiner's office, a defense attorney pointed out that during the fall of 1991, the Tarrant agency sent a body to a neighboring county for burial—a body that turned out to be, not the corpse of the recipient's kin, but that of an unrelated man. In connection with a 1990 killing, when the office could not provide key photos of a strangulation suspect, its chief examiner testified, "Sometimes pictures don't come out. I don't have control over that." He brushed aside an objection by saying, "We don't take Polaroids in the morgue. They are misleading and they are of no value to us." Yet an underling reported that Polaroid photos are routinely made.

In another, unrelated case, a Dallas attorney, Greg Shamoun, is currently suing the medical examiner on behalf of the survivors of a young gunshot victim, Henry Lee Dobbins. Shamoun's suit alleges that in 1991 the coroner's personnel took Dobbins from Fort Worth's charity hospital and shelved him for ninety minutes in a cooler at the morgue—while he was still breathing!

But if the coroner's report on the corpse of Perry Jones can be believed, the Myth of the Door suggests that Koresh and his closest associates lied about the cause of Jones's death. Like the masterminds of the ATF raid, they believed that telling the truth was sometimes a matter of convenience.

The difference between the Mt. Carmelites and the ATF fabricators was that they could not call upon the interests of national security or public safety as a pretext for their falsifications. They had to devise a biblical rationale, and they did. It was one of their more imaginative works of scriptural craftsmanship.

The doctrine of Christ the Deceiver was expressed in the flag that flew over the Mt. Carmel compound during Koresh's reign there. Its design element was a flying serpent, its wings ablaze. In biblical symbolism, serpents have represented deceit ever since Satan, taking the form of a snake, seduced Eve in the Garden of Eden.

Yet according to Koresh and his cronies, the serpent also represented

149

higher truth, or salvation. To make the point, he cited Numbers 21:8–9 and Isaiah 15:29. The more transparent scripture reads, "And the Lord said unto Moses, Make thee a fiery serpent, and set it upon a pole: and it shall come to pass, that every one that is bitten, when he looketh upon it, shall live. And Moses made a serpent of brass, and put it upon a pole, and it came to pass, that if a serpent had bitten any man, when he beheld the serpent of brass, he lived."

Steven Schneider preached that "Satan was the father of lies, a deceiver. But then Christ comes along as a serpent also, is lifted up on a cross as a serpent. In the book of John, it shows why." The relevant scripture is: "And as Moses lifted up the serpent in the wilderness, even so must the Son of man be lifted up." Schneider said that Jesus fabricated "to deceive man back into the truth." During this lecture, he and Koresh also usually added the admonition of Jesus, that "I send you forth as sheep in the midst of wolves: be ye therefore wise as serpents. . . ."

Koresh's handling of the issue was even more complex, for it came from the difficult core matter of the Seven Seals. The text of Revelation (6:5) says: "And when he had opened the third seal, I heard the third beast say, Come and see. And I beheld, and lo a black horse; and he that sat on him had a pair of balances in his hand."

Koresh taught that the balances of Revelation were the same as those referred to in the Old Testament's Book of Hosea (12:6–7): "Therefore turn thou to thy God. . . . He is a merchant, the balances of deceit are in his hand. . . ."

The world outside of Mt. Carmel—its residents believed—was a slice of Babylon, which they regarded, not as bygone Syria, but as a realm where falsity, ignorance, and confusion prevailed. They had their orders from the Bible, and their orders were, Steven Schneider said, to deal with Babylon as Revelation prescribed: "Reward her even as she rewarded you, and double unto her double according to her works. . . ." (18:6). ATF personnel may have lied about whether or not they had fired shots from the helicopters: Mt. Carmel may have added Jones' name to their crimes. The agency may have also lied about firing a barrage of shots through the front door: Mt. Carmel may have lied about the consequences. In telling the Myth of the Door, Mt. Carmel paid Babylon "double unto double" for playing with the truth.

Chapter 17

UP ON THE ROOF AND DOWN IN THE GYM

"I made a phone call . . . to one of the three agents who made entry into that upper level. And I found out just exactly what the time frame was. . . . I said . . . 'How long do you think you were inside that room before you exited the window?' And his answer to me was, '. . . I think it was about a year and a half.' "
—ATF spokesperson David Troy

The plan that the raiders rehearsed at Fort Hood called for seven agents of the New Orleans ATF to scale the roof over the chapel, on the "east" side of Mt. Carmel, in about 22 seconds. Four of them were to enter what they presumed to be the bedroom of David Koresh, on the "north" side of the roof, while three others entered the room on the "south" side of the roof, which they presumed to be an armory. These men were to secure the bedroom and armory, disarm and arrest anyone inside, and rendezvous with agents who had entered the gymnasium below. But the assault didn't work out as planned.

To make their ascent, the ATF teams had brought with them two 20-foot aluminum ladders. Once on the roof, they hoped to gain access to the twin rooms by a technique that they called "break and rake": breaking the window glass and clearing away shards with a special tool. To make sure that no one was inside when they passed through the windows, they planned to throw in "flash-bang" grenades, explosives that give off a bright flash of light, followed by a 175-decibel blast—and which, as courtroom testimony would show, are capable of removing limbs from the bodies of anyone they strike.

Graying Agent Kenneth King took the rear end of one of the ladders, led by Todd McKeehan, twenty-eight. They and two others, David Millen and Conway LeBleu, all four from New Orleans, scrambled up the ladders and across the roof to the "northern" window. As Millen broke the glass, shots came from inside the room, the ATF says. Millen jumped back. King stepped aside, to his left—and was struck by a bullet that entered his right elbow, passed through his chest, then clipped his left elbow. He crumpled onto the roof. McKeehan, a veteran of the Gulf War, fell on top of him seconds later, still clutching his machine gun. McKeehan was "bleeding very heavily. [His blood] was running down on the roof. His eyes were open and fixed," the wounded King recalled. Agent LeBleu, thirty-four, carrying a 35mm camera and wielding a shotgun, fell only seconds afterwards, killed by a bullet through the skull. Either then, or in the momentary blasts that followed, he was punctured by five more shots.

While lying on the roof, Agent King was struck again—this time, he believes, by an assailant in the residential tower. He began crawling for the "northern" edge of the roof. Still under fire, he took four more bullets as he went. When he reached the roofline, he pushed himself over, falling to safety on Mt. Carmel's courtyard.

Agent Millen leapt to the "south" side of the roof, where the other New Orleans team was trying to make an entry. In a scene captured by photographer Dan Mulloney, Special Agent Glen Jordan broke and cleared the window, and Special Agent Bill Buford tossed a flash-bang inside. Then three agents—Jordan, Buford, and Keith Constantino, also of the New Orleans team—entered the room. Guns flared inside, and perhaps also from the residential tower. Millen threw himself down on the roof. Gunfire came up through the ceiling of the chapel, forcing him to the roofline, then down onto the terra firma from which he'd come.

Inside, Jordan, Buford, and Constantino found a set of homemade gun racks, built of 2 by 4 pine. But the racks were empty; the rifles that had been there, the residents later explained, had that morning been taken to a gun show by Paul Fatta.

Buford spied a figure in the dim hallway between the armory and bedroom. It was Scott Kijoro Sonobe, thirty-five, known at Mt. Carmel by the nickname "Snow Flea." A California native who had been recruited while living in Hawaii, Sonobe had been the foreman of the Yardbirds, a licensed California landscaping company run by Koresh's followers, an outfit that, among other things, had installed sprinkler systems in L.A.-area schools. Sonobe was presumably the man who'd been firing at the ATF agents outside the armory and bedroom.

"As I peered through the door I saw the individual was running back into the room, AK-47 at the ready," Buford testified during the San Antonio trial. Buford raised his pistol, and, he said, "shot him in the doorway."

But if Sonobe was hit, he quickly regained his courage. The gunfire returned, coming, the ATF survivors say, not only through the door, but through a wall, and even from the flooring beneath them. Buford was struck. "I could feel the thud, like I had been hit with a baseball bat," the former Green Beret recalled. One shot punctured his right thigh, another, his left leg. Agent Jordan was hit in both legs as well, even though post-raid evaluations indicated that one of his wounds was probably inflicted by fellow agent Constantino. Then a figure appeared in the doorway, firing. "Constantino returned fire and the man fell," the Treasury report on the shootings says. It was Sonobe. "A bullet went through my left hand, between the thumb and the first index finger and it came out of my wrist, and back of my wrist. And it went in my leg . . . my right leg," Sonobe later told the FBI.

As Constantino was exchanging fire with his assailant, Buford and Jordan were on their way out of the room. They edged to the roofline and dropped to the ground. Buford, unable to move, was struck yet again. This time the shot grazed only the bridge of his nose. Comrades pulled him out of the line of fire and began administering the first aid that saved his life. After his partners had fled, Agent Constantino made his way out. He bumped his head on the windowsill as he was clearing it, knocking his combat helmet off. Dazed, he dropped to the ground in an ungainly manner, breaking his hip when he crashed.

The carnage that the ATF raiders suffered on Mt. Carmel's roof and second level roof might have occurred even had the raid gone according to plan. The rooftop raiders did not intend to give the residents a way to acquiesce, by ordering them to surrender. The teams led by Buford and King had no direct radio communication with the other raid teams, and could not have seen if, for example, Koresh had invited the others inside for coffee and a chat. The absence of any plan for a peaceful rooftop entry was revealed during the San Antonio trial, when defense attorney Dan Cogdell questioned Special Agent King.

COGDELL   Did anyone on the roof teams call out, "Police!" "Search warrant!" or "Lie down, ATF!"?

KING   No.

COGDELL   Well then, if David Koresh had welcomed the front door team that wouldn't have changed anything about your mission and tactics? You still would have thrown in flash-bang grenades and completed your dynamic entry?

KING   That is correct.

While the armory raiders were making their withdrawal, the death toll rose. The New Orleans team member whose job had been to provide cover fire from the ground, Robert J. "Rob" Williams, twenty-six, stood up from behind the discarded safe where he'd taken refuge. A bullet struck him. "His head jerked back and he slumped to the ground on his back, face up," eyewitness agent Chris Mayfield says. A third raider was now dead, his 35mm camera put out of action along with his gun.

Down in the gymnasium, another raid team took cover behind furniture stored there, waiting to rendezvous with the roof-entry comrades who would never join them. The architecture of the big room was foreboding, almost more than they could keep under surveillance. Doors at both ends and windows along the walls gave hostile parties openings to enter, and a hallway hung above them, enclosed by paneling. It ran down the middle of the ceiling along the "west-east" orientation of the gym. The hallway came from the second story of the front of the building, through the roof of the chapel, between the armory and its twin bedroom, and out to the "east" end of the gymnasium, where it looked onto a bay window.

The gunfire had stopped and the agents had heard shouts of "cease-fire" from within Mt. Carmel before an armed male figure appeared in the hallway suspended above them, or—nobody has proven details—in the hallway or rooms above the chapel. The figure fired, and they returned fire, the agents say, though their target would survive, seriously wounded, to deny using his weapon. One of the bullets that struck the figure "spun me all the way around. . . . It's like a 250-pound man kicking you in the side," he would recall. His body bore two wounds, perhaps from the same bullet. One bullet grazed his right wrist. It furrowed the skin and severed the nerve to his thumb. The more serious wound was low on the left side of his torso. It took a sliver of the hip bone as it exited through his lower back. The figure retreated as best he could. He recalled that it "took everything in my power to just feel, to crawl, okay? . . . I mean, everything was getting numb." The man whom the gym shooters had floored was David Koresh.

Chapter 18

THE FRONT LINE

"All we know is we needed one minute of surprise, and we didn't get it."

—ATF spokesman Jack Killorin

The assault was equally indecisive on the side of Mt. Carmel that faced EE Ranch Road. Some fifty agents had been assigned to enter the front door, including a contingent of female raiders whose job was to restrain and calm Mt. Carmel's women and children. According to the Treasury report, all fifty came under fire almost as soon as they exited from the cattle trailers. Seven of the raiders, including most of the women, darted behind a white van that was parked beneath a tree that stood between the two ATF pickups, just off the driveway. But even there the fire was intense.

Special Agent Claire Rayburn described what she suffered and saw. "Some of the dogs started to come over the fence area that was in front and when they did so . . . I drew down on the dogs. Lenore [her colleague] shot at them. We were very hesitant to shoot because we had more team members in that same area . . . we were concerned that our agents would be in the crossfire there. Lenore, I believe, did take out that dog.

"We were getting a lot of gunfire from the second floor. . . . We had a body bunker"—a bulletproof shield—"that we tried to stand up to

156

give us some more room because, seven people behind a little van, there wasn't a lot of cover to be taking. . . . The tree branches above our heads were being shot. Eventually . . . I leaned out with Lenore to cover the second and third floor windows. At that time, I was shot in the finger and there was also some, I don't know if it was a ricochet or what. I got two cuts on my left leg . . . and I got a cut on my right ankle . . . and right calf.

". . . We opened up the two rear doors of the van and we got . . . Barbara and Carla in on their stomachs on the bottom of the van. We were very concerned about opening those rear doors because . . . we saw that the entire top front of the van was just covered with gunfire. I mean, there was holes everywhere! So, we got the girls down on their stomachs and had them keeping their heads down. Opening those doors gave us a little more room. . . . We set the body bunker underneath the door on the left so that hopefully not so much would come underneath. . . .

"The other door, we had it opened up. We found two tool chests in there. We pulled them out and put them underneath of that door to hopefully kind of give us some more cover on that side. We then found a sleeping bag and yanked it out and tried to stuff it underneath the middle of the van so that some of the rocks and things wouldn't keep showering us. . . . We were not in a position to be returning fire because . . . we had team members between us and the compound. I did not ever fire my weapon."

The men who squatted up against the picket fence, shielded by its cinder-block base, weren't much better off. And those who had taken refuge behind vehicles on the parking lot were, it seems, most exposed of all. Special Agent Patterson, who had stepped out of the second pickup and drawn his pistol on Koresh, found himself in the line of fire almost as soon as the door shut.

". . . I suddenly started seeing rounds coming out of . . . the door and . . . I saw splinters and fragments of that type. Initially I thought it was our agent shooting at the door but I quickly realized that it wasn't. . . . A shell fragment struck me in the right side of my cheek area just below my eyebrow and right in front of my right ear . . . I immediately dropped to my knees in a safe position" behind a white

157

Honda, one of three vehicles—a pickup, the Honda, and a van—that were clustered near the front gate.

". . . I did observe the rocks on the ground of the driveway were popping as though something were striking them," Joseph Patterson went on. "Whenever I went to my safe position behind the Honda Civic Special Agent Lowell Sprague and Mark Murray had taken cover behind . . . the van that was immediately off to my right, and they began yelling for me to come take cover behind the van with them, which I did. . . . At that point . . . I believe Special Agent Sprague who . . . had an MP-5 . . . semi-automatic rifle was firing into some of the upper windows. . . . Special Agent Steve Willis had made his way to the rear of the van as well, and as you're looking out on top of the van, the rear of the van, it would have been from left to right, Special Agent Sprague, myself, Mark Murray, and then Steve Willis positioned himself in between almost like a diamond, in between myself and Special Agent Murray. And he was on his knees as well."

An exchange of gunfire continued for about fifteen minutes. The shooting was so intense that Agent Robert Champion said, "I couldn't even hear my own pistol being fired." Agent Tim Gabourie later testified that, from his crouch behind the first pickup, rising to fire his pistol exposed him to such peril that "I would just put it on the bed of the truck and empty my magazine"—without drawing a bead! During the fray, however, he did get a chance to take aim on one subject, a dog, whom he killed, he said, for "barking offensively."

Then a twenty-minute lull set in. It was broken, Agent Patterson told the Texas Rangers, when "someone yelled that there was a dog up on the fence area . . . the dog was walking almost on top of the fence down the edge towards one of our agents who I believe was Robert Champion"—who had taken cover behind the cinder-block base of the picket fence. ". . . Whenever they yelled that the dog was approaching and that the dog was in a threatening, growling type manner, uh, I believe it was Clayton Alexander that popped up real quick and shot and, uh, the dog disappeared. It, it had fell on the other side of the fence.

". . . Following that, gunfire erupted once again and we began taking several more rounds . . . suddenly we started receiving fire once again from inside the compound. . . . I turned to look at Special Agent

Willis . . . and as I was looking at him, uh, I heard a kathonk, and saw a, uh, hole in his left cheek. Uh, of course everything slowed down immediately after that. It, it seemed like it took a few seconds but suddenly there was a large stream of blood coming . . . from the hole and, uh, Special Agent Willis collapsed on my legs. . . . He did not show any facial expression whenever he was hit."

Agent Willis, thirty-two—a weekend auto race buff who was a relative newcomer to the ATF—slumped across not only Patterson's legs but those of Agent Sprague, too. "I could feel the blood pumping out of the wound. . . . Then his heart stopped beating," Sprague told the San Antonio courtroom. "His body was still on my legs when I received what, at the time, I perceived to be a shot in the thigh," Sprague recalled. "I thought I had been hit, and I even called out that I had been hit. My first response was to kick. Agent Willis' body rolled off me into the driveway. I checked [myself] for a wound and realized it was only a bruise. Agent Willis had taken another round. It . . . was stopped by the back of his vest. That's what saved me from being wounded." Once he had comprehended the situation, Sprague faced in the direction of the second pickup, where a medic was waiting, and drew his finger across his neck, signaling Willis's death.

In planning their attack, ATF's executives had anticipated that at the hour of assault some of Mt. Carmel's men would be outdoors, working to complete an underground, concrete tornado shelter. The shelter—one of the structures sometimes called "the bunker" by ATF and later, FBI spokesmen and the press—was being built at a right angle to the building, about 40 yards from its "north" end. A third flank of the raiders had been assigned to occupy this area, preventing Mt. Carmel's males from running into the building, where their weapons were stored. The agents whose job it was to secure the tornado shelter arrived in the first of the pickup-trailer rigs, and most of them later said that they heard, saw, or felt disorienting gunfire as they headed toward their destination.

Not only gunfire, but the terrain confused them. Several ditches had been dug in the area as part of the construction work, and the path over which they needed to run was partially blocked by stacks of building material, and by a yellow bulldozer that the residents had rented for the tornado shelter excavations. A henhouse, a well house, and the water tower where Peter Gent died lay between the building and the shelter. The layout in front of them was cluttered, and on the morning of the 28th, the ground beneath their feet was muddy enough to slow a quick run. The situation was so chaotic that, in the skirmish that followed, ATFers had difficulty in determining whether targets were hostile or friendly.

Nobody was working at the tornado shelter when the raiders arrived, though several men were outside, apparently laying in wait. A couple of the agents sprinted into the area, taking cover in ditches when they realized that their assault wasn't a surprise. One of them was Special Agent Eric Evers, a twenty-nine-year-old former El Paso fireman who sports a handlebar mustache. During the San Antonio trial, he told the court that as he ran past the bulldozer and rounded the corner of the building, he came into the area near a chicken coop. Two white males with pistols and a black male with an AR-15 fired upon him immediately. "They had their weapons drawn and when I came around the corner, they just gunned me down," he testified.

Wounded in the shoulder and chest, Evers fell to the ground, but quickly told himself, "Get up! Get up! These guys are not kidding around." He crawled into a shallow ditch, where he huddled for nearly three hours, until a cease-fire was called. During his wait, he says, his assailants fired toward the concrete wall of the tornado shelter, just behind him, trying to ricochet shots in his direction.

Unlike Evers, nine of his peers stopped short, taking cover behind the bulldozer. Because they knew that both agents and defenders were in the tornado shelter area, they weren't sure who to shoot.

"We got off the trailer and . . . we were running the length of the trailer towards the truck, which was in the direction of our assignment," Special Agent Harry Eberhardt told the Texas Rangers. "I began to hear small calibre firing . . . and about that time we started taking rounds around our feet and the dirt started flying up. . . . We took a position behind the bulldozer and for a few minutes, things were sort of chaotic, trying to see where all the firing was coming from. . . . We were really trying to take cover positions.

"About this time, uh, uh Eric Evers . . . was in the ditch next to the underground compound . . . and he stuck his head up . . . and when he did uh, one of the SRT members"—a reference to the ATF's Special Response Team, an elite group of the raiders—"just took a quick shot at him, not knowing that he was Eric Evers. And we said, 'Wait, wait, wait a minute! Don't shoot! May be one of ours.' And then we started yelling down there and he yelled back and said, 'You know this is Eric Evers and I'm hit.' "

Not long afterwards, Agent Eberhardt said, "We observed a subject crawl out from back of the chicken coop area to the ditch where Eric Evers was at, and he was dressed in a black stocking cap, he had on some sort of glasses, he looked like a black male to me, uh, with a black upper clothing on, and he was carrying an AR. . . . He was doing a very low crawl into that area. . . . At first one of the agents on the Houston SRT team said that it looked like someone on the SRT to him, so we didn't fire. . . We finally decided to yell at him and we yelled, 'Are you SRT, are you ATF?' When we did he looked at us and started immediately to crawl back. I fired five rounds at him from my 228, David Opperman fired several rounds from his 228, and . . . Kirt fired rounds with his MP5. . . ." But neither the unlucky resident nor anyone else was killed during the tornado shelter skirmish.

Chapter 19

THE SECOND FLOOR

"My daughter . . . she went to the window and they just started shooting at her because she was at the window. And then, you know, my other daughter, a bullet went like six inches from her head. And my, my son, you know, the bullet went through the floor and it—I mean—I don't know. I, I think it had to be God that kept that bullet from going through the carpet because other bullets did go through the carpet."

—resident Julie Martinez

The black jeans that golden-skinned Sheila Martin, wife of Wayne Martin, was wearing showed that she was still shapely at forty-six, despite having given birth to seven children. Her ebony hair, long and only half-combed, her white sweatshirt, tail hanging outside her pants, and her black jogging shoes testified to the informality that she'd acquired during a decade in the Mt. Carmel flock. But she wasn't casual, she was worried as she stood at the window of her second-floor bedroom, combing the curly hair of her son, Daniel, six, while her four-year-old daughter, Kimmie, clumsily tried to dress herself.

Sheila and her two oldest daughters, Anita, eighteen, and Sheila "Junior," fifteen, had been downstairs in the chapel when Perry Jones told them that lawmen were coming. Sheila and her daughters had returned upstairs with the rest of the women and Sheila found herself giving in to anxiety. Now she was worrying out loud. "Daniel, I don't know if we're going to be living here after today," she told her son.

Before she could fully explain things to him, thirteen-year-old Rachel Sylvia, who lived across the hallway, darted into the room. "Look!" she cried, as she leapt toward the window. "They're coming!" Sheila glanced away from Daniel, out the window that faced the front of Mt. Carmel. She saw men in combat gear running toward the front door, directly beneath her room. Then she heard the shots.

Rachel bolted into the hallway. Sheila pushed Daniel and Kimmie to the floor and kneeled beside them. Shots crashed through the knee-high window, splashing shards of glass across the room. Sheila's eyes shot up to the loveseat that stood in front of the window, its back a few inches higher than the sill. There lay Jamie, her eleven-year-old son, who was no bigger than a four-year-old because he'd been stricken in infancy with meningitis, which blinded and crippled him. Jamie was screaming at the top of his lungs. Sheila couldn't rise to comfort him without exposing herself to fire.

She pushed her two older children to the foot of a bed—one of three in the room—forcing them to huddle. She sat with them in a crouch, waiting for the shooting to stop. A respite came, and she crept to the loveseat, cradled Jamie in her arms, and brought him back to the big double bed. That's when she noticed that Jamie was bleeding. She grabbed a tissue and, kneeling, wiped at his wound, a cut above the left eye. The flying glass had struck him.

Across the hallway and down a little toward the "north" end, the matronly Victorine Hollingsworth heard shots that, she believed, were coming through Mt. Carmel's walls from outside. She heard a woman's voice telling her to take cover in the hallway, and once there, she heard Sheila Martin, Jr., saying something about "the snipers." Hollingsworth, being a British citizen of Caribbean origins, wasn't familiar with the terminology. "So I ask her what is snipers, you know. . . ," she later explained to the Rangers who interrogated her.

Hollingsworth was in many ways typical of the half-dozen older women at Mt. Carmel. Religion had been her life. In a long and personal letter to Texas Ranger Ray Cano, Hollingsworth tried to explain the twists and turns of faith that had led her to the hallway in Texas, essentially in search of a feminine deity.

Her longing wasn't fed by feminist propaganda or education; indeed, Hollingsworth was lucky that she'd learned to read. "I was born in Guyana, South America. . . . My parents were separated and we were very poor," she wrote to the Ranger. ". . . My childhood was very sad and painful, only sickness and death I see. My brother die when I was 5 or 6 years. . . . My sister die when I was about 10 or 11 years old. My mother had twins that die."

At an early age, she had what she would afterwards regard as an inspired vision. "I had a dream . . . that I saw or see a beautiful young lady laying on the sky with the light all around her. I do not know if she was in the sun or the moon, but the light all around her was very, very bright, and very, very beautiful, more than the light we see in the moon or in the sun. . . . She have very long beautiful golden hair. . . . When I grown up and become a woman, I remember that golden hair means Blessings."

For years, she did not know what to make of her vision, perhaps in part because the troubles of adolescence intervened.

> . . . I got engage to a young man when I was 16 years old. I get pregnant, my daughter Patricia born . . . and I never get married. There were days when I did not have anything to eat. At nineteen, I born another child, Richard. He died 9 months old.
>
> I had a man friend when I went to England and live in London, I start looking for a church to go to. . . . When I send for my children, and they came I was determined to start going to church. I told my man friend that I want him out of my life, because I want my children and I to go to church. . . . There was a lot of problems to make him leave me . . . but I pray to my Heavenly Father, and make him a promise that if he let this man come out of my life, I'll serve my Heavenly Father to the end. Our Heavenly Father answer my prayer.

In church, Hollingsworth began walking the path that would lead her to Mt. Carmel. ". . . In 1964 my daughter and I got baptized at a 7-Day Adventist Church. I was very zealous in the 7-Day Adventist

Church. I wanted to become a missionary," she recalled in her letter. "Around 1967 a church brother . . . asked me if I would like him and some other people to come around at my home to study the Bible. Brother Fitzpatrick [one of her visitors] told me that he is the leader of the Branch Davidians and that we have a Prophet in the United States of America, he lives in Waco, Texas, a place named Mount Carmel, and the Prophet's name is Ben Roden. . . . I believe the message . . . and I became a member of the Branch Davidians."

But before long, the figure from her vision returned to haunt—or deliver—her.

> . . . My childhood dream began to come back to me and I start looking for that lady I saw when I was a child, so I went to the Catholic church, because there is a mother figure in the Catholic church, our Lord's mother, the Holy Virgin Mary. I felt very happy going there because our Lord's mother is there.
>
> But one evening there is a knock to my door. When I open my door I saw 2 young white men standing in front of my door. They told me that they are missionaries for the Church of the Latter Day Saints, named the Mormons. . . . They told me about Joseph Smith and that we all have a Heavenly Mother. Well, I feel so happy because more and more my childhood dream began to make more and more sense, so I became a member of the Mormon Church. Just because I have a Heavenly Mother, I was a Mormon for a few years.
>
> Well, Brother Fitzpatrick and his family return back to England. . . . Brother Fitzpatrick told me that the Prophet Ben Roden of the Branch Davidians died and his wife Lois Roden is now the Prophetess . . . and her message is that the Holy Spirit is female and She is our Heavenly Mother. Well, now I feel that I've come to the End of the Road. My childhood dream began to make more and more, and more and more sense, so I think to myself that the beautiful lady that I saw and see is the Holy Spirit and she is my Heavenly Mother.

Torn between two faiths that extolled a feminine deity, Hollingsworth for several months attended Branch services on Saturday, Mormon services on Sunday, before ultimately deciding for the Branch. During the late eighties, she attended Bible studies in England led by Steve Schneider, and later by Vernon Howell. "When I met David Koresh at first I thought he was the king David we read about in the Word," she confessed. In 1988, she came to Mt. Carmel, "to learn more of the 7 Seals."

Heavyset, graying, with poor vision, a bit of a limp, and high blood pressure, Victorine Hollingsworth was not fit to be a combatant. She knew nothing of military hardware—in a deposition she referred to rifles as "long" guns and pistols as "short" guns—and like most of the women, wouldn't have been able to aim a firearm had she been given one. So she bent low over the children who were in the hallway, trying to protect them with her bulk.

One of the mothers cringing there, however, did know a thing or two about guns: Jaydean Wendell, a chubby white woman. Wendell, thirty-four, had been a police officer in Hawaii before her recruitment to Mt. Carmel. Midway into the firefight, Wendell grabbed a rifle—who gave it to her is not clear—went into her room, climbed atop a bunk bed, and while lying there, apparently exchanged shots with the raiders in front of Mt. Carmel. After the firing stopped, Marjorie Thomas, who had been caring for three of Wendell's four children, went into the room to fetch a disposable diaper. She found Wendell on the bunk, Timex on her wrist, wire-rimmed glasses on her nose—dead, a bullet in the top of her skull.

Chapter 20
911

"I've got a law office here. I've got all my law books here. I've got
my diploma on the wall. But I'll tell you something. . . . They
didn't come here to talk to the lawyer that was here."
—Douglas Wayne Martin, referring to the ATF raiders

Within three minutes after Showtime started, Douglas Wayne Martin,
the attorney who lived at Mt. Carmel, reached for his telephone,
dialing the emergency services number, 911. For the next two hours,
Martin and a sheriff's deputy, Larry Lynch, would be at the center of
the conflict, trying to wring peace from the warfare.

Martin would afterwards become the object of a good deal of un-
wanted publicity, not because of his negotiation role, but largely because his motivations puzzled the press. Instead of walking into the
pages of *Ebony* or *Black Enterprise* as a role model for the ambitious—
something he could easily have done—Martin had given his life to a
redneck prophet.

Forty-two, a native of the Queens borough of New York, Douglas
Wayne Martin was the son of a transit authority worker. As a youngster,
he had been known as shy, studious, and perhaps all-too-serious, even
when compared to other members of his striving and somewhat pious
family: his grandfather had been a minister for the SDA. Young Wayne,
his relatives said, carried books with him on family picnics, and no mat-

167

ter what the score, had walked out of Friday pickup basketball games precisely at sundown, because that's when the SDA Sabbath begins. In church on Saturday, Wayne had played piano for choirs.

He graduated from a public high school, then enrolled at City College of New York, where after dallying with a major in sciences, he gave up his plan to follow in the footsteps of his older brother, a physician. Instead, he studied library science, then went to Columbia, where he took a master's degree in the field. At the beginning of his graduate career, he had married Sheila Wheaton, a corporate secretary who'd been reared in Boston. Though he didn't tell his parents as much—they would have disapproved—Sheila was a member of the Branch. Martin had wed Adventist radicalism.

He and his bride moved to Boston, when Wayne finished his master's degree, not to reside near her family (which was Episcopalian) but so that Wayne could attend Harvard Law School. But the self-interest and cunning of lawyering didn't appeal to Martin, and after completing his work at Harvard, he took a job as a law librarian and lecturer at North Carolina Central University, a traditionally Afro-American college in Durham. Associates from Durham remembered him in the same way as childhood friends. "If there was anything unusual about him, he was too nice. He was quiet, mild-mannered," a fellow professor told the *Waco Tribune*. Percy Luney, a North Carolina Central professor and fellow Harvard alumni, recalled that Martin "was so quiet. He would go out of his way to help people."

But Wayne Martin was not entirely content. While at Durham, he had begun expressing doubts to Sheila about the church. His complaint wasn't that the SDA was jettisoning its doctrine, as she argued, but instead, that it was abandoning its younger members to the influence of the secular world. Instead of offering an alternative leadership, however, the quiet lawyer simply gave up. For two years his church attendance lapsed.

Then meningitis struck Jamie, the fifth of the couple's children, their second son. Sheila took the misfortune as a judgment from God, and Wayne relented, promising to return to church. Careful as he was about his image, however, he didn't go back until a year had passed. "He didn't want people to say that God had to touch the child before he'd come back," Sheila recalls. When the couple began attending church again, Wayne became devout. From North Carolina, he watched as Vernon Howell rose in Texas—and was convinced. He believed that he'd found not only a prophet, but one who could bind youngsters to the faith. In 1985, the Martins joined Howell at the Palestine encampment.

After the move to Mt. Carmel, Martin's commitment deepened, even as he became a workaday attorney. His closest friends in Waco's legal circles were a handful of black attorneys who, like him, handled personal injury, criminal, and domestic cases. His associates offered Martin partnerships, but he declined, saying that he wanted to devote most of his attention to his faith. He sometimes met clients in the offices of his friends, but he did most of his legal work from his office at Mt. Carmel.

In Waco, Wayne Martin duplicated his Queens-Durham reputation. "He's a fine attorney. He's always been an aboveboard, moral kind of guy. He's handled his matters here very proficiently," state district judge Bill Logue, a white, told the *Waco Tribune* during the siege. Even El Hadi Shabazz, Mt. Carmel's prosecutor during the Roden murder trial, allowed that Martin was "a thorough, competent attorney. . .genuinely concerned about his clients." But city councilman and black bar association chief Ralph Strother perhaps knew him best. "He was mild-mannered, soft-spoken, polite. . . ," he said, but "thought that the government was keeping tabs on him, wiretapping, bugging him, things like that." Wayne Martin could not win admission to the federal bar, he believed, because Uncle Sam had Mt. Carmel in his sights.

When Martin dialed 911, his call was answered by Jayni Sykora, one of the five dispatchers who customarily worked the line from an office in the Waco Police Department's basement. Sykora deferred to Lieutenant Larry Lynch, a sheriff's deputy who less than an hour earlier had been standing at Showtime's launching point, on the parking lot of the Bellmead Civic Center. Lynch had gone there to establish a method of contacting the ATF once the raid began. He and an agency radio technician agreed that if Lynch needed to talk to the raiders, he would announce himself on the sheriff's radio band, which the ATF technician would monitor. What was foreseen was that Mt. Carmel's neighbors, when they learned that the roads to their homes and ranches were blockaded, would call 911 to find out why. Neither Lynch, nor apparently anyone else, attached any great significance to the assignment. ". . . This is, this is the easy job, OK. Because I'm old and fat, that's why I'm here," he told Martin.

Martin and Lynch would stay on the telephone for some fourteen hours, long enough to revive Martin's politeness. "Is there any possibility that you want me to, ah, move from 911 to another number?" he asked after the hostilities had ended, explaining that "I just don't want to block someone's emergency call." But audiotapes of their talk testify that the emergency and panic at Mt. Carmel were real enough to frighten him out of his mild-mannered role. The quiet scholar was yelling into his speakerphone in a high-pitched voice, darting from the window of his office to the safety of his desk—and perhaps taking shots at the raiders as he moved. The call begins about 9:48 A.M. with alarm and confusion:

SYKORA   9-1-1, what's your emergency? 9-1-1, what's your emergency?

MARTIN   There are men, seventy-five men around our building shooting at us!

SYKORA   Okay, just . . .

MARTIN   Shooting at us!

SYKORA   Just a moment.

LYNCH   This is Lynch. Hello? Hello?

SYKORA   There's seventy-five men circling . . .

LYNCH   Hello? Hello?

MARTIN   Hello!

LYNCH   Yeah, this is lieutenant Lynch, may I help you?

MARTIN   Yeah, there are seventy-five men around our building and they're shooting at us in Mt. Carmel!

LYNCH   Mt. Carmel?

MARTIN   Yeah. Tell them there are children and women in here and to call it off!

LYNCH   Alright, alright, ah, hello?
I hear gunfire.
Oh, Shit!
Hello? Who is this? Hello?

MARTIN   Call it off!

170

LYNCH Who is this? Hello? Hello?

God Almighty!

Who is this coming from?

SYKORA Wayne Martin.

LYNCH Wayne Martin?

Hello, Wayne?

SYKORA He said that there were seventy-five men circling.

LYNCH More than that!

SYKORA And they're shooting.

LYNCH Hello, Wayne? Is this Wayne Martin? Hello? Wayne, hello?

SYKORA Did he hang up?

LYNCH No, he's on the line. I can hear shots in the back.

SYKORA Hope they get the kids out of the way.

LYNCH No, he's hollering there's kids in here and everything, and we know that. They've got some underground.

Hello, Wayne? Hello, anybody! Hello! Hello!

Well, he's, he's still there, I mean I can the background and hear . . . Hello?

Yeah, they have their lines open. Does this tell us what time it came in and everything?

SYKORA Yes.

LYNCH Okay, okay.

SYKORA And you can imagine everybody . . .

LYNCH They're still shooting, I can hear the bullets. God Almighty! I knew this!

Hello?

Are they rolling ambulances out there?

SYKORA I have no idea.

LYNCH Hello, Wayne? Hello?

They're still firing, yep.

Hello, Wayne?

(sounds of gunshots) That was right there by the phone.

SYKORA Maybe he's got a gun, too.

Martin had stepped away from the phone, leaving the receiver off the hook. About ten minutes later, he apparently hung up the line. Lynch immediately dialed Mt. Carmel; Martin's answering machine responded. The deputy dialed again; this time Martin picked up.

LYNCH Hello? Who is this? Is this Wayne? Hello. This is Lynch, sheriff's office.

MARTIN Tell them to call it off!

LYNCH Wayne?

MARTIN Tell them to call it off!

LYNCH Who is this, Wayne?

MARTIN Tell them to pull back!

LYNCH What?

MARTIN Tell them to pull back!

LYNCH Who is this, Wayne?

MARTIN It doesn't matter!

LYNCH Listen. Calm down and talk to me for a minute, okay? Who is this? Calm down and talk, talk to me. Who is this?

Sixteen minutes into the calls, at 10:03 A.M., Martin was yelling, "I'm under fire!"; at seventeen minutes, he blurted out, "We want a cease fire." But Lieutenant Lynch had no authority to grant it. He was not a negotiator for the ATF, he was just a messenger—and his messaging system wasn't working.

Almost since the moment that Martin dialed, Lynch had been trying to reach the ATF. His efforts were fruitless. Twenty-three minutes into the calls, with Martin on the line, shouting, "Tell them to back off!" Lynch in an aside, spat out that "nobody has responded to the damn radio." Martin didn't understand the comment, and apparently in the belief that real negotiations had begun, agreed to pass the word inside Mt. Carmel that a cease-fire was being called. Within three minutes, by Martin's report, the guns of Mt. Carmel had gone quiet.

Another six minutes more would pass—some thirty-one minutes into the gunfight—before Lynch was able to send a message to the ATF. At thirty-eight minutes into the call, 10:25 A.M., Lynch began talking to the raiders' command team. But the indirect negotiations were interrupted, as soon as they began, by renewed gunfire:

LYNCH Okay, Wayne, stand by. They're talking now, so stand by.

MARTIN If they don't back off we're going to fight to the last man.

LYNCH   I understand, I understand, Wayne. Just remain calm. We're
   going to get it worked out. Everything is going to be fine. . . .
MARTIN   I'm as calm as they are. . . .
LYNCH   Stand by, stand by. Just a second. [*sounds of gunfire*]
MARTIN   They're attacking us again! [*more sounds of gunfire*]
LYNCH   Wayne! Wayne! Wayne! Wayne! Listen to me!
MARTIN   They're attacking us again!
LYNCH   Wayne! Cease fire and they'll cease fire! They want to remove
   their casualties, okay?
MARTIN   They're attacking!
LYNCH   No they're not!
MARTIN   Yeah they are!
LYNCH   Stand by.
MARTIN   Don't call me a liar!

By the time forty minutes had passed, Martin and Lynch's discussions were producing lulls in the firing. But no reliable cease-fire was established for nearly an hour, largely because the raiders were out of communications reach. The radio link-up that Lynch had planned to use hadn't worked. Lynch had instead established radio contact with a TSTC campus policeman who had gone to the ATF campus command post to ask the agency to telephone Lynch. Even after telephone talks with the ATF began, the line of communication ran from Wayne Martin, to Lynch, to ATF Agent Comealong, who was posted in the undercover house on EE Road. And Comealong had to relay his messages by radio to the raid team's leaders in the field.

In subsequent congressional hearings, a retired Los Angeles SWAT team commander expressed dismay at the ATF's oversight. ". . . One of the things that we always allow for in the execution of a search warrant," he explained, "is telephone numbers of the individuals inside the place that we are going after, and the team leader has a mobile phone with him so that . . . if something like this were to happen, telephone communications from us to them can occur. . . ." But nobody on the ATF raiding team had a cellular telephone, or even Mt. Carmel's number.

The Martin-Lynch talks toward a cease-fire weren't aided any, either, when at 10:34 A.M.—about forty-five minutes into the raid— David Koresh called Lynch on a cellular phone. For a few minutes, interrupting the negotiations with Martin, Koresh had in a brief cameo appearance injected his bravado and otherworldliness into the scenario.

SYKORA This is who, sir?

KORESH David Koresh, Mt. Carmel Center. We're being shot up all out here.

SYKORA . . .Okay, hang on just a second. . . .

LYNCH Yeah, this is Lynch.

KORESH Hey, Larry.

LYNCH Yeah.

KORESH Hey, Lynch—that is sort of funny name there!

LYNCH (*laughter*) Who am I speaking with?

KORESH This is David Koresh.

LYNCH Okay, David.

KORESH The notorious. What did you guys do that for?

LYNCH Well, David, what, this, what I'm doing is, I'm trying to establish some communications, communications links with you.

KORESH No, no, no. Let me tell you something.

LYNCH Yes, sir.

KORESH You see . . . we told you we wanted to talk. No—How come you guys had to be BATF agents? How come you try to be so big all the time?

LYNCH Okay, David.

KORESH There is a bunch of us dead, there's a bunch of you guys dead. Now, now, that's your fault.

LYNCH Okay, let's try to resolve this now. Tell me this, now, you have casualties, how many casualties, do you want to try to work something out? ATF is pulling back, we're trying to uhm—

KORESH Why didn't you do that first?

LYNCH Okay, all I'm, all I'm doing is handling communications. I can't give you that answer, David. . . .

KORESH Yeah, well, really, let me tell you something.

LYNCH Okay.

KORESH In our great country here, the United States, you know God has given us a rich history of patriotism. We're not trying to be bad guys.

LYNCH Okay.

KORESH The thing of it is, is this. God is sitting on the throne. I know this sounds crazy to you—

LYNCH No, no.

KORESH . . . but you're going to find out sooner or later. There are seven, there are seven seals in His right hand.

LYNCH Alright.

KORESH The question theology has overstepped is that we're the ones that opened the Book. Now, that's what I've done.

LYNCH Okay.

KORESH It's in your Bible, the Seven Seals. Now there's some things in that Bible that have been held as mysteries.

LYNCH Yes, sir.

KORESH About Christ.

LYNCH Yes, sir.

KORESH Now, when it says in Revelation 22, "Behold, I come quickly. My reward is with me." The statement is, what reward did Christ receive in heaven from the Father? He received a book with seven seals.

LYNCH Yes, sir.

KORESH So when I'm told that throughout theological departments that they're going to ruin me because of what I present out of this book, just because they can't present it and I can, there's a meaning to that.

LYNCH Okay.

KORESH In the prophecies—

LYNCH Alright.

KORESH it says—

LYNCH Let me, can I interrupt you for a minute?

KORESH Sure.

LYNCH Alright, we can talk theology. But right now—

KORESH No, this is life. This is life and death!

LYNCH Okay.

KORESH Theology—

LYNCH That's what I'm talking about

KORESH is life and death.

It took the ATF an hour after Koresh's spiel to extract its wounded and dead officers from Mt. Carmel, and to pull back from its property

175

line, as Wayne Martin had demanded. Negotiations took up a great deal of this time, time especially precious to raider Kenneth King, who was still bleeding and fearfully calling for help on his radio headphone.

The minutes were wasted in wrangles that weren't wholly necessary. "The ATF did not have a plan . . . to extract any agents, including wounded agents, from their exposed positions in front of the compound," the Treasury Department report would later reveal. Talks were complicated by a layered chain of command, not only on the ATF, but now on the Mt. Carmel end of the negotiations. Wayne Martin continued his dealings with Lynch, but so, too, did Steve Schneider, talking on Koresh's cellular phone. At one point in the talks, Martin refused to allow the raiders to bring in an ambulance; Schneider countermanded him, but Martin won the wrangle. At another point, Martin forbade the raiders to carry weapons while rescuing their fallen comrades. The refusal was communicated to the men and women in the field, who balked at attempting a rescue unarmed. The rescuers learned, when they finally came to carry away the wounded, that the dispute was of little use: one can't aim a firearm and carry a wounded man at the same time.

A dozen of the ATF's twenty casualties were unable to walk from the field, and four of them were dead. The withdrawing troops called upon whatever vehicles they could find to motorize their retreat. Robert Rodriguez's pickup was brought in from the undercover house, the Bronco belonging to the McLemore-Mulloney television crew was volunteered, and some of the crippled were hefted out on the shoulders of their ambulatory comrades. Photographer Dan Mulloney joined the pedestrian rout. Retreating agents spotted him, encircled him, and while his camera continued to film, knocked him to the ground.

After the bulk of the raiders had retreated and the scene was nearing a state of calm, Robert Rodriguez returned to his pickup, now back at the undercover house. He opened its cab, found the Bible that he'd left inside—and hurled it into the brush, as far as he could see. When offered medical attention for Mt. Carmel's wounded—though it was not clear whether the aid was for those inside the building, or only those who would submit to arrest—Wayne Martin refused. "We don't want anything from your country!" he declared.

176

Chapter 21

THE ELEMENT OF
SURPRISE

"I think obviously it turned out the way it did because of the cult
members themselves. They were willing to die."
—ATF Special Agent Charles Giarusso

Helicopters began circling Mt. Carmel again about 1:30 P.M., within
an hour after the ATF raiders turned tail. Several sightings pushed
Wayne Martin to panic; once, he shouted into the telephone that a
'copter had landed and was disgorging troops onto the roof. Lieutenant
Larry Lynch and the dispatchers made frantic radio and telephone
calls, each time explaining that the 'copters—more than a dozen were
spotted—did not belong to the ATF or other law enforcement agencies.
They were in the service of television stations, every one of them
wanting a unique aerial view of a shoot-out scene. Trusting in the
assurance of Lynch, the inhabitants of Mt. Carmel held their fire and
waited for the media migration to recede. Late on the night of the 28th,
at the request of lawmen, the Federal Aviation Administration declared
that the ten miles surrounding Mt. Carmel's sky were a no-flight zone.

When swift victory is frustrated, Washington officials, pundits, and
ordinary citizens raise questions about the necessity of conflicts and the
wisdom of strategy. Four public servants had been killed during a
questionable undertaking, and the ATF was in for a siege of scrutiny.

Even in an agency as small as the ATF, which had only four thousand employees, about half of them assigned to field duties, ambitions collide every day. When crises arise, inner-agency factions emerge. These internal factions seek to explain agency history in ways that suit their particular interests.

Special Agent Sharon Wheeler provided a grunt's view of the battle in a March 1 press conference when she blurted out, "The problem we had is that we were outgunned. They had bigger firearms than we had. They were able to shoot through doors, and due to that, a lot of our agents were hurt." The statement amounted to a lament that the ATF hadn't brought in artillery, which, sure enough, would have guaranteed victory in the assault. Wheeler's recommendation reflected the vengeful mood of the ATF's raid survivors, but it couldn't withstand questioning from Congress, before whom she would later chalk it up to exhaustion and grief.

A second rationale—and a precursor of the one ultimately adopted—emerged as a byproduct of a television interview on Tuesday, March 2. On ABC's "Nightline," a *Houston Chronicle* reporter told moderator Ted Koppel that "My sources"—ATF agents whom the reporter had known from a beat in Houston—"have told me they think they were set up by at least one reporter and perhaps one local law enforcement official, and that. . . . Reporters for, I believe, the TV station, allegedly were already hiding in the trees when the federal agents arrived." The charges weren't true, but the idea of a fatal leak was full of promise.

In the rumors that began circulating among ATF agents and their friends in the press, *Tribune* reporter Mark England usually got the blame. The charge apparently came from those who had heard about Rodriguez's report to his superiors, saying that Koresh had been tipped by a telephone call "from England."

"The word that spread through the media," recalls Carlton Stowers, who covered the events as a reporter for *Time*, "was that Mark England had somehow tipped the Davidians about the raid. In a matter of days, the story had sprouted and grown. . . . In retrospect, I'd say that the press turning on the press was one of the tragic, though less tragic, elements of the whole scenario."

But for months, the rumors held their own. They were reflected in questions raised by a Pulitzer Prize-winning reporter, and producer of a television documentary on the affair, Wendell Rawls, in an article for *Nieman Reports* (Summer 1993), journal of the Nieman Foundation for journalism at Harvard. ". . . Before the raid," Rawls wrote in his *Nieman* critique, "five telephone calls are made into the Mount Carmel compound from telephone numbers owned by the Waco Tribune-Herald . . . . Authorities say that newspaper officials have explained that the calls were from reporters seeking reaction to the newspaper series. . . . Calling for reaction to Part Two of a series at 8:30 A.M. on Sunday morning? Five times? In an hour?" Of course, ATF officials smiled upon the tale because it placed the blame for the casualties outside of the agency's ranks.

ATF investigators were already questioning Agent Rodriguez and other principals, and what they learned tended to confirm the idea that the agency had lost the element of surprise. While the agency was formulating its public relations strategy, however, its officials denied that surprise had been lost. On March 3, ADLE Hartnett was asked at a press conference whether, "When the undercover agent heard this phone call" (a reference to the ruse that Perry Jones used) "did he realize at the time that this was a tip?" Hartnett said that the agent "did not realize this was a tip at the time." If the residents of Mt. Carmel knew that a raid was coming, the official explanation said, the ATF was unaware.

In Washington during a March 6 broadcast of the NBC television show "Meet the Press," agency director Stephen Higgins hewed to this line, insisting that "this plan was based on the element of surprise. . . . We would not send out agents into a situation where we didn't think we had the element of surprise. . . ."

To make sure that blame stayed outside the agency, on March 15 the ATF issued a gag order, threatening agents with dismissal if they spoke publicly about the raid. Despite the ban, four disgruntled raiders told their stories to the *New York Times*. On March 28, the *Times* reported that "Several Federal agents involved in the violent raid on a heavily armed cult in Texas dispute official descriptions of the operation as well-planned, likening it instead to the Charge of the Light Brigade, laden with missteps, miscalculations and unheeded warnings that could

have averted bloodshed. Contradicting the official version of events
. . . the agents . . . said that supervisors had realized even before they
began their assault that they had lost any element of surprise but went
ahead anyway."

By advancing the theory that surprise was critical, the agents and the
agency helped guard a decision that was critical: That raiding, as op-
posed to arresting Koresh away from Mt. Carmel, had been the appropriate tactic. Officials high and low doggedly defended the line.

In an April 1993 congressional appearance, agency intelligence chief
David Troy argued that raiding Koresh was necessary because "We
never saw him off the compound after we had an arrest warrant for
him, or he would have been in jail." He did not tell his interrogators
that the warrant had been issued on February 25, just three days before
the assault, while the raiders were already training at Fort Hood.

On June 9, ADLE Dan Hartnett pushed back the calendar to a more
reasonable date. He told the Congress that the agency didn't arrest
David Koresh outside of Mt. Carmel because "there was no time—and
I don't have the date in January—from a time in January until the day
of the raid that we had ever seen him off the compound." The date,
had he given it, might have been January 17, when Koresh paid a visit
to the Spoon residence—next door to the undercover house.

But the claim wasn't true, anyway. Logs kept at the undercover
house showed that Koresh had left Mt. Carmel on January 28. During
the San Antonio trial, defense lawyers called to the stand an auto
machine shop operator who brought signed invoices showing that Koresh had been in his place of business on January 29. A rustic character
named Tommy Spangler testified that Koresh had come to the junk-
yard where he worked on February 24, just four days prior to the raid.
And even before Hartnett gave his congressional testimony, the *Waco
Tribune* had reported that general manager Brent Moore and manager
Angela McDaniels had served Koresh at their business, a club called
Chelsea Street Pub, about once a week until mid-February.

Even had Koresh taken a vow not to leave, he could have been lured
outside. He would have been likely to leave, for example, had Robert
Folkenberg, president of the SDA General Conference, challenged
him to a debate at church headquarters in Washington, D.C.; or if

guitarist Steven Vai had invited him to a jam session in Los Angeles; or had any of a dozen starlets called him from a motel in Dallas. David Koresh may have been paranoid, as federal officers would often charge, but he would have regarded any of these invitations as extended by the hand of God—even if the voices inviting him were those of skilled mimics.

Perhaps in desperation, ATF director Higgins excused the raid before Congress by pleading that, had Koresh been arrested outside of the encampment, "instead of giving up, they might have begun to execute people until we freed Koresh." Not only was this charge unsupported—Higgins had no intelligence information to back such a claim—but also blind to the importance of timing: had Koresh been arrested on a drive into town, for example, the raiders could have executed their search warrant within minutes.

During the June Appropriations session, intelligence chief Troy brushed away the wisdom of an off-premises arrest by saying that "following Koresh we didn't feel would necessarily be that important to the investigation, because he himself never got personally involved in acquiring those items"—items, meaning prohibited firearms. But if that was the case, why arrest Koresh at all? The presumably guilty party, disciple Paul Fatta—who was eventually convicted of firearms crimes—could have been arrested on any Saturday or Sunday as he left Mt. Carmel to attend gun shows.

In its last word on the subject, a 500-page September 1993 report by the ATF's parent Treasury Department, officialdom explained: "The chief attraction of a raid scenario was that it offered the possibility of catching Koresh and his followers by surprise. . . . If agents could sweep into the area at 10:00 A.M., they would find the Branch Davidian men working in the pit outside the Compound, without access to the weapons that Koresh kept under lock and key. . . . The men could be detained, the arsenal secured, and Koresh arrested." The plan, the agency reported, called for the men of Mt. Carmel to be unarmed and at work on the tornado shelter at the hour that the raiders arrived.

But in accounting for the failure of the raid, the report's authors found that among other things, all the men at Mt. Carmel didn't work in the "pit," or tornado shelter, all of the time. "Over the life of the undercover house operation . . . the surveillance logs refer to the men working in the pit on only 14 out of the 36 days for which surveillance was maintained. . . . On those days that the surveillance logs did indicate the number of men observed working in the pit, the number was never more than 13." The report also found that "there was not . . . a plan for postponing the raid" in the event of untoward signs, that "sufficient thought was not given to what ATF agents would do if they . . . were met with either an organized ambush or scattered pockets of resistance," and that in general, an "absence of contingency planning" characterized the raid.

In obedience to the reasoning that said that surprise was critical to success, the agency later dismissed two of the raid's commanders, Phil Chojnacki and Charles Sarabyn, who could have aborted the assault. They were probably sacrificial goats; both were eventually reinstated by a civil service appeals court. Any close look at the evidence indicates that the ATF opted for a raid because it was accustomed to raiding. Maintaining "the element of surprise" was an entirely secondary, even inconsequential consideration.

Had the agency's planners felt that surprise was absolutely critical, they would have followed the advice given to them by police manuals, the Green Berets who assisted them at Fort Hood, and even by the Treasury Department's evaluation team: They would have raided at night. "Even though most dynamic entries are executed shortly before dawn—when most suspects are likely to be asleep," the Treasury report noted, "the planners' confidence that the men would be in the pit led them to give up the predawn advantage in exchange for finding the men in the pit area at 10:00 A.M."

As the attorney for one of the dismissed agents noted in pleading for his reinstatement, "the fact of their surprise was not one of the two key elements of this raid. For the agency to contend that 'surprise' and 'activity in the pit' were the focus of Agent Sarabyn is to misstate the decision to proceed with the raid. . . . Persons at the scene with knowledge about the raid did not consider the men in pit to be significant . . . persons at the scene . . . knew before the morning of February 28 that, in all likelihood, the men would not be working in the pit. . . . During the briefing at Fort Hood, Special Agent Robert Rodriguez . . . and Dale Littleton, who supervised the undercover agents, reported that it had been raining and there was water in the pit. They advised that there probably was not going to be anyone in the pit."

Judging from their past success, the raiders believed that they had no great reason to fret. Somewhat reluctantly, the Treasury report's authors admit this conclusion. The raiders, it says, "knew from their own experiences leading countless similar operations [that] things might not go as planned, but ATF could still successfully achieve its objectives."

Raiding is the expertise of the ATF, and statistically, it's not as dangerous as one might think. In the thirty-six months prior to the failed Waco mission, the agency had called out its SRT or SWAT teams 578 times, executed 603 search warrants, mostly against dope dealers, and had seized some 1,500 weapons. It had encountered gunfire on only two of its raids, and the only fatalities (three of them) had been among suspects. During the prior decade, it had lost only one agent in the line of duty, and he was destroying fireworks at the time of his demise.

ATF raiding teams had routinely succeeded because ordinarily, when suspects look out their windows and see an overwhelming show of force, they throw up their hands. Survival is their paramount concern. Ordinarily, when raiders go into action, they don't know whether their quarry has been forewarned or not: that's the kind of detail that they usually learn only after a raid is over, from the confessions of defendants, for example. That forewarning does not doom a raid is a point sometimes championed in ATF literature with references to an action in which one hundred and fifty members of a California motorcycle gang surrendered uneventfully, despite knowing that a raid was imminent. The element of surprise isn't necessary to the kind of success that the somewhat unheralded ATF has known, largely because the dope dealers who are its quarry are pragmatic and streetwise souls.

Not so the residents of Mt. Carmel, mild-mannered Graeme Craddock, for example. Craddock, thirty-one at the time of the raid, was a pale, slightly built Australian, about five feet nine inches, and soft-spoken—truly a man who gives the impression that, as his defense attorney Stanley Rentz says, "you'll die quicker from eating white bread than from being around my client." An electrical engineer by training,

Craddock was until 1992 a physics teacher in an Australian high school, still single and living with his parents. He was also a senior deacon in the SDA.

In March 1992, Craddock received a telephone call from Steven Schneider, telling him in a general way that prophecies about the End Time were soon to be fulfilled, and that Koresh wanted him to come to Waco. Craddock was somewhat surprised: his understanding of the doctrine taught at Mt. Carmel was that the prophecies wouldn't be fulfilled until 1995. Nevertheless, he packed his bags, arriving in Waco in less than a month's time.

"We were under the understanding that we were about to be investigated by welfare workers . . . and our understanding of the biblical prophecies is that we would undergo a long siege," he later explained to the grand jury that investigated the Mt. Carmel events. ". . . There were some suspicious activities that were observed outside the encampment itself, and during the visit from the welfare workers, we felt or we thought there were SWAT teams stationed at various points around the camp. . . . This was more or less . . . what we had learned in the past was about to come to fulfillment."

Craddock, who had visited the United States several times since his first contact with Vernon Howell in 1988, came back to America because he believed that a siege—and more—was in his future. The residents of Mt. Carmel expected that a corrupted and hypocritical nation would attack them, that they should resist the assault, and that some of them would suffer what secularists regard as death. Their belief in the virtue of bloodshed set the residents of Mt. Carmel off from mainstream American Christianity, but Professor Cohn's medieval messiahs would have found in it nothing strange.

In examining the exemplary life of Jesus and his own future as a Messiah, Vernon Howell had found, just as East Texas redneck culture would have told him, that turning the other cheek wasn't really the Christian way. As the authorities closed in on Jesus, he pointed out, the Saviour told his disciples (Lu 22:36), ". . . he that hath no sword, let him sell his garment, and buy one." A subsequent scene from the New Testament, in which Jesus is arrested, was merely an episode from a shoot-'em-up, in Howell's retelling of the text. ". . . Peter jumped the gun and chopped off the centurion's ear," he said. "He was a bad shot, wasn't he? He was going for the guy's head!" According to the doctrine that the Waco Messiah taught, the disciples who fled when the throng came to bind over Jesus were cowards. Howell expected better of his apostles.

They looked forward to their role. Like Craddock, the others "were there for some event to take place, the siege. A lot of people were tired of waiting around for something," Craddock said. "We had been there a year almost, and nothing had really happened, and a lot of people . . . made the comment, 'When is something going to happen?' " When the *Waco Tribune*'s "Sinful Messiah" series began on February 27, Craddock told the grand jury, David pointed to its lead story and said something like, "It's going to be soon."

Government witness Kathy Schroeder recalls that when the raiders dismounted the cattle trailers, she and others didn't think (as dope dealers do) of surrendering in the face of overwhelming force. ". . . Fear was not our foremost thought," she says. "First and foremost in everyone's mind was that, as we believed, prophecy was being fulfilled in that we were being attacked. That thought can be quite elating (happy). To see what we believed was fulfillment of God's words, spoken thousands of years ago, was very exciting."

Koresh had taught Craddock, Schroeder, and most of the others that two outcomes were possible for the siege he foresaw, and after it began, he added a third. "The best scenario for us was we were to get translated out of this earth into heaven without seeing death, taken alive, that sort of thing," Craddock told the grand jury. "The [second] possible scenario, which really he didn't speak too much about until after the siege began, was that we would be taken into custody, into the prison system, to allow the Father, God the Father, to come and deliver us. The third situation is we would all get killed either by bullet or whatever means. . . . We were expecting a military force or some sort of attack."

The most exotic of these possibilities—translation—was not an oddity of Mt. Carmel's doctrine, but a teaching familiar to both Jewish and Christian theologians. The Old Testament records two cases in which living mortals were swept into heaven, that of Elijah (II Kings 2:11), who, after the appearance of a chariot of fire, "went up by a whirlwind

185

into heaven," and that of Enoch, of whom the New Testament (Heb 11:5) says, "By faith Enoch was translated that he should not see death. . . ."

When the bullets began to fly, at least one resident was dismayed that translation didn't instantly take place. Tapes of Wayne Martin's conversations with Lieutenant Lynch on the afternoon of February 28 show how Koresh turned his follower's disappointment into a new call to faith and dedication:

LYNCH Are you okay? You sound, is there a problem?

MARTIN No, there's no problem.

LYNCH You sound upset. Are you? What's happening? Talk to me now. You sound upset.

MARTIN Well, everything is, uh . . .

LYNCH Everything is what, huh?

MARTIN When you, when you study the prophecies, you see, you see two possible ways this could have worked out. . . . But because it happened the way it did, I feel responsible. . . . We've been a burden to him. . . . We've learned truth from him that nobody else could teach us, and in spite of it all, we still couldn't follow a few simple rules that he gave us. And so, and so, we feel responsible. . . .

LYNCH Well, let, alright, bring me up. You said that due to not following his rules, his simple rules, what, I mean, what have you not done?

MARTIN Well, take a look at me. I'm overweight. I'm not supposed to be that way. I was supposed to, to get in shape and . . . try my best. But I still came short. . . .

In a word, the residents of Mt. Carmel weren't translated because many of them had fallen short of God's discipline. Wayne Martin had failed to lose weight, David Jones wouldn't quit smoking—there were a multitude of sins. Who was responsible for David Koresh's wounds? In Martin's view, not the ATF—whose assault was foreordained—but the prophet's backsliding followers.

The text that had been used to prepare Mt. Carmel's faithful for the raid was Nahum, an Old Testament work that instructs God's people to "keep the munition, watch the way, make thy loins strong, fortify thy power mightily" (Nah 2:1). Nahum is a controversial writing. "No book in the Bible has been maligned as much as this one," a Protestant commentary says. "It is frequently described as a vengeful, nationalistic expression of glee over the destruction of a bitter enemy. . . . Nahum has been described as ethically and theologically deficient, even the work of a false prophet." A two-page book, accounting for only some 1,600 of the Bible's total of about 850,000 words, Nahum tells the story of a battle by God's people against a hated enemy. Victory leaves the enemy's camp "empty, and void and waste," and God's people, in good Old Testament fashion, plunder the place. Despite its content, scores of theologians, including Martin Luther, have defended Nahum's inclusion in the Christian canon. "The book teaches us to trust God and to believe," Luther wrote, "especially when we despair of all human help. . . . The Lord . . . shields His own against all attacks of the enemy, be they ever so powerful."

Koresh taught that when Nahum was played out at Mt. Carmel, it would not necessarily come to a victorious end. If his followers fell short in their study or discipline, barring a miraculous intervention, God's people would suffer the fate prescribed for their enemies. Surveying the future, Kathryn Schroeder writes, she decided that Mt. Carmel would probably be on the receiving end of the terrors of Nahum, that ". . . we would lose the battle. (See Dan 11, esp. v. 33–41). But . . . this battle was only the beginning of the end for this 'enemy.' " In a word, her interpretation was that even if the raiders won the military encounter at Mt. Carmel, the demise of the government's authority would also be sealed. Mt. Carmel's residents were doomed, in worldly terms, perhaps as much as the agents of the ATF—but a glorious future awaited Carmelites once the siege began unrolling the events of the End Time.

Graeme Craddock told the grand jury that on the morning of February 28, he was outdoors washing his clothes when someone warned him that Robert Rodriguez had come in. Leaving his washing behind, Craddock joined the group in the foyer. There he witnessed the entry of David Jones, the call to the telephone room, Koresh's apparent nervousness—Craddock thought that he was shivering from the cold— and the undercover agent's departure. Craddock placed no particular

187

importance on these events, and was returning to his chores when Peter
Hipsman cornered him in the hallway to warn that a raid was afoot.

Craddock says that he then "did what I think was expected of us." He
went to his first-floor room, where he kept an AR-15 and a 9mm pistol.
He strapped an ammunition vest around his torso, went to a window,
and watched. Koresh, he says, stopped by the room and instructed him
that "no one was to fire unless he gave the go-ahead."

During the fifty-one-day siege, government agents and the press
repeatedly described Mt. Carmel as a "fortified compound," and in one
particular, it was. The summer before the raid, men who lived there
had cut six-inch openings in the sheetrock walls on the building's
"west" side, the side that the front door faced. The openings were made
at a height of about two feet from the floor. Cement was poured into
them, filling the space between the sheetrock and the outer wall.
Graeme Craddock's room was one of those that had been fortified in
this fashion.

When he saw the raiders dismounting from the cattle trailers, Craddock told the grand jury, "I let the curtain go and got down on the
floor, and then the next thing I heard was a volley of gunfire. . . . It
appeared to come from the outside. . . . It was coming from the left or
the southern portion of the building . . . I heard nothing coming from
down the hallway. Just out the window . . . and that was the initial
stages of it, and then—just everything." Craddock testified that because
no order to fire was given, throughout the raid he cowered behind the
concrete fortification, never discharging his weapons.

Whether or not his denial can be believed, his testimony and that of
others who were indoors on February 28 clearly shows that even had
the element of surprise been preserved, the ATF might have suffered
casualties just the same. Like the apostle Peter, when the captors of
Jesus came, Koresh's followers might have raised their swords to prevent the arrest.

But most residents, including government witness Schroeder, think
that an armed exchange was not inevitable had the forces of law conducted themselves in a more orderly manner. "If any law officers had
come in Mt. Carmel as one of only a few (no more than half a dozen,
I guess), I know that David would have gone with them," she writes.

"Now if they handcuffed him right there inside Mt. Carmel, it is very possible that some rescue of some kind could have happened, but I just don't know. I doubt very seriously if DK would have ordered any firing if there were only a few officers."

The agency would have known what risks it faced with any entry plan, had it waited a couple of weeks to launch its raid: Koresh had invited Robert Rodriguez to take up residence there on March 1, and a room had been prepared for him, surviving followers say. The ATF would also have known that the residents' weapons were not "under lock and key" as it had mistakenly presumed. But had the agency waited for more extensive reports from Rodriguez, its March 10 budget hearings would have passed.

Rodriguez, had he moved into Mt. Carmel, would also have learned that theologically, the residents of Mt. Carmel were averse to throwing up their hands before a show of overwhelming force. So unpragmatic and unstreetwise were they—so much unlike the usual quarry of law enforcers—that, on the morning of February 28, shortly after the raiders extracted their wounded and withdrew, Wayne Martin felt that it was necessary to explain to Larry Lynch that obstacles would confront any negotiations for Mt. Carmel's surrender. Transcripts of the conversation show Martin saying that "we're looking at our options at this point." Lynch asks what those options might be. "We want God to come and help us," Martin explains. Flabbergasted, Lynch asks what other possibilities the residents are considering. Wayne Martin only sighs.

David Koresh, interpreting the Book of Nahum, had already shown his flock the next line of the divine script: ". . . The chariots shall be with flaming torches in the day of his preparation, and . . . shall rage in the streets, they shall jostle one against another in the broad ways: they shall seem like torches. . . ." (Nah 2:3–4). Those chariots with "flaming torches," Koresh had said, were armored vehicles, military tanks. No such weaponry was yet in sight, or even en route—but Mt. Carmel already knew that it was coming.

Chapter 22

THE SECOND SHOOTING

"I asked him why anyone in their right mind would be going into a firefight where people were being shot and killed. Nash said he was going to help his people defend themselves."
—Special Agent Charles Meyer

The raiders who withdrew from Mt. Carmel carrying their wounded weren't the only federal forces on the property. Some 200 yards away, at the back of Mt. Carmel, on its "east" side, a half-dozen "forward observers" or snipers were posted, four of them behind the walls of a cement-block building in which motorcycles—Mt. Carmel's toys— were parked. Two other snipers were hunkered behind a tractor chassis between the garage and Mt. Carmel's "northeast" side. Though a few bullets had come whizzing in their direction, and a dog had confronted them, the snipers were unscathed in the gunfire, and except for Special Agent Roger Guthrie, thirty-seven, of the Detroit ATF office—one of three agents who would claim credit for Peter Gent's death in the water tower—they apparently didn't try to kill anyone.

The truce negotiated by telephone called for the ATF troops to withdraw beyond Mt. Carmel's property lines. By radio, the snipers were ordered to pull back, into a hay barn that lay about 300 yards west of the cement-block motorcycle garage, on land of the neighboring Perry ranch. The six snipers were soon joined by another half-dozen lawmen, part of a contingent of fifteen, including two snipers from the Texas Department of Public Safety. A couple of hours earlier, the group had come from the TSTC command post to back up the agents in the motorcycle shed. At the time, one of the ATF reinforcements explained, ". . . It was our information that a helicopter had been shot and was inside the compound and . . . some of our agents had been injured and were pinned down."

The dozen men who gathered in the hay barn soon concluded that they were in for a long siege, and would need sleeping bags and other supplies. They sent two of their number back toward the road from which the reinforcement group had come, further east on the Perry ranch. When the pair returned, about 4:00 P.M., they brought a third agent with them, a member of a rear guard. About the time that the supply-scouting party came back in sight of the barn, they spotted a white male, clad in a light blue ski or stocking cap and a faded jean jacket. He was about 20 yards in front of them. The lawmen took cover.

The three agents weren't sure whether the man in the stocking cap was friendly or hostile. Their immediate presumption was that if he wasn't a lawman, he might be one of Koresh's grunts, fleeing the scene, perhaps after emerging from one of the tunnels that they believed branched out from Mt. Carmel. The agents were wrong on both counts.

The man they had spotted was a short, stubby patriarch of Mt. Carmel, Woodrow "Bob" Kendrick, sixty-two, the former father-in-law of David Jones. He had not come out of any tunnel, nor were there any tunnels leading out of Mt. Carmel. Kendrick did not live at Mt. Carmel, had not been there in weeks, and wasn't fleeing: he was trying to get in!

He was one of three men who slept and ate at an auto repair shop that Mt. Carmel operated about four miles west on Farm-to-Market Road 2491, closer to Waco. Some of the agents at the barn—before the plan was canceled—had planned to raid the auto shop that day. It was indicative of the controversy surrounding the whole affair that the authorities would refer to Kendrick's shop as the "Mag Bag"—a slang term for ammunition vests. The "Mag Bag" was the trade name of Paul Fatta's gun show operation, which was registered to the shop's address.

The Mag Bag consisted of two beige steel buildings, rented from a local banker. Mt. Carmel's carpenters had erected sheetrock partitions inside one of the buildings, creating office space, a rude kitchen, and a bedroom. Kendrick slept in one of its rooms, and Michael Schroeder in another.

Schroeder, twenty-nine, was a small-framed man with the talents of an artist and musician, who wore a golden ring in his left ear. He was strong-headed and romantic, "the kind of mechanic who threw his wrenches," an attorney would later say. As a child "he'd do exactly what I told him, but be hollering, 'No! No!' while he was doing it," his mother recalls. After graduating from high school in Florida, he'd worked as a supervisor on a crew that maintained mall landscapes, and in the mid-eighties he'd developed a passion for religion. Raised as a Lutheran, he joined the Baptist Church, then the Church of God, and like Victorine Hollingsworth, passed through other denominations in a search to match biblicism and intimation. His wife and former high school sweetheart, Kathryn, was that morning at Mt. Carmel with her three children by a previous marriage, and with Bryan, age three, the son she'd borne for Michael. Kathy had brought Michael into the SDA.

The night before, the three men at the shop had installed a 454 cubic-inch engine in a 1982 Chevy one-ton truck. Schroeder was putting finishing touches on the job that morning when Kendrick beckoned to him, urging him to take a look at the helicopters he'd spotted in the skies. Schroeder took a peek through Kendrick's binoculars and guessed that the 'copters—probably air ambulances for the withdrawal—were hovering near Mt. Carmel. He went inside and repeatedly dialed Mt. Carmel's number until he got through to Steve Schneider, who told him of the assault. Schroeder decided to go to Mt. Carmel. As Kendrick later said, "If you know Mike, he's going to do whatever he wants."

Schroeder, who had no authority over them, told Kendrick and the shop's third resident, Norman Allison, to pile into a red Ford Ranger pickup with him. Clad in a hooded gray sweatshirt and wearing a dark blue stocking cap, Schroeder took with him his 9mm pistol. Kendrick joined them with two handguns that he owned, a .32-caliber revolver, and a 9mm semi-automatic, a 1991 purchase from Hewitt Handguns. But Allison didn't quite fit the plan, in several ways.

Norman Allison, twenty-eight, was a thin, deadly handsome Afro-Britisher, who in his hometown of Manchester had been a taxi driver. Though he was an SDAer, he was also something of a ladies' man, a part-time singer, a "microphone composer," or rapper, in godless night-clubs. He had come to Waco during the fall of 1992 at the urging of his friend, resident Derek Lovelock. But after spending a few weeks at Mt. Carmel, Allison surmised that Koresh didn't like his singing and wasn't going to make him a member of his band. So Allison asked Koresh to keep his passport in Mt. Carmel's safe, while he went on the road, bound for Hollywood. Koresh warned Allison that if he left, he might miss out on the confrontation that would open the events of End Time. Allison's reply became a Mt. Carmel legend: "That's all right, I'll watch it on TV," he said. Government witness Victorine Hollings-worth, when asked by authorities to sum up her impression of the handsome rapper, said, "Norman didn't know anything about the Message. He only came there because of the music."

Allison had discovered neither fame nor fortune in California, and in late January he came slinking back. Too penniless to hire a car, the former taxi driver had covered the six miles to the Mag Bag on foot. Koresh didn't want him back in Mt. Carmel, but Schroeder and Kendrick offered to let him sleep on a discarded bus seat at the auto shop. Allison became a hanger-on. He was without means of support and didn't own a firearm. As he was heading toward the Ford Ranger, one of his companions handed him a homemade leather pouch; inside was a Jennings .22-caliber semi-automatic—a $65 dollar pistol, a real Saturday night special. Kendrick had bought it for his wife, years before.

Since the roads leading to Mt. Carmel were blocked, the three men drove to the mobile home where David Jones's mother lived. They parked the pickup there, and set out on foot toward Mt. Carmel, about three miles southwest. As they moved down the roadside, an unmarked police vehicle passed them a couple of times, and then stopped. Its occupant, a highway patrol officer, asked the three if they'd seen a

vehicle bearing personalized license plates, a question apparently unrelated to the assault. Kendrick said that they hadn't, and the lawman
wheeled off. Schroeder decided that they had best take a cross-country
tack, to avoid meeting more cops. The trio set off into the brushlands.
As they were walking, Kendrick slipped into a gully that was waist-high
with water, but he managed to climb out, wet but unhurt.

Kendrick's physical condition was almost as great a problem as Allison's lack of commitment. The patriarch wore thick eyeglasses, usually kept a hearing aid in each ear, and had already been the victim of
four heart attacks. His condition forced him to walk slowly, behind the
other two. As they neared the hay barn on the ranch neighboring Mt.
Carmel, he fell back. Schroeder stopped and waited, to check on him.
". . . I gave him the 'high sign' with my head, I was fine," Kendrick
testified at a bond hearing. "And then he started to ticker, because he
knows I have heart trouble. He says, 'Are you okay?' and I said, 'Yeah,
it hurts, but I'm fine.' " But Kendrick continued to lag until, he claims,
he lost sight of his comrades.

He did see two of the three lawmen who were returning from their
supply foray. "I heard a walkie-talkie click, and I looked around
. . . and here are these two officers that went right by me," Kendrick
recalled. "One is a tall slender fellow and the other one is not quite as
tall and heavier-set. And I froze in my tracks, because what was I
supposed to do?

". . .The taller guy had a gun in his hand and he went like that,
slapping, as if they were kind of joking and talking to each other. . . .
And then they kind of walked a little while . . . and then they kind of
veered off to the left to go over the fence to go to this barn." But before
the agents got to the barn, they spotted Kendrick. Ducking, they lost of
sight of him, and seeing nobody, about ten minutes later they resumed
their trek.

Back inside the barn, the returning agents learned that none of the
two dozen lawmen who were on the Perry ranch was wearing a light
blue stocking cap. A few minutes later, they were ordered by radio to
return to the command post. The lawmen filed out of the barn as a
military patrol would, in formation and on the alert. Special Agent
Jimmy Brigance reported: "We cut one fence . . . climbed over that

fence, which put us in a field. We went, oh, probably thirty or forty yards into this field, so we were downhill from the compound out of the line of fire. . . . About midway or three-quarters of the way across that field . . . I saw one male, what appeared to be a male, with a dark blue, looked like a ski cap or a toboggan cap. . . . Meyer and Pearce and myself and Savage then began yelling in his direction, telling him to come out with his hands up. I remember Pearce saying, 'Federal agents, come out with your hands up.' We got no verbal response."

The agents had spotted Michael Schroeder, on the edge of a brush-lined drawl or gully. Thirteen armed lawmen, with pistols, sniper's rifles, and a shotgun, were arrayed against Schroeder, though perhaps he could only see eleven of them—two of the ATF snipers were dressed in extreme camouflage that made them "look like something that crawled out of a swamp," one of their peers later recalled. More than half of the lawmen were too far away to be in pistol range, though their rifles could deliver accurate fire. Schroeder's position was indefensible.

But the only eyewitnesses (all lawmen) say that Schroeder opened fire on them. "I would say 30 seconds passed and then a shot was fired at us, and then two more shots were fired at us. . . ," Special Agent Brigance told the Rangers. "After the third shot was fired, I returned fire and then there was sporadic fire as different agents were able to determine exactly where he was . . . I believe that continued for, I would say, in the neighborhood of thirty minutes."

Bob Kendrick says that though he didn't see the shooting, from his position, chest to the ground and closer to the barn than to the gully where Schroeder stood, the first shots sounded as if they came from the government's side. "I heard the number-one shot from the barn. Then I heard two that sounded like they came from a little to the left of it. After the third, all hell broke loose. Those first three shots weren't from a pistol. The first one was definitely from a large-caliber rifle or a shotgun. I'd lay my life on it." His impression was collaterally confirmed by one of the Special Agents who, when interviewed on March 5 by the Texas Rangers, said: "Now, the fire sounded, sounded to me like what I know as rifle fire because it had that, that familiar crack at the end. . . . It didn't sound like 9mm fire. I know what 9mm rounds sound like."

As the uneven gunfight continued, Special Agent Brigance told the Rangers, " . . .At some point while I was firing, I could tell that the target had been hit. He made a jerk movement. . . . He stayed up, there was more rounds fired . . . but he was still in the same basic position as he was when it started. It appeared to me that he'd been hit at least two or three times by the way he was moving. . . ." No one can know for sure, but perhaps that's when the astounding aim of Special Agent Wayne Appelt came into play. From a distance he estimates at about 100 yards—a long shot with a pistol—Appelt claimed in his statement to the Rangers that "I fired my handgun until I saw the subject or suspect drop.

"I watched the subject after he went down," Appelt continued, "to make sure that he wasn't trying to fire upon the snipers. We watched him for several minutes. We ceased-fire when he went down and then watched the suspect for several minutes to make sure that he wasn't attempting to fire at our snipers or any other agents."

A much different story leaps out from the pages of the coroner's report. It shows that four shots struck Michael Schroeder's torso and limbs. One of the four was a mere graze, across his left rib cage. Another entered his left thigh and traveled downward, lodging about three inches above his knee. A shot that entered his right shoulder, however, punctured a lung, and another, which struck him just above the waist on his right side, punctured Schroeder's iliac artery. Perhaps it was because of these last two wounds that the medical examiner's office ruled that the cause of his death was "internal injuries due to multiple gunshot wounds."

Schroeder was gravely wounded, and it must have taken superhuman devotion to remain standing. But he did stand, perhaps even long enough to take a shot to the brain. It is, however, not likely that Schroeder remained on his feet until the three holes noted by the medical examiners were put into his skull. Two were on the right side of his head, going through the brain; the third, at the back of his head, was apparently an exit wound from one of the other two bullets.

All the lawmen on the hillside gave statements to the Texas Rangers, but only six of their narratives have been made public. According to those statements and to the trial testimony of the six agents who gave them, none of the lawmen approached Schroeder, or his corpse, to make sure that he was dead, or, for example, to offer him custody in a guarded hospital room. They walked away from his body, the lawmen say, without taking a close look—and without delivering any shots to his head from close range, an act that would have guaranteed his demise. The medical examiner's report seems to confirm their claim: the powder discharge that examiners usually find in or around close-range wounds was not found in the bullet holes in Schroeder's head. But that's to be expected: his stocking cap would have acted as a filter.

Schroeder's body lay where it fell, unstudied and presumably, unmolested, until March 3, when sniper Guthrie and several FBI agents viewed it. The following day, the Rangers took photos of the body and the scene, and the corpse was carried away. On March 4, Schroeder's dark blue stocking cap was inside the hood of his sweatshirt, just inches back from his head. It was not in his body bag, and was nowhere to be found when his corpse reached the medical examiner's hands. Nor did it turn up when Rangers returned, trying to assess the second shooting.

The Rangers had been appointed to investigate the leak that gave away the assault's element of surprise, and to check into the deaths at Mt. Carmel, both because federal officials wanted—or said they wanted—an independent inquiry, and because they had jurisdiction in their own right, murder being a crime in Texas. But in regard to Schroeder's body and several subsequent incidents, the cooperation they expected from the federal officials who took charge of the scene was either not forthcoming, was denied, or mooted.

The authors of the Justice Department report on the Mt. Carmel events made a troubling admission. Ranger Captain Alan Byrnes, they wrote, "recounted a specific event in which the FBI's failure to cooperate may have impeded the search of the crime scene." Jeffrey Jamar, Special Agent in charge of the FBI's effort, ". . . allowed the Rangers to recover Schroeder's body and perform a limited crime-scene analysis. Later, the Rangers asked to be allowed to complete the crime-scene search by casting footprints. . . ."—a measure that might have determined whether or not any of the thirteen lawmen walked up to Michael Schroeder, or his body. "Jamar refused the request, and did not allow them back onto the crime scene for ten days. By then, rain had severely eroded the footprints they had hoped to process."

After Schroeder collapsed, Special Agent Appelt told the Rangers, ". . . there was some yelling from in the area where he was firing at us from. At that point, one of our agents yelled to come out with your hands up and a black male came out with his hands up, wearing a green army-type ski cap or beanie with a little visor on it, and I believe, a green and blue jacket and blue jeans." Special Agent Mark Mihalec "was instructing the guy to come up toward him," ATFer Marvin Richardson said in a statement to the Rangers. "So he starts working his way up the hill with his hands up . . . Mark tells him to work his way on up toward him on his knees, gets him there, asks him if he has a gun. He says, 'Yeah, I got a gun.' He points to his pocket and Mark reached into his pocket while I was covering the suspect."

His captor found Allison's Saturday night special, still in its leather pouch. A quick field check showed that it had not been fired. Interrogated on the spot, and knowing that his passport was locked in Mt. Carmel, Allison told the lawmen that his name was "Delroy Nash," a stage name he sometimes used. Though he claims not to have seen the killing, he told the lawmen that Schroeder was dead, and also that Kendrick—who was out of sight—was wounded.

But Kendrick wasn't wounded. He was over a hill, perhaps 100 yards away, and still in command of his senses. The agents knew that he was near. "I could hear the man in the ravine and I could hear him breaking branches when he appeared to be making a great deal of noise going through the ravine," Special Agent Jeffrey Allen Pearce recalled. At least one of the agents reported that Allison called out to Kendrick, telling him to surrender. But Kendrick, who wasn't wearing his hearing aids, could not be spotted, and the party of thirteen, with their prisoner, arms strapped behind him with nylon handcuffs, moved on.

When the thirteen lawmen and Allison/Nash reached the roadway, they were whisked away by three vehicles. As they hauled the captive to jail, Special Agent Charles Meyer perhaps spoke for all of the lawmen. "I told Nash that no one believed that he and the others were trying to get into the compound. I told him that it made no sense if everyone was getting shot and hurt, then it was time to leave the compound." And Allison spoke for all of Mt. Carmel's denizens. "He said he didn't care if we believed him or not," Meyer reported.

Woodrow "Bob" Kendrick, meanwhile, was still walking, keeping his mind on his weak heart and his eyes peeled for police cars. It took him four hours to reach the mobile home, where he would remain. On March 9, a Texas Ranger called, saying that he wanted to talk to him. "Come on out," Kendrick said. When the Rangers arrived, the patriarch invited them inside, showed them his two pistols, and calmly submitted to arrest.

Chapter 23

TALKS

"In Nebuchadnezzar's day . . . Daniel and them were subject to the Babylonian kingdom, weren't they? . . . But when it came [time] for Nebuchadnezzar to make that image and command all people to bow to it . . . well, the acid test came. They threw those boys in the fire didn't they? But who protected them? God did! Now, we're in the fire now."
—David Koresh

"I'm not a theologian, David, I'm just a policeman."
—ATF agent

By the time the sun had set on February 28, Wayne Martin was talking to sheriff's deputy Larry Lynch on one telephone, while David Koresh and Steven Schneider negotiated with someone whom we shall call Agent Comealong, a graying, pudgy ATF agent, on another line. Their talks would within hours bring about the isolation of several children from the zone of armed conflict.

But the talks were flawed almost from the outset, destined to fail in their ultimate objectives because mutual understanding was absent, bureaucracy stood in the way, and neither side was disposed to concede on key points.

Larry Lynch and most other lawmen understood the post-withdrawal situation at Mt. Carmel as a standoff, in which the government lacked the ability to vanquish its opponent without risking public censure. The object of negotiations, from this point of view, was to secure the voluntary surrender of those inside Koresh's kingdom. This negotiating strategy proceeded from the assumption that universally, the highest value is human life.

Mt. Carmel's children, in this perspective, were neutrals to the conflict, the sort of victims who classically become refugees in time of war. More than once the government's press conference spokesmen— and the press—would accuse Koresh of holding the children as hostages. The children were the key to public support.

Seen from within Mt. Carmel, the talks were not about arranging a surrender, or even about saving lives, though those of the children were worthy of special concern. "The highest value for us is not human life, but the human soul. That's the viewpoint of all Christians," Livingstone Fagan declares. He and others cite several scriptural sources to back their view, including Matthew 10:28, "And fear not them which kill the body, but are not able to kill the soul; but rather fear him which is able to destroy both soul and body in hell." Whether or not the adults at Mt. Carmel were to surrender or were to die was, for them, a question for God to decide. The issue could not be resolved until a divine mandate came in, and when and if God spoke, His orders could not be questioned or altered. Negotiations were merely a means of avoiding collateral conflicts; for example, the gunfire that would have resulted had Mt. Carmel's residents not been able to learn, by telephone, that the helicopters buzzing their home were creatures of the media, not the police.

Most of the parents at Mt. Carmel believed that children born under its influence, regardless of age, had been guaranteed eternal life. Some of them who survived cite Isaiah 49:25 as proof of that: ". . . for I will contend with him that contendeth with thee, and I will save thy children." Since this doctrine held that the children were saved regardless of their deeds or fate, there was no reason to expose them to death; they could not, as the parents could, gain anything by martyrdom. With that in mind, the parents began sending their offspring out of Mt. Carmel almost as soon as the assault on February 28 had ended, even

201

though some already suspected that if they were ever to see them again, it would be, as one mother put it, "on the other side" of mortality.

But the children of David Koresh were not shielded by the same consideration. The unique status of Koresh's children and the fearlessness of Mt. Carmel's adults were two sides of the same coin, whose inscriptions the federal authorities never learned to read. The fate of all combatants at Mt. Carmel, as far as its inhabitants were concerned, was governed by the doctrine of "quickening," a concept mentioned some two dozen times in the Holy Writ, though too presumptuous or obscure to be included in most reference books. Even in Koresh's long sermons with negotiators, he mentioned it only in passing. He did, however, try to introduce it by referring the negotiators to an eerie popular film, whose script he thought they could understand. They apparently ignored the tip.

Koresh told the negotiators that they should view *The Lawnmower Man*, a 1992 flick that has become an underground classic. Based on a 1975 short story by Stephen King, it tells of a mentally retarded yardman whom a scientist persuades to participate in a work of cerebral transformation. During a series of lab sessions, the scientist feeds computer software—history, mathematics, and the like—into the young man's brain. As his competence improves, his behavior changes, too: he becomes a lover and ladies' man in the suburban neighborhood where he tends grass. But before long, the yardman is taking revenge on those who mistreated him during his Mr. Retardo days. After several former abusers are found maimed and dead, the scientist tries to dumb-down his subject. The yardman, now a gigagenius, knows what's afoot, and warns the scientist that any effort to return him to a lower existence will backfire: he'll respond by passing his consciousness into the brain of a central computer, from which he'll control all of the globe's wired devices. Ultimately, the scientist ignites firebombs in his lab while his subject is inside, stuffing his brain with yet more software. The yardman dies in the fire, but as he does, every telephone in the world starts ringing. The caller is the master computer.

Lawnmower Man was shown at Mt. Carmel to explain Koresh's 1985 experience in Israel. According to its faithful viewers, Vernon

Howell is the retarded yardman, the Merkabah is the lab, and God is the central computer. Mt. Carmel's inhabitants, unaware of King's short story, believed, not that the movie's plot coincidentally paralleled Koresh's 1985 transformation, but that it reflected it. "Today's prophecy is tomorrow's common knowledge," says Clive Doyle.

David Koresh had not taken either a King short story or a Hollywood film as his text. The basis of the doctrine of quickening was at least arguably biblical. The concept shows up in such scriptural passages as Psalms 119:37: "Turn away mine eyes from beholding vanity; and quicken thou me in thy way"; John 5:21, 24: "For as the Father raiseth up the dead, and quickeneth them; even so the Son quickeneth whom he will. . . . Verily, verily, I say unto you, He that heareth my word, and believeth on him that sent me, hath everlasting life, and shall not come into condemnation; but is passed from death unto life"; and John 6:63: "It is the spirit that quickeneth . . . the words that I speak unto you, they are spirit, and they are life." One of the few commentaries that mentions the quickening renders John 6:63 as saying, "Those who (truly) hear the Son and believe God avoid judgment completely . . . and come immediately into eternal life."

Protestants have traditionally held the view that when we die, we are inert, "know not anything," until the day of Judgment. Catholics, on the other hand, believe that upon death, the soul and consciousness ascend, either to Judgment or to Purgatory. Mt. Carmelites believed something in between: That those who have experienced quickening experienced a "special" or prior resurrection, while all others are shelved, to "know not anything" until Judgment Day. Mt. Carmel was, in the view of its inhabitants, a quickening lab. Its work had consequences in this life as well as the next.

Quickening, theologian Fagan explains, is a process of deification. "The thoughts of God," he writes, "are not as human thoughts. We are dealing in an entirely different spectrum of thinking (Isa 55:6–9; I Cor 2:7–16). Appreciating God's thinking, requires man to go beyond himself. Mt. Carmel was designed of heaven for purposes of accomplishing the above transcendence . . . the residents at Mt. Carmel, were able to hear God's word, while blocking out the artificial noise of humanity."

This is what the government labeled "brainwashing" and the residents of Mt. Carmel called "quickening." They believed that it gave them a special intelligence, and a special destiny.

Any casual conversant with Fagan will note the references he makes to "humanity," as in, "Humanity does not have ability in itself to understand the future; it is stuck in space and time." He speaks of the species as if it were a thing apart. In his view, it is. "We all have a measure of the spirit of God," he admits. But "Mt. Carmel built upon that and proceeded to a point . . . that an individual could bring himself to that point that he's a divine reality." Residing at Mt. Carmel gave people insight into God's Word, allowed them to partake of His Spirit, and enabled them to transcend mortality, Fagan says. The apparent threshold for achieving this effect was mastery of, and acceptance of, the first Four Seals. Once a believer had passed that stage of the indoctrination process, his future was no longer that of the human order. All of the Mt. Carmel residents who survived the February 28 assault, Fagan says, had already transcended humanity. "We are angels, but still in human flesh," he declares. "The difference between us and God is that He got there before us."

But not all deities were equal, either at Mt. Carmel or in the chambers of God. Mt. Carmel's adult residents were immortal, like God, but God seems to have claimed the right of prior occupancy and rank. That left Mt. Carmel's defenders at the mercy of His command. God spoke to them through the Bible, and through David Koresh, its interpreter. Like God, Koresh had become immortal, and had claimed the right of prior occupancy and rank.

And so his children were different, as Koresh made plain to the FBI in one of his telephone chats:

KORESH   . . . But these are my biological children.
FBI   And we are all God's children.
KORESH   To a degree.
FBI   Well, what degree?
KORESH   Some greater than others.

Koresh held that his children were special either under a doctrine positing the inheritance of acquired characteristics—Christian Lamarckianism!—or under the terms of theoretical work-in-progress. According to the Lamarckian doctrine, David Koresh's quickening had taken place at the hand of, and in the laboratory of, God, and had produced as thorough a transformation as the human flesh and brain could withstand. Mt. Carmel's lesser deities had never gone "beyond Orion" or ridden the Merkabah or spoken directly with God. They were of lower rank, incapable of fathering genetically angelic children.

But according to an interpretative doctrine-in-development discussed by several of the residents, the scriptures indicated that Koresh's children were divine. Passages like Isaiah 8:18, 11:5, and 29:23, which say things like "the children whom the Lord hath given me are for signs and wonders," were cited to show the children's superiority, with the implication that their father must have been genetically different from other people even while still in his mother's womb. Koresh's children "were born with God's DNA," Livingstone Fagan proclaims. Koresh had God's genes.

His children, the theologically advanced residents of Mt. Carmel believed, weren't actually children. Their personalities had what pop psychologists would call "an inner adult." The children were really the twenty-four elders or judges mentioned by Revelation in connection with the approaching Judgment of mankind. They had chosen to live on earth, much as God the Father chose to live here through the medium of Jesus the child. The other children of Mt. Carmel—Wayne and Sheila Martin's children, for example—may have been granted eternal life. Koresh's children had been alive in the heavens for thousands of years.

Subject to a couple of codicils, what those residents of Mt. Carmel who were well versed in doctrine expected, once the first shots were fired, was that the government would kill Koresh, that he would ascend to heaven with the "wavesheaf" (Mt. Carmel's residents and others who had experienced angelic transformation since the ascension of Christ), and that the whole bunch of them would later return to gather 144,000 followers at Mt. Zion, thereafter to judge the living and dead. The children who were sent out of Mt. Carmel would either ascend with the wavesheaf, or be gathered into the 144,000. Koresh's children-judges, on the other hand, had to ascend with him and the wavesheaf.

205

"No one will get my DNA," Koresh had declared to assault survivor Catherine Matteson. If as a result of the brewing conflict, he triumphed over the world's unbelief and was accepted as the Messiah, his children might live. But whenever he died, they too would die. This was not a matter of choice, it was a matter of prophecy.

Any attempt to bridge the vast chasm between the theological objectives of Mt. Carmel and the policy objectives of the negotiators was complicated by both horizontal and vertical bureaucracy—and by the false perception of it. On the government side, the division of tasks produced conflicts so chronic that the Justice Department, in its report on the affair, would conclude:

> . . . It was the FBI's overall strategy to negotiate a peaceful exit from the compound, while also conducting certain tactical operations designed to tighten the perimeter around the compound, to demonstrate to those inside that Koresh was not in full control, to make the lives of those inside increasingly uncomfortable, and to provide greater safety for everyone involved. Ideally . . . these two approaches work in tandem to bring about a successful resolution to a situation . . .
>
> In the case of Waco, the negotiators felt that the negotiating and tactical components . . . were more often contradictory than complementary. The negotiators' goal was to establish a rapport with the Branch Davidians. . . . By contrast, the negotiators felt that the efforts of the tactical personnel were directed towards intimidation and harassment. In the negotiators' judgment, those aggressive tactics undermined their own attempts to gain Koresh's trust as a prelude to peaceful surrender.

ATF Agent Comealong, from his post in the undercover house, handled the first negotiations with Koresh, those which confirmed the pullback whose details Wayne Martin and Larry Lynch had set. Agent Comealong also spoke in the talks which secured the exit of four Mt. Carmel children late on February 28. The prophet apparently enjoyed parrying with the easygoing officer, and as always in his dealings with lawmen, tried to turn the centurion into a convert. His lectures would have made sense to a Bible scholar, but much of what Comealong heard was Greek to him.

"In the book of Daniel, Daniel was shown," the preacher told him, ". . . while under the Chaldean captivity, he was shown the nations of the earth that shall rule over God's people, will be symbolized as one great image. And the image will be head of gold, arms of silver, belly of brass, legs of iron, feet part of iron and of clay."

Practically word for word, Koresh was reciting the Writ's account of the event that the biblically literate know as "Nebuchadnezzar's dream."

"And Daniel says to the king, Nebuchadnezzar," he continued, ". . . 'Thou, oh King, art this head of gold. And after thee shall arise another kingdom inferior to thee, and yet a third kingdom of brass'. . . And then there shall be a kingdom that shall be as ten toes, partly strong and partly broken.' So when Rome split up under the nomadic kingdoms, it fell into many different kingdoms. We know it as Europe."

Here Koresh was expounding a standard SDA interpretation of Daniel 2, identifying Babylon, Medo-Persia, Greece and Rome as parts of the image from Daniel's dream. As many other SDAers do, Koresh identified the United States as one of Rome's ten toes. His sole addition to existing Christian interpretations came when he told the befuddled Comealong that the stone which, in the biblical version of the dream, smites the feet of the image, was the Seven Seals. In the jargon that was his customary form of speech—the jargon of propheteers—Koresh was warning the Special Agent that smiting, and not surrender, was what he perceived as his mission in life.

By merely listening to discourses like these, Agent Comealong gained the favor of Koresh. After the FBI took control of the negotiating process, it named new negotiators. Koresh learned of the change early on March 1, and threw a fit, demanding the ad hoc negotiator's return. When Comealong was briefly brought back, Koresh, in high spirits, reviewed the catechism that he'd given him the day before:

KORESH   . . . God sits on the throne in heaven, right?
COMEALONG   Man, I'm really worried about you.
KORESH   Listen, . . . , does he or does he not?
COMEALONG   Would you let me ask you this?

207

KORESH Question: does he or does he not?

COMEALONG He loves you, sure He does.

KORESH No, does He sit on a throne or not?

COMEALONG Sure, He does.

KORESH Alright, does He have a book with seven seals?

COMEALONG Yes, He does.

KORESH Is Psalms 45 the first seal?

COMEALONG Well, I'm not sure. But if you say so, I'll take your word.

KORESH You can't do that! That makes you like a cult follower.

The rapport between Comealong and Koresh was smothered under the new order of things. No longer alone in the undercover house, Comealong made his March 1 calls from the FBI command center burgeoning in the old ATF offices at Texas State Technical College. In the new setting, Comealong's negotiation bids were subject to immediate review. "I've got all kinds of bosses and commanders and generals around here," he complained to Koresh. "I mean, I've got guys with scrambled eggs and gold leaves and badges like you wouldn't believe, and they're all heavyweights, from Washington to the governor, you know. And, and everybody—I mean, think about me. I get pressure. I've got the news, I've got the governor, I've got the President, I've got everybody in the world. . . ."

When Comealong left the telephone on March 1, a squad of FBI men, plus psychologists and negotiators from the Austin Police Department, took his place. The talk teams would at first work twelve-hour shifts, then eight-hour shifts, four to eight negotiators, note takers, and supervisors on each shift. Koresh and his aides were negotiating with a relay team. During the fifty-one-day siege, he and Steve Schneider would deal with more than two dozen negotiators, including five men named John who identified themselves by numbers, as "John-1," "John-2," and so on. "Is there someone there I haven't spoken with yet? Maybe I can go for some new number?" Steve Schneider would complain.

But Koresh and his crew didn't immediately understand what bureaucratization meant. They presumed that the negotiators, as they thought Comealong had done, were offering handshake, man-to-man deals. Koresh was startled when an FBI agent deftly tried to modify a

208

bargain that the prophet had struck with Comealong. "You're saying your bosses, your bosses," Koresh protested. "I mean, I mean, this is not Burger King management here, you know. You're the negotiator, you're the one's that's got a lot of, a lot of power, don't you?"

Circumstances time and again made it clear that faraway powers, and not the talkers, were indeed in charge. "You've got to understand," one negotiator explained, "that this is a multi-agency effort and if I were the boss, you and I could probably work this thing out perhaps a lot faster." Another pleaded, ". . . we're getting, you know, we get some heat from the, from the other guys. Additionally, you know, the, the bosses back in D.C. look at this thing on TV or USA Today . . . and they don't see anything happening." Said a third, ". . . They've got things being re-layed all, 1,000 or 1,500 miles back to D.C. It's not a simple chain of command." Koresh finally caught on. ". . . That's what you people are, you're professional waitresses," he snapped in a fit of ill humor.

On Mt. Carmel's side of the telephone, David Koresh and Steven Schneider did most of the talking. Schneider, whom the press and police would alike describe as Koresh's "lieutenant" and "second-in-command," was a quiet-spoken man, given to folksy Midwesternisms like "How's yourself?" He was the son of a salesman, and according to Marc Breault, a fairly good salesman himself. "This guy could sell you smog. He's that good," Breault told the *Waco Tribune*.

Forty-three, Schneider had spent most of his adulthood in transit between Hawaii, his preferred residence, and Wisconsin, his home. In common with the FBI men, he found Waco nearly unbearable. "I don't like the fire ants, I don't like this changeable weather, and I don't like the city," he told the men on the other end of the line.

His childhood, he said, had been spent in a family "where they tuck the children into bed, myself and sisters, and they'd always have get-togethers. Very close-knit family, a lot of support." But like Koresh, he'd been stricken by wonder at an early age. ". . . Right from the time I could comprehend, I was always looking out at the stars and wondering how I got here, where I was going, why all the problems in the earth, why not peace, why this, why that." His mother was a member of the SDA, and in a Wisconsin Adventist high school, Schneider began to learn answers to his questions.

He didn't learn completely, or all at once. One of his fortes, as a go-between, was in telling the secularized, mostly Catholic negotiators how he, too, had strayed from God's path. The story was partly true. As a young man, he enrolled in an SDA college in England near Nottingham, Newbold College—alma mater of Livingstone Fagan—only to be expelled after a bout of drunkenness. During one of his sojourns in Hawaii, he tried what he regarded as the swinging bachelor's life. He even attended parties, he told the FBI, where film stars were in attendance: Pat Boone and Clint Eastwood and a couple others who, in SDA circles, qualify as really risqué men of the world. Then, "I got to know a, a quarterback," he recalled. "He was going to be a quarterback with the Rams, and he gave up his career to get into Hinduism. . . . That's what kind of got me into searching out a lot of eastern religions, seeing what they were about. . . . Then after that, I just pursued studying a lot of the holy books and the philosophies of men, trying to find a weight of evidence, and I was always moving onward. And then I ran into David in '86, through this Marc Breault. . . ."

Along the way, he picked up a wife, Judy Peterson, a shapely strawberry blonde two years his junior. The couple had met at a Madison, Wisconsin, dance hall in 1970, and, Steve would say, "right from the beginning we were into the same things, backpacking, hiking. We liked studying the Bible together, we liked, you know, the same kinds of foods"—no small coincidence in an era before vegetarianism was widespread.

Judy, a Lutheran, adopted Steve's Adventism and accompanied him on one of his extended migrations to Hawaii, then returned there as his wife in 1981; they were wed more than ten years after their first kiss. In Hawaii as a married man, Schneider resumed his education and harnessed his interest in Asian faiths to a University of Hawaii program in comparative religions. He was pursuing graduate studies there, and working as a teaching assistant, when Marc Breault brought Vernon Howell into his life.

Breault knew Schneider from their common association with Honolulu's Diamond Head Seventh-Day Adventist Church. "Steve was the only person I respected in terms of biblical prophecy," Breault told Mark England. "I went to Hawaii to get his thoughts on whether

Vernon was true or not. To my surprise, Steve accepted his theology. I guess I recruited him, but in another sense his acceptance cemented my belief that Vernon was true. I thought if anyone could refute Vernon, it was Steve."

Schneider had initially doubted Koresh, he claimed. For nearly a year he remained in Hawaii, spending thousands of dollars on telephone calls to Vernon, arguing with him. Then he made a trip to California, where for five hours he listened to the mechanic-holy man. Still, he was undecided: not until he took Vernon to spar with a professor did Steven Schneider decide that the redneck was Christ. After his conversion, he said, he saw that his talents as an SDA evangelizer didn't compare with those of the new Messiah. ". . . It's like I sold them a toothbrush and he comes along and sells the house that goes with where a toothbrush hangs," he said.

Yet in numerous conversations with the FBI negotiators, Schneider tantalized them with the proposal that, if they could bring to Mt. Carmel an expert capable of holding his own with Koresh, he'd renounce the Waco Messiah. When a negotiator, apparently working from media sources, told Schneider about Cyrus Teed, Schneider begged to see Teed's writings—but the Bureau refused to comply. There wasn't much likelihood that Schneider would turn, at least not toward any mainstream faith, in part because his standards were higher than those of most Christians. "Religion is a bad thing," he admonished a G-Man, "when you can do what you want to do, and just go to a religious social club once a week, where you go through a yo-yo experience, stand up, sit down, stand up, sit down . . . Christianity two thousand years ago wasn't that way."

Koresh no doubt valued Schneider as a friendly face for presentation to secular men, and no doubt knew that deep in his soul, Schneider could not stray from the path of devotion. Three statements from Schneider told who he was. ". . . I really don't like this world, I really don't," he said, echoing the deepest commitment of End Timers as far back as Ellen White. "The wisest man who ever lived, Solomon," he instructed his FBI counterparts, "once said, it's better to spend your time at a funeral than at a party. . . . If you're at a party, the next day you wake up . . . might have a hangover. It was all for . . . vanity, it passes away, it's hardly a memory. Those that go to funerals, that could be your loved one laying there, that could be you in the casket. It brings the issues of life and death before one. . . ." "I am an idealist," he declared. "I look for absolute truth. But where is there absolute truth? One thing that's absolute, as far as I can see, and that's death."

Steven Schneider was a peer to the negotiators on the other end of the line because like them, he was not "second-in-command" or even twenty-fourth in command. He had no command. He was a message runner, nothing more. Unlike his federal counterparts, he did not have bureaucratic understudies, aides, or proxies. Other residents sometimes chatted with the G-Men over the telephone, but when Koresh could not, or would not, attend to the calls, nobody was assigned to spell Schneider on the line. For fifty days, he slept by the phone, lest some emergency arise in the dead of night. His last words before retiring each night, usually about 2:00 A.M., were spoken to an FBI man, and negotiators woke him with calls, usually at 6:00 A.M. The Hades that Schneider came to know was invented not by Dante or the prophets, but by Alexander Graham Bell.

Mt. Carmel's tiny bureaucracy was both a blessing and a curse to the negotiating process. Feeling pinched by Koresh's primacy and obstinance, the G-Men a few times tried to persuade Schneider and even Rachel Jones, Koresh's legal wife, to make decisions when the Messiah was indisposed. They refused, saying that only Koresh could speak for God. But most of the time, the negotiators praised Mt. Carmel's simple flow chart as more workable than their own. ". . . You have the perfect chain of command," one of the Numbered Johns said. "It's you and Steve and you get things done. We don't have the perfect chain of command here. There's an awful lot of folks, including way back on the East Coast."

The government negotiators were crippled not only by bafflement and bureaucratic infighting—the talkers and fighters worked at cross purposes—but also by glitches of a technical kind. Mt. Carmel's residents claimed that for months before February 28, every time rain fell, their telephone lines would go dead. That seemed to be the case during the siege, and rain fell on February 28, and intermittently thereafter. Immobile for most of the fifty-one-day siege, Koresh spoke through a

50- or 100-foot extension cord, spliced at several places. Residents walked on the cord, sending static down the line, cats played with the splices, disconnecting calls, and a surviving dog once chewed the cord in half.

But the chief problem that hung over the negotiators was that neither party had many cards in its bargaining hand. The FBI negotiators could not promise that the ATF raiders would face arrest, too, as Koresh and Schneider demanded. The G-Men could not even discuss the events of February 28. "That involves the ATF and, and I'm with the FBI, okay," John-4 explained. Nor could they say what criminal charges were awaiting any residents who came outside: that was an affair for the U.S. Attorney's office.

Late on March 12, Koresh requested through Schneider permission to send resident Greg Sommers out of Mt. Carmel to feed the community's two dozen chickens, which were kept in a coop that David Jones had built. A negotiator relayed the request to the Bureau's field command, which snubbed it. Yet the field command had only minutes before asked that Mt. Carmel send someone out to pick up a set of videotapes that the agency had prepared for viewing by those inside. Exasperated, the negotiator practically urged Schneider to evade the chicken-feeding ban. "The decision on the chickens is going to be yours, if you understand what I'm saying to you," he suggested. ". . . Why don't you be ready to send Greg out to get the tapes . . . maybe you can handle something else at the same time. . . . You're probably going to kill two birds with one stone, per se?. . . That's about as clear as I can make it."

The government negotiators couldn't authorize a chicken feed, and Koresh's willingness to talk was devoid of what the Bureau and the public considered substance. The key element in any negotiation—shared values—wasn't present. Understanding none of Mt. Carmel's theological obsessions, negotiators dangled proposals before Koresh and Schneider, and congratulated themselves when their promptings were accepted. Their first success after the cease-fire came about sundown on February 28, when Koresh conceded to Agent Comealong that if announcers at Dallas radio station KRLD would read over the airwaves a brief message that he'd penned, he would start sending children out,

213

two by two, a pair following each broadcast. Government spokesmen would afterwards say that Koresh was using the children as a bargaining chip, but his followers believed he was obeying an impulse to give all of the unsaved—including the government agents arrayed against him—an opportunity to hear and accept his message.

When Comealong returned to the telephone on March 1, he proposed a new deal: national exposure for Koresh—he suggested an appearance on the Ted Koppel show—in return for the surrender of everyone inside Mt. Carmel. Steve Schneider listened to the pitch, then passed the telephone to Koresh, whose only comment was, "Can't do it." Koresh wanted everyone inside to have a chance to make an individual decision, Schneider explained. Some ninety minutes later, while Koresh was reporting sounds that he took for those of raiders on the roof, and simultaneously discussing Isaiah 13, Joel 2, Rome's ten toes, Hezekiah and Eliakim, among other things, a negotiator renewed the offer of coast-to-coast publicity. This time, Koresh inexplicably accepted. The terms of the new deal were that Koresh would make an audiotape, which the Bureau would persuade a national radio network to play. When it was broadcast, everyone inside Mt. Carmel would surrender. Koresh was suddenly sanguine about the opportunity. "Do you know how much money I've spent trying to get churches to, to look into these things? I've spent over a million dollars," he said. Then he offered to pay for the air time.

The Bureau's proposal was to disseminate Koresh's message through the Christian Broadcasting Network (CBN), a radio link-up that had an affiliate in Waco. To secure cooperation, FBI agents would that night roust CBN executives from their beds in Phoenix, the network's headquarters city. As a condition of the deal, the negotiator required that an adult bring the audiotape out of Mt. Carmel. Koresh chose the seventy-seven-year-old Catherine Matteson to do the job; her septuagenarian friend Margaret Lawson agreed to accompany her. As soon as the deal was struck, the Bureau went into hurried action. Transportation, booking facilities, child care, and medical accommodations were arranged for the some one hundred ten people whom the G-Men expected to emerge. But in Mt. Carmel, there was only chaos and talk.

Chapter 24

THE SUICIDE PACT

"So I was praying and asking . . . my heavenly Mother if she could take me away. . . ."
—Victorine Hollingsworth

On the night of March 1, while making plans with the negotiators, David Koresh lay upon blankets spread in the hallway that led from the second-floor bedrooms to Mt. Carmel's residential tower, where he customarily slept. His abdominal wound was still seeping, and he was subject to spasms of pain and lightheadedness. Perhaps because they wanted to show concern, or to protect their agreement, the negotiators consulted with one of two nurses among Mt. Carmel's residents. "You would recommend that he get medical attention, would you not?" a negotiator asked. "Well, just a minute please," the nurse responded. The negotiator then heard her ask for Koresh. After consulting the patient, the nurse returned to the telephone. "Well, at the moment, we don't think it's necessary," she said. Yet Koresh's blood pressure was 85/40, dangerously low, and he refused any medication, even aspirin for his pain. Unless the Messiah received hospital care, it seemed likely that he would shortly expire.

Koresh apparently believed that he was dying. No sooner had he struck the surrender deal than he called the adult residents to his side, to say goodbye, in case either looming death or looming imprisonment might separate them. The men and women of Mt. Carmel formed separate lines, and one by one—men first—they passed to speak what they feared were last words to their saviour. Many of them believed that their own deaths were near, either because the end of human existence was at hand or because, if not, the FBI would prophetically slaughter them once Koresh's fate was cast. At least a few found the scenario unbearable and began making plans to die. If the testimony of government witnesses Victorine Hollingsworth, Marjorie Thomas, and Kathryn Schroeder is true, talk of suicide was in the air.

"The plan," Schroeder said in her confession, "was for David Koresh to tape a message for release to the world, and a 58-minute tape recording was made. Koresh believed at that point that he was about to die. Once he did, he was to be carried from the building on a stretcher. . . . The members were to follow him and once outside they were to fire upon the FBI agents, drawing their fire, killing and being killed. Some of us were given hand grenades to use in the alternative; we were to stand together in small groups and pull the pins, blowing ourselves up. The plan involved taking as many of 'the beast' with us as we could. I worried about whether I would have the courage to carry this out; women were told to arrange to be shot by another member, if necessary. Neil Vaega agreed to shoot me. . . ."

Suicide is not accepted by most Christians, even though Jesus surrendered to a certain death. "Everyone is responsible for his life before God who has given it to him. It is God who remains sovereign Master of life. We are obligated to accept life gratefully and preserve it for his honor and the salvation of our souls. . . . Suicide is contrary to love for the living God," the *Catechism of the Catholic Church* rules.

But suicide crops up time and again in Christian sects—the Jonestown People's Temple and the Euro-Canadian Solar Temple are contemporary examples—because, though church doctrines may forbid it, the scriptures do not rule it out. In a work devoted to the scripturality of suicide, A *Noble Death* (1992), Arthur Droge of the University of Chicago and James Tabor of the University of North Carolina review six self-inflicted deaths recorded in the Old Testament. Especially noteworthy is the case of Samson, who, brought as a prisoner to a temple, blinded and bereft of his legendary powers, asks God (Judg 16:23–31) to give him the strength to level the building with his tormentors, the Philistines, inside. "Unlike the previous cases, Samson is not mortally wounded . . . ," Droge and Tabor point out. "At the moment of his death he is facing humiliation. . . . God is directly involved in his death in that he must grant Samson the supernatural strength for the last feat. In other words, God must approve it. Samson makes his choice, God concurs, and it is done. Again, as with the previous cases, the text gives no indication whatsoever that Samson's choice to take his own life was viewed with disapproval."

Jews have for centuries extolled the death of at least one group of believers who, under circumstances of persecution, sought death. ". . . Nine hundred and sixty Jewish men, women and children," *Houston Chronicle* writer Richard Vara summarizes, "died rather than submit to Roman conquest in A.D. 73. Jewish rebel leader Eleazar ben Yair conquered a Roman-held mountaintop fortress named Masada in the Judean Desert in A.D. 66. The site was nearly impenetrable to Roman forces who began a three-year siege in A.D. 70. Finally, as the Romans penetrated the last line of the fortress defenses, 10 men were selected by the Jewish fighters as executioners. They, in turn, killed the others and then themselves."

From their review of the literature on the judicial fate of early Christians—including sentences to the pyre, and to gladiator duty and scuffles with the lions—Tabor and Droge conclude that "the evidence, such as it is, suggests that very few Christians were sought out by the Roman authorities. As de Ste. Croix has shown, 'nearly twice as many (if not more) were volunteers.' " Lay Christians were not the only ones who took themselves to the sacrifice; "early in the second century Ignatius, bishop of Antioch, gave firsthand testimony to the motives that led some Christians to die voluntarily for Christ. Condemned to death in 107, Ignatius was led as a prisoner from Antioch to Rome, where he was to fight with the beasts. On his journey Ignatius wrote letters to various churches. . . . In his letter to the Christians of Rome, Ignatius pleaded with them not to make any effort to save him, and so rob him of his crown of immortality."

217

Dicta from the Vatican carried no weight at Mt. Carmel; the scriptures and accounts of the early church era did. Some of the surviving residents insist that they made no suicide pact—but their denials don't rule out its possibility. "There was never any suicide pact or plan," Livingstone Fagan declares. "There was, however, an expressed reaffirmation amongst certain individuals in the course of events, of their willingness to die for what they believed, rather than surrender to the authority of their persecutors."

Fagan's phrase "amongst certain individuals" is apparently the key to discerning what happened. Not everyone signed onto the plan. Some members stood aside. "I told people that if everybody was going out the front door, I thought that was dangerous, and that me and my daughter, Shari, were going to wait, off to the side of the building. We wanted to see what would happen to those who went out first," Clive Doyle says. Sheila Martin reports that she was upstairs in her room at the time any suicide pact would have been discussed, and if it was talked about, she didn't know of it, nor would she have agreed. "I never heard that David had such a plan, or approved of such a plan," she explains.

The suicide pact (or pacts) was developed during and after a meeting downstairs, in the Mt. Carmel cafeteria. The meeting, in turn, arose as people came down, one by one, after their farewells to Koresh. In this atmosphere, with involuntary death or imprisonment drawing near, the residents exhibited an emotionalism that was highly out of character. "People were singing and praying so loud that it was almost like a Pentecostal meeting," one of the attendees says. "Then Steven Schneider came down," Kathryn Schroeder recalled in her confession, "and told us that we were making too much noise and we should hush so that David could talk to God." The meeting broke up. The subject of suicide had not been discussed in a formal way, Schroeder reports. "Nothing was ever said in a meeting. . . . It was just spoken of (only what little was necessary, I guess) between people."

If Koresh talked to God on the night of March 1, it was a one-sided conversation. The Heavenly Father didn't reply. Shortly after dawn on March 2, movement toward the surrender began. The FBI brought buses to EE Ranch Road, ready to carry the residents away. People inside Mt. Carmel packed their bags; Clive Doyle says that he and his daughter even packed a picnic lunch, in case hunger should strike while they were awaiting processing. Koresh sent out Catherine Matteson and Margaret Lawson, along with the 58-minute audiotape and two of Sheila Martin's children, Kimmie and Daniel. The authorities took the tape from the pair—and arrested them. A few hours later, Special Agent Earl Dunagan signed an affidavit alleging that the ATF has probable cause to believe that the two senior citizens "did knowingly and willfully use weapons, including machine guns, to commit the violent crimes of murder and attempted murder of federal law enforcement officers." Yet Matteson is far-sighted, incapable of aiming a gun, and the ATF's investigative records regarding Lawson bore the notation, "Margaret is probably the most harmless woman around."

On the telephone, Koresh reviewed details of the plan with negotiators. The women and children would go out first, and "we said we was going to put them like, in a vista, so you can see them," Koresh affirmed. ". . . That way you'll know there ain't no bombs on them or something like that. . . . And then the guys, we'll bring those out one by one, with their hands up. That will be good for TV."

Koresh's 58-minute tape was broadcast locally between 1:00 and 3:00 P.M. Mt. Carmel's faithful listened, and many were dismayed. In the space of an hour, he tried to explain his Messiah's role, the first of the Seven Seals, and what the gunfight at Mt. Carmel signified in God's plan. Not only did he fail to make a clear exposition, but many of his hearers weren't prepared. A transcriber for the *Fort Worth Star Telegram*, for example, rendered the audio's "the Lion of the Tribe of Judah" as "the lion in the trial of Judas," and "God is the one who has written" as "God is the one who is ridden." The 58-minute lecture presented only one clear message: That for the obscurest of reasons, David Koresh thought he was special.

Nevertheless, Koresh had promised to emerge. He placed the wounded Scott Sonobe—"Snow Flea"— by the telephone, while Steve Schneider helped the Messiah prepare to exit. For nearly two hours, messages from the FBI were relayed down the hallway to Koresh by the limping and shouting Sonobe, who reported that Koresh was changing

219

clothes, or was being lifted onto the stretcher that would carry him out, or that he was being hoisted down the stairway. Greg Sommers, who had been Mt. Carmel's patron of dogs as well as chickens, came onto the line to ask a special favor: a litter of eleven puppies was left motherless by the February 28 assault, and Sommers wanted to bring them out in a box. His request was first denied, and then granted, but neither Sommers nor anyone else came out the front door. The Bureau brought ATFer Comealong to the telephone when the deal seemed to have been lost. "I've got commanders who do not trust me. I said, 'Look this is going to happen.' And they're starting to doubt me," he explained. But not until after four o'clock was a definitive explanation of the delays given: ". . . There was a voice," Steven Schneider came to the telephone to say, "that . . . said nothing else to him but 'wait.' " God had replied to the prayers of David Koresh. The mass exit plan was indefinitely postponed.

"We later learned," Kathryn Schroeder confessed, "that we had sinned immediately after the raid, by indulging in whiskey, cigarettes and prohibited foods, and should we die then, we would not be saved." In a word, if there ever was a suicide or exit plan, Koresh called it off. The residents of Mt. Carmel were to keep themselves alive, so that they might atone. Those who had binged in the hours following the raid, including Schroeder, who had reverted to smoking (the cigarettes were pilfered from Koresh's stash, she says) would later be exiled from the community's ranks. God had decided that His faithful should gird themselves for events grander than anything that had happened yet.

Inside Mt. Carmel after the exit/suicide plan was nixed, no one doubted that Koresh had acted sincerely. The view taken was that negotiator Comealong, for example, had his superiors, who could tell him when to talk and when to cease talking; Koresh had his superior, who could countermand expectations and promises, too. But outside of Mt. Carmel, a different story was true. "David Koresh kissed the kids goodby. He was going to go outside and commit suicide in front of the TV cameras," FBI spokesman Bob Ricks said, "and at the last second, he chickened out."

Chapter 25

MILK AND OTHER
HASSLES

"I'll tell you what does bother me. This is a big fuss over nothing.
These people have been here a long time and never bother
nobody."
—Mt. Carmel neighbor Billy Atkinson

". . . Here's an Army tank over here now, armored carrier vehicle
of some sort . . . there's this, there's that. I mean, what is this
going to be, World War II or something?"
—Steven Schneider

Seven weeks of wrangling began after the aborted mass exit from Mt.
Carmel. Most developments were mere verbal events, incidents in a
log of discussions. Though every minute of the Bureau's chats with Mt.
Carmel was recorded, the public learned only what the FBI wanted to
disclose. As in an international conflict where a friendly and an enemy
force are defined by Congress, communication was forbidden with
those on the other side of the barricades. A cold war developed from the
stalemate of the shooting war, and the new conflict's victories were won
through television and the press, recorded not in body counts, but in
public opinion polls. While the picture that government spokesmen
drew of the standoff highlighted federal patience and rationality, secret
transcripts of its negotiations reveal that the federal agents didn't always
shoot straight with either Mt. Carmel or the press.

221

Before the raid, television signals had come through a satellite dish mounted on the roof of the room that the ATF had mistakenly taken for Koresh's abode, the bedroom that McKeehan and LeBleu died trying to enter. Helicopters had strafed the room before the ground gunfight began, Koresh and Schneider claimed, and the bullets, the two said, had penetrated the dish's processing unit, disabling it. With neither an antenna nor a working dish, Mt. Carmel received the signal of only one television channel, and reception was poor. Mail delivery was halted with the raid, and despite contrary claims by the FBI's spokesmen—and the efforts of some members of the negotiating team— the Bureau refused to supply the residents with printed accounts of the siege. Radio was Mt. Carmel's chief source of information about what was going on outside, and on some days, there was no news at all: after the FBI disconnected the community's electricity lines and batteries grew weak, reception became an aleatory and happenstance affair. On days when government spokesmen wanted to send a public message to Koresh, its technicians reconnected the power lines during Bureau press briefings, and dutifully, if spitefully, the residents of Mt. Carmel tuned in. Koresh and his followers were confined in an environment of controlled information flow.

On the morning of February 28—while telephone lines still linked Mt. Carmel to the world—Wayne Martin had dialed fellow attorney Ralph Strother in Waco. He asked Strother to inform the media about the raid. During his 911 calls, he made repeated requests for contact with the press. But the government wouldn't oblige. "Wayne, we can't endanger the media," Lieutenant Lynch had explained. In the interests of protecting the media, within hours of the shoot-out the authorities were halting all reporters at a spot that became known as "Satellite City," some two miles southwest of Mt. Carmel. Its distance was chosen because, the government said, Mt. Carmel's gunners were in possession of .50-caliber weapons with a range of 9,000 feet, or just under two miles. ATF records, however, showed that the rifles had a range of 5,900 feet, or about a mile. And as several members of the press would complain, in other conflicts, including the Gulf War, authorities had not kept photographers and reporters out of gunshot range.

The federal cops had more than safety in mind when they barred the press from the scene. As a negotiator explained to Scott Sonobe's wife, Sita, on March 3, ". . . We feel that it's in your best interest and everybody's best interest that a lot of information doesn't get out." Three days later, the same negotiator told Koresh, ". . . We've been ignoring the press because we don't want the press to know what we are or are not doing. . . ." At the same time, the FBI held out contact with the press as an inducement to surrender, promising time and again that if Koresh came out, the media would hear him speak. ". . . The media is very interested in your side of the story," Agent Comealong advised the preacher. "Yeah, I understand that," Koresh replied. "That's, that's why you all have locked me off from the outside."

A committee from the Society of Professional Journalists (SPJ) in its report issued at the end of 1993, essentially sustained Koresh's complaint. "While . . . concern for safety is understandable," the committee reported, "journalists have long chosen to accept physical danger as part of their role in covering important stories. . . . Access to the heart of a story, to the front lines of any battle, is essential. . . . In the case of Waco, journalists were kept so far away from the front lines that they were not able to properly scrutinize the actions of the law enforcement agencies and negotiators."

Suppression of information was not limited to keeping reporters at a distance from Mt. Carmel. During the siege, the SPJ committee found, "Court appearances were held secretly. Hearings were closed to the press. Key documents ranging from motions to government responses to arrest and search warrants were sealed." The committee also lamented that "In case after case there was no meaningful protest from the news media. . . ."

The residents of Mt. Carmel did not think that the hundreds of reporters assigned to the story were capable of comprehending their world view, since it was based on theology and faith. But they wanted the press within reach, to witness the FBI's ostensible military tactics. For example, two of Mt. Carmel's outbuildings were leveled by tanks on March 3. That same day, tanks rammed a 1990 Chevrolet Cavalier station wagon that was parked on EE Road, next to the undercover house. The vehicle, reduced to a shambles, belonged to the *Waco Tribune-Herald*, whose reporters had abandoned it on February 28.

The destructive act didn't appear in telephoto views of the area, and wasn't made known to the public for days. In its effort to clear the field for a new assault, FBI tank pilots also halved a mobile home, interred a dozen motorcycles, crushed two dozen go-carts, tricycles, and bicycles, knocked out the windshield of a bus, and flattened Paul Fatta's pickup. They carried away the fence from Mt. Carmel's front yard, flipped a bass fishing boat, and overturned a bulldozer that the community had rented—for some $3,000 per month—from a local building supply house.

The government's tracked vehicles also planed the surface of the Mt. Carmel cemetery, leaving Anna Hughes, among others, to await Judgment in an unmarked plot. Texas Rangers secretly protested some of these moves as destroying evidence that they needed for reconstructing the events of February 28, and Schneider and Koresh also complained. But the negotiators said that they had no command over the tankers. "Well, who's controlling these guys? Are they their own nation?" Schneider snapped. An answer was given at a press conference, when a reporter asked about the *Tribune* vehicle, two weeks after its destruction. FBI spokesman Bob Ricks replied—or quipped—that "We are not professional tank drivers. We are FBI agents who are driving tanks."

On March 8, the FBI men entered the two Mag Bag or "shop" buildings in tanks 12 feet wide. Since this armored action occurred away from Mt. Carmel, it was filmed and reported. The building's owner, local banker Gary Welch, told the *Waco Tribune* that he was aghast. "I don't understand why they had to do that. I offered yesterday to give them the key," he said. The forced entry was necessary, Federal agents claimed, in case the Mag Bag was booby-trapped. After the smashing entry, ATF agents, Rangers, and G-Men swept and combed the ruins for evidence. Just as they suspected, they found evidence of guns: six shotgun shells!

If the government's acts of destruction incensed Mt. Carmel's inhabitants, the fate of the children who were in government custody gave them even more cause for doubt. Their parents complained on two levels: about milk, and about custody.

Ellen White had not forbidden milk to her followers, but had predicted (CD 411) that "in a short time the milk of the cows will also be excluded from the diet of God's commandment-keeping people." Mt. Carmel's residents, drawing on White and on the counsel of contemporary nutritionists, had decided that, as a general rule, cow's milk was useless, even harmful, to adults, and was to be regarded as of less value to children than maternal milk or goat's milk. So ingrained was their worry that when the first children were sent into authoritarian care, they carried with them a few quarts of goat's milk and $1,000 in cash, a sort of Milk Fund for the unusual circumstances that lay ahead.

But not all of the children went outside, and inside Mt. Carmel, an unforeseen phenomenon was noted: nursing mothers quit lactating, apparently in reaction to stress. Just after midnight on March 4, Koresh reported this to a negotiator, demanding that milk, even cow's milk, be sent inside. He and the agent were arranging the exit of Heather Jones, age nine, when Koresh made his demand. ". . . Let's get her out and then let me send you the milk," the March 4 negotiator said.

Heather Jones, one of the children of David Jones, emerged at 8:39 A.M. the following morning. Later that day, and the next day, and on March 7 and 8, Schneider, Koresh, and several of the mothers renewed the demand, citing the Bureau's promise. But no milk came. Instead, on March 7, FBI spokesman Ricks told a press conference: "They got a number of individuals on the phone and talked to us about how they needed milk. We said we're ready and willing to bring the milk in, and they rejected the offer to deliver milk."

Transcripts of March 6–7 telephone conversations show a different development. The FBI's negotiators, overlooking the March 4 promise, offered to send six gallons of milk in exchange for the exit of four more children. Koresh responded to the 6x4 offer by invoking the March 4 pledge, and in a humored—or sarcastic way—formulated a counterdemand. He told the negotiators to better their offer by sending in not six gallons of milk, but six gallons of ice cream—accompanied by the return of two children. Sticking to seriousness, the FBI talkers reiterated their 6x4 position. Koresh then sent word through an aide, telling them "to go have a milk shake." After some ninety minutes of this kind of banter, Koresh refused to bargain further, leaving instructions with Rachel, his wife, to tell any callers that he wasn't at Mt. Carmel: he had gone, she told the negotiators, to "Waco to buy milk."

225

Spokesman Ricks construed these exchanges, not as a refusal to accept the 6x4 deal, but as refusal to accept a delivery of milk.

On Monday, March 8, Sheriff Jack Harwell came to the FBI command post to speak by telephone with Koresh, who lost no time in raising the issue of milk. "I heard about the $1,000, David, and that didn't surprise me at all. . . ," Harwell said, as if he hadn't known about the reported refusal. Then he promised to "see what I can do about getting that milk out there to you. . . . I want those babies taken care of." The county sheriff apparently persuaded the big Bureau to cooperate: six gallons of milk were delivered to Mt. Carmel before sundown. Shortly afterwards, in discussing the FBI's change of mind with one of the Numbered Johns, Koresh learned that the denial had not been an unquestioned tactic, even inside the government camp:

KORESH   Hey, we appreciate you all finally coming around with this. We, we just could not understand why you all were, you know, punching at the kids, you know, for something like this.

FBI   Neither can I, neither can I, okay?

KORESH   . . . I gave you $1,000, you know.

FBI   Yeah, that had nothing to do with it. It's—you know and I know who it is, and it's not us. I'll just leave it at that.

The government's concession created a public relations quandary. The FBI could not admit that Koresh, through Harwell, had persuaded the agency to honor the March 4 promise, since its negotiators had been ignoring the pledge. Moreover, the agency's spokesman had already declared that Mt. Carmel "rejected the offer to deliver milk"; the Bureau could not admit that it had lied. So it held the news to its chest. Not until March 9 did it reveal that Harwell had spoken to Koresh, and in explaining the visit's outcome, it pictured Harwell as having prevailed on Koresh, not the agency. The press reported what it was told. The government's strategy of speaking through Harwell "seems to be working," the Waco Tribune observed. "Authorities were able to deliver six gallons of milk for the remaining children late Monday." Though Koresh and his crew had won the dispute—no additional children were sent out in exchange for the delivery—in the press, the milk for Mt. Carmel's children was credited to the FBI. As polls would show, readers and viewers were convinced that their government was demonstrating patience and humanitarian concern.

Schneider, Koresh, and the mothers inside Mt. Carmel would go to the telephones a dozen times more, haranguing negotiators about the need for milk, even after they discovered that listening devices had been placed in the plastic bottles in which it was sent. Their demands grew especially frequent after authorities began interrupting Mt. Carmel's electricity supply on March 9; not having electricity meant that milk went sour.

From the start of the children's exodus, mothers who stayed behind put notes in their offspring's pockets, instructing the reader to turn the child over to the care of relatives, whose telephone numbers were inscribed on the exit messages. But nothing like that happened. Instead, the children were housed in a facility operated by the Texas Department of Protective and Regulatory Services. The parents' overriding worries were that their kids would be fed pork, that their uncut locks would be shorn, or that other taboos they associated with their religion would not be respected. To put them at ease, the FBI sent a videotape into Mt. Carmel, showing the children in their temporary home. Parts of the tape were made available to the news media, who included clips in televised reports from Waco. But the film only inflamed Mt. Carmel's mothers. The children, Judy Schneider concluded after viewing it, were "eating candy all day long, drinking soda pop . . . hyper as heck. . . . Watching tv, acting like wild nuts." "The kids were all going wild, jumping around," Lorraine Sylvia pointed out. "They seemed to be eating and drinking continuously and we don't do that," Teresa Nobrega complained.

The videotape, and another sent in by the FBI, in which five negotiators showed their faces to those inside, gave rise to an idea: that Mt. Carmel would make a tape of its own. On March 8 and 9, tapes were prepared and sent out to the FBI. In one of them, Koresh appeared in a tank top shirt, stubble on his face, a scabbed wound on his wrist, a seeping one in his side. Though obviously in pain, he made a great effort to introduce his children, waving their hands at the camera, and telling one toddler, for example, "Say thanks for the milk, too." He also went out of his way to be macho on film, introducing his concu-

227

bines and talking tough. "This is my family and nobody is going to come in on top of my family and start pushing my family around," he declared. "Being an American first," he blustered, "I'm the kind of guy that I'll stand in front of the tank. You can run over me but I'll be biting one of the tracks!"

In the other tape, some two dozen residents took seats, singly and in family groups, in front of the camera. In their own words, they told the photographer (Steve Schneider) why they came to Mt. Carmel, and why they had decided to remain. Bernadette Monbelly, thirty-one, a coffee-colored young woman from England, declared, "This is where existence is for me in the world. There is no existence outside this vicinity. This is where David is, he is revealing the Seals, and this is what the world should have been waiting for." "I came here with my grandma, when I was five," mumbles a doe-eyed teen-ager, Abigail Martinez, seated on a couch with other girls her age. "I came here when I was seven years old, and my grandma brought me here," says her sister Audrey, twelve. "I didn't come for the truth. I came with my husband," Sita Sonobe confesses.

Livingstone Fagan's wife, Evette, dressed in what appears to be a braided hairdo and an African smock, breaks into tears as she tells the camera that although she sent her children out for safety's sake, it embittered her. "They would be better off here, even if they died here," she declares. "They'd be safer than being in the hands of Babylon." Ofelia Santoyo, a sixty-two-year-old Mexican-American—grandmother of the Martinez children—asks the viewer to send word to her family "not to worry about me because these prophesies have to be fulfilled." Her grandson, ten-year-old Joseph Martinez, talks about a bullet that on February 28 "went through the carpet" where he was cowering "and stopped in the carpet, in the wood."

Whatever disagreements one might have with the residents of Mt. Carmel, the film humanizes its subjects. In their post–April 19 investigation of the Waco affair, Justice Department investigators reported: "The negotiator's log shows that when the tape was reviewed there was concern that if the tape was released to the media, Koresh would gain much sympathy." Though the document was news, and would have been ideal for television, it wouldn't have served the agency's public relations goals. Instead of presenting it to the press, the Bureau sat on the videotape. On March 26, Koresh sent out a third film, showing new scenes of himself and the children who remained inside. This, too, was suppressed.

Throughout the siege, every investigation found that, in contrast to the lurid charges raised in the *Tribune*'s "Sinful Messiah" series and elsewhere, Mt. Carmel's children had been safe inside. On March 8, *New York Times* Texas correspondent Sam Howe Verhovek reported that "Despite allegations by former cult members that Mr. Koresh sexually abused girls, there is considerable evidence that the children were, in at least some respects, well cared for. None show any signs of physical abuse, and most seem consumed with a wish to see their parents." The *Waco Tribune*, on March 12, quoted Bob Boyd, a Child Protective Services division spokesman, as saying, "I think we're seeing the same thing from these kids and any child that's taken away from their own home. These kids are the same. . . . They're coping very well."

Even after the April 19 conflagration, when reports on the children could no longer influence negotiations, the news didn't vary. On April 11, Bruce Perry, chief of psychiatry at Texas Children's Hospital in Houston, a doctor who studied the kids during their confinement, told the Associated Press that the children "are in very good condition and show no signs of abuse." "The children have not confirmed any of the allegations or described any other incidents which would verify our concerns about abuse," Texas child welfare executive Janice Caldwell reported on April 23. In an interview published on May 5 by the *Dallas Morning News*, Dr. Perry said, "We have no evidence that the children released from the compound were sexually abused." After breaking from the group, apostate Alisa Shaw, who left Mt. Carmel about a month before the February 28 raid, told an interviewer that "All the women had so much support because of being mothers and living with each other, they all had so much help raising their children. There were a lot of children that weren't David's but it really did seem like one big family." In the wake of the April 19 fire, even FBI chief William Sessions confessed that the Bureau had "no contemporaneous evidence" of misdeeds toward children. The abuse charges lobbed against Koresh and his followers were repeatedly shown to be false.

229

Yet Texas authorities, perhaps for public relations reasons of their own, treated the charges as real. On March 9, with twenty-one children in hand, the state Department of Protective and Regulatory Services, through its Child Protective Services division, decided that it could not be merely a baby-sitter during the siege. Instead, it stripped parents of custody of the children they'd sent into its care. The agency's action meant that even if the parents came out of Mt. Carmel, and were not charged with any crime, they would not be able to resume their family lives without first passing tests of parental fitness. The same requirement was levied, ipso facto, onto those relatives whom the parents had chosen as guardians. Though those inside Mt. Carmel believed that they might die before the conflict ended, they did not intend to cede their parental authority while they lived. The assumption of legal custody by the state deepened their anxiety over the machinations of Babylon. "David had an agreement with them that the children would go to their grandparents and other relatives," Sheila Martin recalls. "When we learned over TV that the state was going to take our children, we realized that they had lied. We knew that we couldn't believe them then. I just prayed that God would take care of the whole situation."

Among those affected by the state's child custody decision was petite, brown-skinned Juliette Martinez, thirty, the mother of six children, five of whom, ages three through thirteen, lived with her at Mt. Carmel. Juliette and her children belonged at Mt. Carmel, perhaps in ways that outsiders could not fully grasp.

Juliette's grandfather, Epigmenio Acuña, a Mexican immigrant, had been working as a landscaper in California in 1931 or 1932 when he ran into a Spanish-language tract explaining Ellen White's ideas about the Sabbath. He checked what he read against the Bible and decided that White's interpretation was correct. Not knowing how to get in touch with her followers, he'd begun observing the Sabbath on his own.

The Depression years, for Mexicans in California, were a time of unemployment and deportations. Like many others, Epigmenio in 1932 took his family back to his home country. With him and his wife,

230

Concepción, had gone Ofelia, their one-year-old daughter, born in the United States. Back in Mexico, Epigmenio was one day commuting from the countryside into the capital city when he saw a fellow bus rider reading a book by Ellen White. The rider was an SDA missionary, and Epigmenio promptly joined the church. Concepción, however, stood by her native Catholicism; Ofelia learned Adventism only at her father's knee.

During the late forties, Ofelia went to the border, to work in garment factories on the north side of the Rio Grande. In El Paso and Juárez, she paid little mind to matters of faith. On one of her jobs she met Jose Luis Santoyo, a secular American, whom she later married. The couple ignored religion. "When we used to go to Mexico, my father would talk to us about it, but as soon as we came back to the U.S., we'd forget about it," she recalls. Her husband began drinking heavily, Ofelia claims, after a tour in the Army during the Korean War. Ofelia left him, taking with her the two sons that he had fathered.

Another secular man came into her life, but after a few years, this liaison ended badly, too. Ofelia bore two children—one of them Juliette—to this man, whom she never married. In California during the sixties, distraught with life, Ofelia turned back to religion, joining a congregation of the Reformed Movement, an SDA splinter group. While on a family sojourn in Arizona, Juliette, then in her late teens, met and married a young man who was a Reform Movement deacon. Juliette bore three children to him, and then, as if repeating her mother's history, sued for divorce, alleging infidelity. So embittered was she with churchiness that Juliette turned her back on Adventism. Her next liaison was with a man whom she described as "just a junkie" from El Paso.

During Juliette's marital storms, her grandfather died, her widowed grandmother joined the SDA, and her mother accepted the call of David Koresh. Concepción and Ofelia, Juliette's grandmother and mother, had reunited at the encampment in Palestine, Texas. When Juliette could no longer cope with her growing brood, she sent two of her three children to them. Financially stranded and with nowhere to turn, in 1990 she joined her grandmother, mother, and two daughters at Mt. Carmel. ". . . I didn't come here because I wanted religion or

231

anything," she told the FBI. "I was, you know, I was all, you know, strung out and everything, and this is where they helped me."

Koresh took a special liking to her children, informally adopting them as his own; the kids called him "Dad." Though the community's life was unorthodox by almost any standards, Mt. Carmel gave Juliette's brood the stability that she had been unable to arrange on her own. It provided four generations of her family with a common faith and a home.

In early March, FBI negotiators realized that the exit of Juliette Martinez's children would be a watershed: only Koresh's children, and Juliette's children, remained inside. But Juliette resisted, and the objections that she raised spoke for almost everyone inside:

> FBI   . . . You're concerned about your children as good mothers are. I know you want to leave. I know you want to send your kids out. Please send your children out. David will let you send—come out. David has repeated that you're all free to go and that if you stay it's your choice. . . . But your children are not old enough to make those decisions. Send them out.
>
> MARTINEZ   . . . They want to be with me.
>
> FBI   Well, you come out with them. You come out with them. There's no reason you can't—
>
> MARTINEZ   If, if, if I go out, I mean, you know, being here is the only way that we could be together. If I go out you guys are going to separate us. . . . You won't let me be with my children if I go out. . . . They'll put me in jail and they'll take them away.

Her expressions were tentative, not adamant. She asked the agents to let her consult an older brother in Arizona. "I know every time I had a problem or decision to make I always talk to my brother," she pleaded. A husbandless woman wanted to talk to a trusted male, but the agents balked. "You can talk to your brother as soon as you come out, but right now, send the children out," the negotiator demanded. Juliette refused to give in.

When the hard sell didn't work, the negotiators, sensing her indecision, had agents in Arizona track down Juliette's brother. They recorded an interview with him and played it for her on March 8. He told her he wasn't capable of taking care of her children and urged her to surrender.

After playing the tape, the negotiators pressed harder. "I don't know what more you need to hear, Julie," one argued. "Bring the children to safety now. . . . Why wait until the situation may get worse? Come out now while you still can walk directly into full safety." "How can I believe anything you say? Everything on the radio is lies, too," she retorted. "You know, all they're doing is getting the public ready to come and, and, and do away with us." Her accusation touched a nerve with her interlocutor.

FBI   Wait. With all the media that's watching—The world is watching this via satellite, you know. How could the government, the ATF, the FBI, anybody now with all this spotlight shining on us do anything improper to you or anyone else?

MARTINEZ   They're going to do it.

FBI   No, nothing improper, nothing illegal.

MARTINEZ   Yeah, they're going to come and get rid of us all.

FBI   Get rid of you? Why would we want to do that? Why would we want to harm you?

MARTINEZ   Because that's what they, that's what they came over here for in the first place. You know, they came shooting at us and climbing all in our windows and everything. . . .

FBI   . . . There were some things that shouldn't have been done. That was—that's over a week ago. What has happened in the last week? . . .

MARTINEZ   If we go out, we're going to, we're going to have to go to jail . . .

FBI   . . . Nobody knows that you're going to have to go to jail. . . . You said you didn't do anything. And if you did not do anything, then there will not be any charges filed against you. That's not the way it works, especially with the world watching, with the media watching.

MARTINEZ   Well, the media is not watching. They won't let them.

FBI   Look, everybody cares. . . . Everybody knows the names of the people that are in there and they will be covered by the media and the results of what happens will be covered by the media. . . .

MARTINEZ   Only what the FBI wants them to see.

233

FBI   No, no, no. No, no, no. We're talking about the courts, the justice system.

MARTINEZ   There's no justice. . . . Once I go and fall into you guys' hands, that's it.

FBI   No, it's not a matter of falling in anybody's hands, it's a matter of walking to the safety of the free world.

MARTINEZ   Free world?

FBI   And the justice system and the media.

MARTINEZ   There is no free world.

The conversation ended on a futile note, with the negotiator telling Martinez, "How would you want this to be resolved? Huh? How? What would you want to happen?" Her reply was, "For God to come and deliver us all from our enemies."

On March 21, Ofelia, Juliette's mother, sixty-two, came out of Mt. Carmel. She wanted to join Concepción, eighty-three, who was living with David Jones's mother, Mary Belle. Had the two been placed together, they would have been able to care for Juliette's children. Though she was never charged with any crime, Ofelia was denied bond, like all the other residents, and just as Juliette had predicted, her mother spent the next few months in jail.

For its final arguments with Juliette Martinez, on March 25, the Bureau chose a female negotiator who mentioned her own motherhood in the chitchat that led into the serious talk:

FBI   . . . I've heard no one say that anyone there hasn't been a good mother to their children. But I think the situation, as it is now, it's not going to get any better, it can only get worse. And I would think, as a mother, I would think you'd want to get your kids out of that situation. . . .

MARTINEZ   This is our home.

FBI   I beg your pardon?

MARTINEZ   This is our home. You know, why do they want to take us out of our home?

FBI   Well, it's important that you leave there. That, that can't be your home now. We have to get you out of that situation.

MARTINEZ   Why did they do this to us?

234

FBI   I can't talk to you about that, you know, the events of the past. . . . I assure you that nothing bad is going to happen to your children.

MARTINEZ   No, just end up in a foster home somewhere and they get abused and slapped around. . . . Giving them junk food and, and pork. . . .

FBI   . . . That should not be a concern because that's not true. They always want to keep the children with their parents.

MARTINEZ   Hey, that's what they've been saying over the radio, that, you know, they're going to be put in foster homes. They weren't even . . . going to allow them to be sent to their relatives.

FBI   . . . We have to give them to a relative. And the way the relative is determined, it's determined by a judge. He has an independent study done of the home that they would go to and he makes the decision. . . . It has to be someone who is responsible, who has the love for that child, and also has the financial capabilities of taking care of the child.

Martinez wasn't convinced that "an independent study" would grant either her jailed mother or her aging grandmother guardianship of her children—or that she would wind up with custody of them, either. Her negotiator seemed to be speaking for Babylon.

FBI   . . . This has been going on almost for a month. It's not going to get better. Do you think so?

MARTINEZ   If God does something, yes.

FBI   It's not going to get better.

MARTINEZ   Do you believe in God?

FBI   It's not going to get better. It's only going—

MARTINEZ   Do you believe in God up in heaven?

FBI   I'm not going to discuss religion with you, okay?

Unconvinced, Juliette Martinez stayed inside. She and her children died in the April 19 blaze.

Chapter 26

ALLIES

"... They had the right to defend themselves against excessive, deadly force."
—defense attorney Dick DeGuerin

"I realized that something was happening there that would have historic significance."
—agitator Gary Hunt

Despite the general disfavor with which Americans viewed Koresh and his clan, the publicity generated by the standoff drew allies to Mt. Carmel's cause. But the community's allies didn't become heroes inside. Its theologically advanced residents had only a vague notion about the efforts being made on their behalf, and they spoke of them with a mixture of approval and condescension. Their teachings were aimed at steering believers away from preoccupation with the secular world, and reentering it, even to form vital alliances, was not a prospect they hailed.

A chasm stood between David Koresh, a handful of theologians, and everyone else at Mt. Carmel, largely because religion is never a matter of dogma written in stone. Believers always individualize what their clergy impart; even Koresh, who claimed to be merely a medium for the Bible, had done that. In many circumstances, the faithful person-

236

alize their credence in pagan ways, as when Latin American Catholics, for example, place folk saints upon family altars. Among Protestants, believers frequently claim that despite what the scriptures might enjoin, in prayer God has provided them with a unique dispensation or insight. Dogma always exists, but it is only one, competitive element of religiosity, and David Koresh knew that his dogma had to compete.

Rather than trying to impose a monolithic orthodoxy, Koresh had always tailored his teachings to different levels of comprehension, taste, and interest, even creating auxiliary, or flanking doctrines, that, like the walls of a theological maze, eased his followers toward the gate whose keys he alone held. After the February 28 shoot-out, for example, he gave the nod to three scriptural interpretations of what lay ahead, all of them gradients of a thought. Koresh systematically made room for other people to play supporting roles in his messianic scheme, and he made room for allied doctrines as well. In doing so, he opened the door to something that he probably did not expect: that he, and not his allies, would become the convert.

The first, and simplest, of the theological interpretations he advanced to explain the siege—intelligible even to FBI negotiators—was that of Noah's Ark. "So, see," Koresh told them, "salvation does not depend upon a person being good . . . just like in Noah's day. You didn't have to be a saint to be saved. You had to get into the ark, though." His rendering pictured Mt. Carmel as the antitypical salvation ship. Noah, Koresh pointed out, had gotten into his ship when he thought the time was right, though that turned out to be seven days before the rains began. The residents of Mt. Carmel began waiting for an antitypical flood to begin on February 28, though, for scriptural reasons, they expected the destruction to come this time by fire. Not only would they be saved from the conflagration, but those who did not join them—like those who snubbed Noah's invitations—were likely to die. ". . . This is a probationary period," Steve Schneider explained to a negotiator, "where you and others have an opportunity to hear and see something about the Seals. . . . Those that reject the truth, you're going to have to experience the truth . . . like in the days of Noah."

A more sophisticated prediction was advanced by Kathryn Schroeder in a confession written from jail, which cites Nahum 2. A great conflict

237

had begun, God's people would probably lose the initial battle, but their martyrdom—perhaps like that of the defenders of the Alamo—would win the war. The interpretation from Nahum was not only based on a more obscure scripture than the Noah text, but was also more advanced in that it raised the possibility that the faithful would perish, too.

The most advanced of Koresh's prophecies was that the looming future would be a fulfillment of Revelation 6:9–11, the Fifth Seal:

> And when he had opened the fifth seal, I saw under the altar the souls of them that were slain for the word of God; and for the testimony which they held;
>
> And they cried with a loud voice, saying, How long, O Lord, holy and true, dost thou not judge and avenge our blood on them that dwell on the earth?
>
> And white robes were given unto every one of them; and it was said unto them, that they should rest yet for a little season, until their fellowservants also and their brethren, that should be killed as they were, should be fulfilled.

The residents who had died on February 28, Mt. Carmel's preacher reasoned, were now under the altar in heaven, in the company of history's martyrs, crying for a vengeance that could not begin until those remaining were dead. The interpretation was a new one to some of the flock, whose training had covered only the first Four Seals. Though tied to Nahum 2 in the details of its interpretation, the Fifth Seal stood out from the simpler texts because it asserted in seemingly certain terms that none of the faithful would survive. It was a text, or an interpretation, that some followers were reluctant to accept.

Koresh and his flock were not entirely isolated from Babylon, nor from its hopes, including longevity, and it was unlike the Waco Messiah to say that anything was just so, unqualifiedly. Instead, he taught that "God always leaves a way out." He said that, for example, hell was not eternal, even for the most sinful souls. Circumstances could combine to save even mortal lives—in particular, those of the residents who stayed inside Mt. Carmel during the siege—however unlikely such an outcome might be. Though he believed that their doom was probably sealed in heaven, Koresh knew that some of his followers found the prospect of death nearly unbearable, and he did not wall out all external influences, or all residual hope.

Because they hoped that a break would come, several residents kept their ears tuned to radios. A March 5 broadcast offered them what they thought was a way to foil the barricades. It was the first of four strategies that allies would foist upon the encampment.

The broadcast was of a morning talk show on a Dallas AM station, KGBS. An area communications technician, Ken Fawcett, had called to report what he'd seen on raw television feeds of the siege. Signals beamed from cameras near Mt. Carmel were being bounced by satellites back to reception centers on the ground for editing, and Fawcett was picking up the unedited transmissions. What he had been seeing—and most viewers didn't see—disturbed and intrigued him.

Fawcett's involvement began early on the afternoon of February 28. He was watching a televised basketball game when his mother called to tell him about the Waco events, he says. Fawcett switched channels, viewed a bit of the reportage, concluded that it described a foreign locale, and informed his mother as much. But she called again, insisting that he pay closer mind. The technician tuned in a second time, and before the day was over, he was recording both the raw feeds and ordinary programming.

"My initial impression," he recalls, "was that these people were getting what they deserved. I thought that religion was the cause of all the problems in the world, and these people were probably like Libyan terrorists." A discrepancy between the raw feed and the programming, however, caused him to doubt. "The report that the media put out at the time was that more telephone lines were being laid for Koresh. But I worked for the telephone company for thirteen years, and I knew that wasn't right, from the trucks and linemen that I saw on the feed. You can tell a splicer or an installer man by the tools he carries, and I knew that they weren't installing." As he suspected, the linemen were severing Mt. Carmel's links to the world.

As the days passed, other things stuck in his mind, too. "The thing about the feed is that you can hear the cameramen, the sound men, everybody, talking to each other, things and people you don't hear on regular TV. Once, after they had moved the television crews, I heard a cameraman saying, 'Hey, we can see from here better than we could last night.' Immediately, the DPS"—the Texas Department of Public Safety, or highway patrol—"told them that they had to move again." The images of tanks moving onto the property, contributed to his unease, too. "When you start getting tanks out to use against citizens, like in Bosnia or Tiananmen," he remarked, "it's kind of chilling."

A detail he picked up from his monitoring inspired a plan: the TV dish at Mt. Carmel hadn't moved in all the hours that he'd been watching, he told a talk show host from KGBS. Even if telephone lines weren't working, Fawcett suggested, the dish could serve as a yes/no signal. To test the suggestion, Fawcett's interviewer, Ron Engelman, allowed him to address those inside. "David, if you can hear my voice, move your satellite dish from Galaxy 6 to Galaxy 1," Fawcett said over the airwaves.

Ron Engelman, a thin, gray, chain-smoking, bearded announcer, veteran of twenty-two years in the radio trade, had left a job in Boston to chair the KGBS program only a month before the shoot-out. Though he claims, "I let the show go where the callers wanted," Engelman was what he calls a "Constitutionalist" when the Dallas job began, and the topics his listeners picked usually followed in the same vein. Some of Mt. Carmel's residents were listening to the show, both because it was sympathetic to their cause and because they were learning to sympathize with its political line.

"Constitutionalism" is not a term in the vocabulary of electoral buffs or the daily press, but as the events in Waco would reflect, a trend of anti-government sentiment worthy of such a name was burgeoning in non-partisan politics. The current's central tenet, as stated in the manifesto of a California group that calls itself the Constitution Party—which did not exist at the time of the ATF raid—is that "Our lack of knowledge of the Constitution is what allows the powers in federal government to proceed and strip us of our God-given freedoms. . . ."

Those whom Ron Engelman terms "Constitutionalists" have traditionally taken unto themselves labels like "patriots" and "sovereign citizens." Some are political descendants of John Birchism and other movements of the ultra-right. But a younger crowd, often loyal to the

240

Libertarian Party, also falls into the category that Engelman named—
the category, numerous in Dallas, from which he drew callers to his
show. Though wide differences separated these Constitutionalists—
some are pot-smoking heathens, some demure Christians—one issue
unites them: Opposition to gun control. When the ATF raided Mt.
Carmel, the telephone lines in Engelman's studio exploded with voices
of protest.

Neither Koresh nor Schneider had listened to the KGBS show before
February 28, but now Mt. Carmel's ears bent to its message, which, its
inhabitants thought, reflected their own point of view. In Christian
fundamentalist circles, deciphering prophecies about oppressors—the
King of the North, the King of the South, Babylon, Assyria, the Beast
of Revelation—has become practically an industry over the past fifty
years, and the usual decodings identify the United States, the United
Nations, the papacy, the Trilateral Commission, the Council on Foreign Relations (or some combination of these) as the Bible's bad guys.
Koresh's innate radicalism led him to opinions of a similar kind, and so
did his heritage from the SDA. In a contemporary work published by
the church, *The New World Order*, for example, SDA lecturer Russell
Burrill, referring to a prophecy of Revelation 12, notes that "In order
to fulfill this prediction, America will need to repudiate her constitution and the bill of rights, which guarantee freedom of religion. . . .
Yet this is the inevitable future of the United States, as foreseen by John
the Revelator."

David Koresh, however, had been only superficially interested in
politics. ". . . As long as man controls man, the difficulties and problems of the world as it is now witnessed . . . are going to remain," he
declared, in words reminiscent of Ellen White. Steve Schneider's older
sister, Sue Johnson, had given him a subscription to *Spotlight*, an
ultra-right weekly Washington tabloid, and from it, and perhaps from
gun show associates as well, both men had learned to put a conspira-
torial twist on the Constitutionalist line. Their Constitutionalism was
far more radical than anything that radio host Engelman professed.

"The way that your nation, the United States of America, works,"
Koresh told the FBI, "is that it puts on its currency In God We Trust.
Now, on the one dollar bill you have a pyramid there. . . . Let me tell

you, the God of Egypt was not the God of Moses," he admonished. Koresh alleged that the bill's pyramid-and-eyeball design, the obverse of the Great Seal of the United States, represented, not the symbolism of Masonic Founding Fathers, but that of the Bavarian Illuminati, an organization that he believed to exist still. The Illuminati, says the *Encyclopaedia Britannica*, was "a short-lived movement of republican free thought founded on May day 1776 by Adam Weishaupt, professor of canon law. . . . Their founder's aim was to replace Christianity by a religion of reason." From 1778 until the organization's forced, and presumably, final dissolution in 1785, the Illuminati courted Masons as prospective members. A pyramid-and-eyeball motif occurs in relics from both groups, making its origin difficult to fix. On esoterica like these, conspiracy theories thrive.

". . . I see your agency and other agencies like yours," Steve Schneider told the FBI, "as Big Brother. I really do . . . I believe that there is a Trilateral Commission and a Council on Foreign Relations." Making reference to Revelation 18's predictions about the End Time, he declaimed: "The Bible says merchants would be the great men of the earth and by their sorceries they deceive all of mankind." "The Constitution . . . ," Schneider averred during a harangue to its ostensible servants, has "been run over by all these powerful merchants that now control these little puppets that are called politicians": most Constitutionalists and, indeed, most voters would have agreed. His predictions, of course, were dire. "This country of America that I've loved all of my life," he lamented, ". . . very powerful, very strong, based on freedom of speech, religion, all that, it's going to be brought down as an example to the world." Constitutionalism, Koresh and Schneider assumed, was a secularized and therefore nearly useless version of the present truth.

When Ken Fawcett made his appeal, one of Mt. Carmel's listeners moved the building's satellite dish to Galaxy 6, and a chain reaction began. Fawcett reported the switch to Engelman, who already had an idea about what to do next. "When we're at war and we get a POW, and that prisoner is wounded," he says, "we send him to get medical care right away. And here we were, with prisoners in our own country, and the FBI was using medical care as a bargaining chip." The residents of Mt. Carmel, he huffed, were being treated more harshly than Viet Cong.

Engelman's complaint was heard by members of a short-lived Dallas suburban group, the Constitution Foundational Association, or CFA, who were acquainted with two medical practitioners in Portland. They called their Northwestern friends, and both volunteered to go into Mt. Carmel, if consent could be obtained from inside. Fawcett wasn't available on Monday, the 8th, but Tuesday he was on the line and watching a raw television feed. Engelman asked his Mt. Carmel listeners to move their dish again, this time in assent to the entry of medical personnel. The dish moved. Engelman also relayed a truly unusual request, typical of the schemes dreamed up by soldiers in the Constitutionalist crusade.

Gary Hunt was a tall, gray-bearded, forty-six-year-old Florida land surveyor and Vietnam War veteran who on March 7 had come to Waco to cover the developing story for the *Outpost of Freedom,* a tabloid monthly that he published himself. Hunt had studied business law as an undergraduate, and he thought that he could serve Mt. Carmel's interests, not only as a journalist, but as a double for Koresh, through a power of attorney. If a dying or paralyzed man could assent to representation by a nod of his head, a wave of his finger, or a blink of the eyes—movies and legal legends told Hunt that it had been done that way—appointment could also be gained through a TV dish, he reasoned. So he sent a fax to Engelman, urging Koresh to tap him by wagging the dish. The host relayed Hunt's request over the air, and it, too, was granted by the machine atop Mt. Carmel. In order to confirm Fawcett's report of these sightings, Engelman asked his Mt. Carmel listeners to hang a banner from one of their windows—and a new tactic was born. During the next thirty-six hours, they hung several bed sheets in view of the cameras at Satellite City. The first carried no message, but the second was inscribed, "God Help Us: We Want the Press." A third said, "Send in the CFA." Before the siege had ended, others would be unfurled, citing scriptures and proclaiming, "Rodney King We Understand."

On the morning of Thursday, March 11, Engelman, an associate from KGBS, two CFA honchos, and two medical men left Dallas for

Waco, two hours away. The talk show host says that he didn't know until they were en route that the healers whose entry he'd arranged weren't family physicians, but podiatrists, foot fixers. In Waco, Hunt had already tried to serve papers on ATF and FBI potentiates as a stand-in for Koresh, and had been roundly rebuffed. But about the time that Engelman was reaching town, Hunt was entering the federal courthouse, legal briefs in hand, a new tack in mind. "I, along with David Koresh, and Eric Lighter"—another of the Constitutionalists—"am confessing to murder and other crimes, the same crimes committed by the ATF and FBI against the Branch Davidians," he told a deputy clerk. "As a friend of the court and a material witness, I am asking you to enter these papers into the court's file." The papers that Hunt wanted to file, on behalf of Koresh, called for a grand jury investigation into the events of February 28. The astonished clerk stepped away from the counter that separated the two, and seconds later, G-Men blocked Hunt's exit from the room.

Meanwhile, out on FM 2491, federal lawmen and state troopers were at that moment denying the podiatrists and CFAers entry to Satellite City, and warning Engelman and his colleague not to go farther than the barricades that kept the press away from the road to Mt. Carmel. On television, Bob Ricks was scolding the media—he meant Engelman— for establishing independent contact with Koresh. "They're going to try to reach you and try to divert our efforts to get the matter settled. . . . Allow us to do our job . . . let's have the press do its job," he lectured. When a Satellite City reporter advised that state troopers were preparing to oust him from the zone, Engelman fled back to Dallas, to invoke TV dishes no more.

The radio host's adventure did not bring medical care to Mt. Carmel, but it apparently did turn the FBI's attention to the question. On March 12, the negotiators brought a physician to the telephone with a request to talk to Mt. Carmel's wounded few. The doctor's conversations would add to what the Bureau already knew, and elucidate what its agents would later learn about the medical needs inside.

At least one of Mt. Carmel's walking wounded, David Jones, had hardly been injured. "I stood in a window . . . and I watched those people come out of there," he told the men on the other end of the line. "And it was quiet, except for I could hear what sounded like a train or helicopters behind us. . . . And I heard somebody start talking out at the front of the building. I don't know what they said. But they started shooting . . . and bullets flying all around me, dust hitting me all over my body you know . . . glass, wood, bits of metal. . . . I turned . . . to dive on the floor, and something hit me in the bottom and knocked me on the floor.

"But within ten minutes, I started moving myself and I noticed I could move . . . I looked back . . . and I could see just some threads torn on my pants pocket in the back. . . . I thought it was just threads tore, so it was like three days before I pulled my britches down and . . . on the inside of the pocket . . . there's a perfect round hole, and in my underwear was a perfect round hole. . . ." Jones had been struck squarely on the tailbone. The bullet made a shallow entry, and as he put it, "anyway, they dug it out." The bullet caused more laughter than pain.

Scott Sonobe, who was shot in the hand and thigh, was having difficulty with his hand. "When I first got shot," he said, "[it] felt like I had somebody else's hand strapped to my wrist." Sub-freezing temperatures prevailed on the day when he spoke to Haigman from unheated Mt. Carmel, and Sonobe complained that he couldn't stick the swollen hand into a glove. He'd been soaking it in Epsom salts, and taking a form of tetracycline to limit infection, he reported. Though his thigh wound was shallow and was causing him no pain, "if I twist my arm in a certain way," his hand pained him, as did lifting objects heavier than a sheet of paper. The doctor advised him that bones had probably been shattered inside the hand, that Sonobe needed to be X-rayed, and that his wound required surgical cleaning. The believer confessed that only a three-day antibiotic supply remained, but said that when it ran out, he was going to trust in God, staying inside.

Judy Schneider also spoke to the doctor. A bullet had passed through her right index finger and grazed her shoulder, she said. ". . . At first the finger fell right down," she recalled. "I couldn't hold it up and then after the tape bandaging it, I can hold it up now and move it, so people don't think I broke it." She had been treating it with Epsom salts, taking megadoses of vitamin C, and rubbing garlic directly onto the wound,

245

in the hope of aiding a cure. On the videotape that had been sent out earlier in the week, Schneider had displayed her finger, enlarged and discolored, and the physician had viewed the tape prior to the telephone chat. He wasn't optimistic. He advised her, as he had Sonobe, to get surgical attention, but she was adamant that she wasn't coming out. "Unless you can come in, unless you can give me some kind of stuff to dissolve that dead tissue, well, I don't know, I guess I'll just die here," she told him. But the doctor's mission was to gain intelligence and argue for surrender, not to provide care; he could not promise that doctors would come. When he stressed the potential dangers of Judy's condition in a subsequent conversation with Steve Schneider, her husband reported that "she's just asking me now, what about cutting off the finger?"

The most gravely wounded soul in Mt. Carmel was, of course, David Koresh. He had nearly died between February 28 and March 2 when, according to the reports that he and his aides provided, his blood pressure dropped, even if his pulse remained at a jogger's sixty beats a minute. He urinated blood after the shooting, and he continued to suffer maladies beyond pain. On March 4, noting that the wound in his wrist wouldn't close, he'd asked for a suture kit; the FBI sent the first of its bugging devices into Mt. Carmel, concealed in the first-aid supplies.

On March 8, a severe headache began, and it didn't let up for nearly three days. During that span, Koresh's abdominal wound was seeping a pinkish fluid, and from time to time renewed bleeding was evident. The preacher reported that his thumb was numb, that he experienced pain when defecating, coughing, or laughing, and that he was having intense dreams about birds, helicopters, and running. Dick DeGuerin says that his client was trembling and sometimes fell out of consciousness during their talks, and Steve Schneider noted that Koresh complained of seeing spots before his eyes; on March 28, the Messiah told the FBI that he was having spasms or tremors. The day before the doctor's phone consultation, a negotiator had pressed him about the state of his health. He was drinking orange juice, eating green vegetables, taking spoonfuls of liquid iron, and applying garlic to his wounds, the Messiah said. That and God's will, he insisted, would be enough to work a cure.

The doctor and the negotiators warned that infections could set in, and asked Steve Schneider to be on the lookout for signs of septicemia, including severe headaches. But Koresh wouldn't talk to the physician, and even though his symptoms returned—bleeding on March 21 and a severe headache on March 25–27—he staunchly refused aid. Perhaps out of fear for his leader's life, Steve Schneider twice asked that antibiotics be sent for Koresh, but the FBI's job was not prescribing medications over the telephone. Nor did the Bureau's negotiators offer to send in physicians, despite a March 18 press conference claim by spokesman Ricks that "We have said that if you show us a sign of good will, and that is by allowing children and other adults to come out, we will allow those who need medical treatment to return back inside the compound if they so wish."

When Ron Engelman's mission to Mt. Carmel failed, allies of a second kind attempted what the Constitutionalists had been too timid to try. The first of them was twenty-five-year-old Louis Anthony Alaniz, a Houston telephone operator. In early March, while riding a metro bus near his home, he recounts, "I'd been hearing all of these people talking bad about the Davidians, and it just hurt me to hear them be so prejudiced against people that they didn't even know." Alaniz didn't know the people at Mt. Carmel, either—his last religious affiliation was with a Pentecostal congregation—but he felt that his fellow riders were out of line. Getting up from his seat, he walked to the back of the bus and began to pray. During his communication, he says, a vision came to him, an image of "hands and arms crying for help." Alaniz didn't know exactly how he was to help the besieged Mt. Carmelites, but the image returned repeatedly for days, until he could ignore it no more. On the morning of March 4, he jumped on a Greyhound, bound for Waco.

The Greyhound station in Waco is located squarely in the middle of downtown, some ten miles away from Mt. Carmel, whose circumference was sealed for more than a mile around; even people who lived in the vicinity had to pass checkpoints on their way home. Alaniz asked station employees to help him reach the besieged site, telling them, "God wants me there." His invocation inspired a series of cooperative efforts that indicated little support for the federal presence in town. A

Greyhound driver, he says, gave him a ride to a closer spot, still six miles distant from his goal. Then he set out on foot, waved at the helicopters that were looming overhead, flagged down a driver, asked for directions, and confirmed them with a boy who was passing by on a bicycle.

After he'd penetrated the roadblocks that circled Mt. Carmel, still a mile from its front door, the Houston pilgrim approached a farmhand who was leaving his house. The man had a pickup, but was wary. The young believer told him that God had sent him on a mission of peace, and, "I asked him, 'Would you like to have your life back to normal?' " The man relented, and pointed out the road that ran past Mt. Carmel. "I need to go through the woods," Alaniz pressed. The farmhand told him to jump into the back of his pickup, and he drove toward the battleground. At the treeline, he dropped his passenger off, pointing and telling him how to proceed.

Like Bob Kendrick, Louis Alaniz had a hard time inching toward Mt. Carmel. He, too, lost his footing on a muddy creek bank. "God, You said that if I'd put a foot forward, You'd give me a way," he reminded his patron at the bottom of his slide. Promptly he was shown how to get going again, but after crossing a culvert, he came face to face with a Brahman bull. After ducking that obstacle, he spotted men in combat garb, cruising in a truck. Alaniz took cover at the bottom of a ditch; red ants bit his arms. He jumped up, spied the truck again, and returned to his bed of ants. This time they stung his legs. "God, You said if I put a foot forward, You'd provide a way," he whispered again. The truck disappeared and the young Christian bolted across an open field. As he came near one of Mt. Carmel's ponds, the sound of a diesel engine caught his ears. A tank emerged from behind a bus. Then it turned, as if its drivers didn't know that he was near.

Alaniz sprinted toward the besieged building. Rounding a corner, his eyes captured scenes that are still vivid in his mind. "Every single window was destroyed, and the bullet holes made trails, like a celestial star map," he says. Rushing for the front door, he glanced at the two cattle trailers, still parked where they'd stopped on February 28. "It struck me kind of odd; I could only see one bullet hole in them," he recalls. He rapped on the front door, as hard as he could. A voice inside asked for his name. ". . . The Spirit of the Holy Ghost sends me," Alaniz blurted. The door didn't open, and by now the tankers had him in view. A voice from a loudspeaker barked, "Return to the building! Return to the building!" "Let me in! Let me in!," Alaniz cried to the faceless door. "Either they're going to shoot me, thinking I'm one of you, or ya'll are going to shoot me, thinking I'm one of them," he pleaded. The door slowly opened: God had given Louis Alaniz a way. So dumbfounded were the press and the FBI by his entry that initial reports claimed he'd ridden in on horseback!

Alaniz was dirty. His hosts brought him water, soap, and fresh clothes. They showed him into the telephone room, placed food at his side. A nurse stopped by, to ask if he needed help picking thorns and splinters from his scratches. A limping Koresh shook his hand. "What's going on here?", the young Christian demanded. "Two subjects, religion and politics," the preacher drawled, and the visitor's first lesson began, more than six hours on the Seals. "I'd been going to church since I was real little, and nobody had shown me the Seven Seals. . . . It got pretty deep," Alaniz remembers.

Morning came, "nuts, applesauce, and raisin rolls," he says. "Bible study began at eight or nine." After that, communion, more Bible talk, a break for lunch, and at two or three o'clock, exegesis again. Usually the talks lasted past dark, Alaniz says, with an unsteady Koresh at the helm. Day after day rolled by in this way. During breaks in the study sessions, Alaniz sometimes watched and listened to the tanks as they circled outside. One of the tanks, he reported—and videotapes confirm—was flying a flag with a white field crossed by red diagonals, a standard whose significance was (and is) known only to the tankers; in other military conflicts, the design symbolizes only the letter V, or in some systems, the message: "Need assistance." Alaniz could only guess at its meaning. "To me, a white flag means surrender. Red has always meant blood, and an 'X' cancels out. So to me, the flag was saying to us that they wouldn't let us surrender."

The tank drivers, Alaniz says, mooned the residents and made obscene hand signs. "Why don't ya'll just get the hell out of here? Why are ya'll making us stay here?", they yelled over their loudspeakers. "Once," Alaniz asserts, "they didn't know that they hadn't turned off their speakers. I heard one of them say, 'Why don't we just kill them all?' "

Louis Alaniz had been inside about two days when another visionary appeared, a man who also said that he'd come on a mission of peace—a middle-aged hippie who called himself Jesse Amen. Peeved that the barricades had been breached again, federal negotiators put the new visitor through an interrogation by telephone.

FBI   . . . Where are you from?
AMEN   . . . I travel from God.
FBI   Oh, is that right? Well, why—where do you, where you live at?
AMEN   . . . I live in the wind. . . .
FBI   Well, obviously, you came from somewhere, Jesse.
AMEN   Well, I'm telling you the truth . . . I'm a witness from God, and God's my witness.

Amen *was* telling the truth. He was a pilgrim, making his way by bicycle across America under a light that shone from above. The feds saw in the celestiality of his responses only the common signs of criminal evasiveness—"obviously, you're afraid of something," his negotiator chided—and soon quit trying to squeeze information from him.

During the week of his stay, his surviving hosts report, the guest with the navel-length beard told them about Lord Lightning Amen, and his companion, Cherry Lightning Amen, counterparts to Mt. Carmel's God and Holy Spirit. He also presented the besieged Christians with a plan. All the Old Testament prophets, and the rest of Lord Lightning's 50,000-man army, were in readiness along the banks of the Colorado River, ninety miles away. They'd march to Mt. Carmel's rescue if only Koresh would hang a red flag outside his door, Amen said. But the Adventist Messiah snubbed him, citing John 18:36: ". . . if my kingdom were of this world, then would my servants fight." Even when he wanted to be doctrinally inconsistent, the preacher always had a scripture in hand.

Jesse Amen left Mt. Carmel on April 4. "He told me," Alaniz recalls, " 'Louis, whenever you go to a Thanksgiving or Christmas dinner, people keep offering you all this good food, but you know, you get to where you just can't take no more.' " Within a week, in a light-hearted moment of negotiations, the FBI tried a new threat on Steve Schneider. "We're sending Jesse back to you," one negotiator jibed.

Despite pinched conditions—water rationing began in early April inside Mt. Carmel—and the strictures of the Adventist diet, Louis Alaniz stayed inside until April 17. When he emerged, he was jailed with Brother Amen. Like emissaries whose credentials aren't in order, both made futile efforts to convince their jailers that Koresh and his flock could be subdued with words.

The two Christian pilgrims were relieved by a new set of allies who came openly, thanks in great part to the Constitutionalists who had gathered in Waco. North Carolina attorney Kirk Lyons, a stout man in his thirties, given to red suspenders and other retro accessories of dress, had come to Waco in early March to assess the legal needs of exiting residents. Realizing that the job would be more than he could handle, he telephoned Dick DeGuerin of Houston, easily the second most well known criminal defense attorney in Texas. DeGuerin, fifty-two, is a remarkably youthful figure who, when he steps out of his Mercedes, gives the impression of a preppie in cowboy boots. Satisfied with the list of lawyers whom Lyons had already recruited, DeGuerin agreed to take up the cause—but only if he could claim the Messiah as a client. Lyons relayed the offer to Bonnie Haldeman, Koresh's mother.

On the night of March 10, DeGuerin and Haldeman drove to the FBI command post at TSTC, presented their credentials, and asked to speak with Jeffrey Jamar, the agency's Special Agent in Charge, or SAC—top man on the scene. After waiting about two hours, DeGuerin says, he left his telephone number with lower-ranking agents and went back to his hotel. No call came that night or early the next morning, and renewed attempts to reach Jamar by telephone were fruitless. But DeGuerin didn't give up. "I knew that with all the press in town, I wasn't hopeless, and that if I had to, I could make the FBI pay us mind," he says. He and Haldeman drove out to the checkpoint through which the press passed on its way to Satellite City, requested permission to enter Mt. Carmel, and were barred. The TV cameras rolled. After the televised snub, the attorney went downtown to the federal court-house, where he filed a petition for a writ of habeas corpus.

In his petition, DeGuerin argued that since Koresh could not freely

251

leave town, he was already in custody; people who've been arrested have a right to a lawyer. Even if Koresh wasn't in custody, the attorney said, like anybody else, his client had a right to consult a lawyer. Federal District Judge Walter Smith, Jr.—who would sit in judgment at the 1994 San Antonio trial—denied the petition on March 5, ruling that "One simply cannot point a gun (literally or figuratively) at constitutional authority, and at the same time complain that constitutional rights are being denied." Or in other words, the judge found that presumed rebels have no rights.

Having drawn the government's attention, DeGuerin shuttled back to Houston, where he wrote SAC Jamar a letter, arguing that he and the agency had parallel interests. "I told him that I wanted a client who is alive and in the criminal justice system, because that's where I work," he recalls. "It seemed to me that they would want the same thing that I did." In late March, the Bureau okayed the attorney's plan. During the seven days of March 29 through April 4, DeGuerin would visit Mt. Carmel five times, accompanied on two of his trips by attorney Jack Zimmermann, who had been hired to represent Steven Schneider.

Inside the encampment, the lawyers interviewed eyewitnesses, inspected bloodstains and bullet holes, and advised the residents to videotape the front door and the tower's ceiling. They also talked to their clients about fees. "David said that they had between forty and sixty thousand dollars in cash inside Mt. Carmel, but I told to him that that would be just a small part of what defending him would cost," DeGuerin says. The attorneys did not bring the cash or videotapes out of the besieged building, DeGuerin maintains, "because I wanted to play by the rules." The FBI searched them upon each entry and exit.

Their financial demands concerned Koresh and Schneider, but DeGuerin proposed a solution that partially resolved their unease. A book would be written, telling the preacher's side of the assault story. Film and publication rights would be sold to finance the defense effort. DeGuerin in fact engaged a literary agent, who felt that he could auction the rights for a minimum of $2.5 million, a figure higher than the attorneys' fees.

But even that was a mixed blessing. "David was upset," DeGuerin recalls, "because his mother had taken some money for an interview

252

with a tabloid television program, though really, she did it just to get those people away from her door. He was afraid that people would think that he was trying to make money out of the situation." To blunt that perception, DeGuerin agreed to form a trust fund for Koresh's children, and to make them, not his client, the beneficiaries of any profits from the scheme.

While the lawyers were presenting and revising contracts for their clients—and before any full agreement on surrender was reached—a fourth set of allies came over the hill, Philip Arnold and James Tabor, both holders of doctoral degrees in religion. Like the others, these two experts had their own plan for extracting both the Bureau and the attorneys from the stalemate.

University of North Carolina Professor Tabor had been intrigued by a reference that Koresh made to the Fifth Seal in his February 28 CNN interview. Trying to discern the upstart Messiah's message, Tabor wrote later in *From the Ashes: Making Sense of Waco* (1994), "I realized that in order to deal with David Koresh, and to have any chance for a peaceful resolution of the Waco situation . . . one would need to enter into the apocalyptic world of David Koresh and his dedicated followers. It was obvious that they were willing to die for what they believed, and they would not surrender under threat of force." Tabor's first move was to telephone his friend Phil Arnold, the director of an institute of religious studies in Houston.

On March 7, Arnold went to Waco to offer his services to the FBI. Like DeGuerin, he was able to make contact only with lower-level Bureaumen, from whom he learned only that the negotiators were ignoring their Bible studies from Koresh. Arnold attended a couple of the press briefings at Waco's downtown convention center, and after one of them, he approached spokesman Bob Ricks, hoping to persuade him that Koresh's intentions might be clear under the light of a theological review. Arnold claims that Ricks brushed him aside, muttering, "There is nobody who can understand what this man is saying." After this encounter, the Bible scholar was barred from reentering the briefing sessions.

He returned to Houston where, he recalls, "I was almost banging my head on the table, trying to figure out what to do. 'If I can't get the FBI to let me get to David,' I told myself, 'how can I get a word to David?' People's lives were at stake here." Then he remembered Ron Engelman. Arnold made arrangements with the talk show host, and then by telephone rehearsed a presentation in which he and Tabor addressed Koresh on the subject of the Seals. Their epistle aired live on April 1.

Tabor and Arnold concentrated on two points from the Book of Revelation. The first was that the Fifth Seal's instruction "to wait a little season" could be interpreted in several ways, as setting forth a period that could last for months, even years. They also suggested that a passage in Revelation 10:11, dealing with a sealed book, tells its holder, ". . . Thou must prophesy again before many peoples, and nations, and tongues, and kings." It was not clear from the scriptures, they urged Koresh, that the standoff at Waco had to end with the Fifth Seal's soon closing.

The interpretations that the new allies proffered weren't acceptable, Mt. Carmel's theologians believed. As Livingstone Fagan points out, "The Book makes it very clear that only the Lamb can reveal the Seals. If David was the Lamb, who did these guys think they were?" But the message from Tabor and Arnold was joyously received because it indicated that the Messiah was finally reaching an audience he'd long sought. Attracting adherents had been a difficult and costly process, and the community's more adept interpreters had been disillusioned by the recruitment of some believers who, they thought, weren't intellectually prepared to understand the doctrine. For years, they had longed for a shortcut: If only Koresh could enter into talks with Bible scholars, he could quickly make his points. Recognizing him as the Lamb, the scholars would announce their findings to the world, greatly speeding God's work of salvation. Since Tabor and Arnold could understand what Mt. Carmel's Messiah was prophesying, Koresh and his followers hoped, the pair might become beacons to the world.

In talks with defense attorney Dick DeGuerin and practically anybody else he could buttonhole, Philip Arnold began predicting that if Koresh were to come out of Mt. Carmel, or were to decide what to do about surrender, he would make his decision during Passover. He had formulated this conclusion entirely from his readings of scripture and tradition; nobody inside had confirmed his guess. But the scholar's prophesy was confirmed on April 4, when DeGuerin and Zimmermann made their last visit to the besieged camp. Koresh and Schneider announced to the attorneys that they would not decide until after Passover. The community was having trouble in setting precise dates, in part because Passover is calculated from the lunar calendar, and the job of reckoning it had, in the past, been done by Perry Jones. But they finally fixed their eight-day observance as opening on April 7 and ending at sundown, April 14. DeGuerin says he was convinced the group would come out at that time; to prepare for its exit, he began recruiting attorneys for the other adults inside.

During Passover, David Koresh, like a prophet from the Bible, went into an intensely spiritual mode, the sort of mental state that secularists equate with insanity. The outside world first saw evidence of this in a letter that Koresh sent to the FBI on April 10. The nine-paragraph document, typed by an aide, purportedly came from God. "You're not rejecting a man by fighting against David, My servant, no, for I have given and revealed My name to Him," its second paragraph declared. "Learn from David My seals," cautioned the eighth paragraph. ". . . I forewarn you, the Lake Waco area of Old Mount Carmel will be terribly shaken. The waters of the lake will be emptied through the broken dam."

At the letter's close, God signed His name in Hebrew as "Yahweh Koresh." In the eyes of those who were interested, this signature solved a mystery of a minor kind, though the authorities would later obscure the light. Vernon Howell had told his followers that "Koresh" means "Death," federal prosecutors would allege during the San Antonio trial, styling their ghostly defendant as a "prophet of death." But according to the teachings at Mt. Carmel, "Yahweh" represented the first sounds a newborn makes and "Koresh" represented the sounds of the death rattle: Yahweh Koresh, the name that Mt. Carmel's Messiah attributed to God, was but another form of Alpha and Omega.

The reference to Lake Waco was a prediction of a flood, though for several days the FBI and other law enforcement agencies treated it as threat, putting the area under surveillance. As Koresh would later explain, "I was shown a fault line running throughout the Lake Waco area. An angel is standing in charge of this event," which Mt. Carmelites had been predicting since Houteff's day. The apparent meaning of the warning was that if Koresh's mission to earth was ignored, Waco would be inundated by natural forces beyond anyone's control—including those of the local Messiah.

When Koresh had worked his way out of his mystical Passover cocoon, Steve Schneider informed the FBI that "the picture is finally coming together as to what's happening, when and all that." During his audiences with God, David Koresh had been told how the crisis was to be resolved. What he had learned, his instructions and orders, would be set forth just after sundown on April 14, in a letter addressed to his attorney outside.

The April 14 letter revealed that "I am presently being permitted to document, in structured form, the decoded messages of the Seven Seals. Upon the completion of this task, I will be freed of my 'waiting period.' I hope to finish this as soon as possible and to stand before man to answer any and all questions regarding my actions." Koresh added that "I will demand the first manuscript of the Seals be given to you. . . . As soon as I can see that people like Jim Tabor and Phil Arnold have a copy, I will come out and then you can do your thing. . . ." Along with the letter went a request for writing materials.

During his Passover visions, David Koresh had adopted Arnold and Tabor's interpretations. He had decided to "prophesy again." He set no deadline for his labors, but the Bible scholars estimated that it would take him two to three weeks to write an exposition of the Seals.

For reasons that barristers, Constitutionalists, and Christians, both zany and orthodox, could not understand, Koresh was resolved to do what the secular world demanded of him. He was coming out, and so was everyone else. The plan to write the Seals gave Koresh a new shot at recognition as the Messiah, and the surrender exonerated the patience of his allies. It was all very convenient. Babylon and Jerusalem were now on the same map.

The upcoming surrender could only be derailed if the government got antsy, or if God went back on His word—and of course, His reputation for truth and veracity is better than that—or if Koresh confessed to lying about his Passover conversations with the Man Upstairs. Government spokesmen would later point out that Koresh had gone back on his word on March 2, and indeed he had. But Koresh was not God. He was the Word of God, and when there was no word from God, what David Koresh said could be edited or spiked on high. When, on March 1, Koresh had promised Mt. Carmel's surrender for the following day, he had not spoken with God about the issue, or made any claim to that. He was speaking for David Koresh, and the surrender plan was in the works, the survivors insist, until God put it on hold. This time, Koresh said that he had cleared his strategy with the front office.

When DeGuerin informed the FBI of Koresh's new plan, he says, second-in-command Bob Ricks snarled, "And then what's next? He's going to write his memoirs?" The defense lawyer claims that SAC Jamar cut short his subordinate's sarcasm by declaring, ". . . We've got all the time it takes." "This latest business with the Seven Seals, we have intelligence that it was just one more such stalling technique," FBI spokesman Jeffrey Jamar would maintain on April 20. But that wasn't true. Koresh had gone straightway to work, scribbling and dictating notes. According to the accounts that Steven Schneider gave to the FBI, the Waco preacher had completed his text on the First Seal (now available on computer disc) and had drafted a Second Seal exegesis by the morning of Sunday, April 18. That was the day when the FBI finished preparing its final assault.

Chapter 27

THE PSYWAR

"Are you a patient person? Well, you're going to see patience, because the only thing that we're going to do is sit and wait."
—FBI negotiator John-1.

"Mr. Koresh . . . refuses to engage in the normal negotiations process."
—FBI spokesman Bob Ricks

When the FBI assumed command on the morning of March 1, the Bureau's best minds had expected the standoff to last for a week or ten days. Time, they thought, was on their side. "We're prepared to do whatever it takes and stay here as long as it takes to settle this matter without any further bloodshed," SAC Jeffrey Jamar declared. Even after the debacle of March 2, the Bureau kept on a happy face, promising patience and a resolution that its planners could not envision. They had little choice. The Bureau's Hostage Rescue Team had come away from its last highly publicized standoff, a July 1992 action against white separatist Randy Weaver, with a reputation as a gang of trigger-happy Rambos. And during the Waco siege, due to the change in presidential administrations, the Justice Department was headless. No Attorney General had been named. From a bureaucratic point of view, March was not a time for taking decisive action.

258

Instead, the agency's Waco commanders adopted a set of harassment tactics and attitudes that are sometimes sold under the somewhat glorified name of "psychological warfare." At the same time, they continued their efforts to win the real psywar, waged on their superiors and the public through the media.

One of the Bureau's first psywar tactics involved bargaining over the body of Peter Gent, whose fate the residents did not discover until Friday, March 5, on a clandestine venture outside. Clive Doyle says that on that day, "Mark Wendell found Peter's body in the water tower, and lowered it down with a rope. Then Jimmy Riddle and I took his body, zipped it up in a sleeping bag, and laid it in the concrete room at the bottom of the tower." Apparently, their movements weren't spotted by the FBI.

Having heard by radio that Gent's parents had come to Waco from Australia, Steven Schneider asked that the FBI take the body to town for burial. His negotiator readily agreed to a plan whereby two residents would carry the corpse to EE Road, then return to their home. But within minutes, the negotiator doubled back. He was bargaining now. "I'm saying that you could take the body of Pete out with two adults, one adult of whom will have to stay with the body to, to explain to the coroner the circumstances surrounding why the body was there . . . for this period of time and that sort of thing," he said. Koresh and Schneider balked at the demand, for it meant that at least one more resident would be jailed.

Gent's body lay in the concrete shed all weekend, despite pleas and demands from Schneider. On Sunday, March 7, he told the negotiators that three residents were going to bury Gent the following day, regardless of consequences. The G-Men acceded to the ultimatum, and press reports gave no hint of the underlying acrimony. "Ricks said negotiators and Howell had agreed for the cult to conduct a funeral and bury the body of a cult member. . . ," reported the *Waco Tribune*. "Federal agents have allowed them to do a burial and some sort of memorial service," a television reporter said.

The day after Peter Gent's body was laid in its grave, a public address system that the Bureau had erected on Mt. Carmel's grounds began blaring noise, night and day. During the next six weeks, it would blast the sounds of sirens, seagulls, bagpipes, crying babies, dying rabbits, crowing roosters and dental drills. The sound of an off-the-hook telephone was also broadcast, as were Buddhist monastery chants, Muslim prayer calls, Christmas carols, even the rumble of a train passing through a tunnel. Selections from the faded rocker Alice Cooper, and a recording of a best-forgotten Nancy Sinatra hit, "These Boots Were Made for Walking," were added to the list. Sometimes the broadcasts caused panic. "At one point they were playing helicopter sounds, and we thought that we were being buzzed again," Doyle recalls. "The music that's been played has been specifically selected for its irritation ability," FBI spokesman Bob Ricks told the press. "It will give them many hours of wakefulness to ponder many things," echoed his colleague, Richard Schwein.

The noise that the Bureau broadcast had at least one effect. Robert Cervenka, a farmer whose lands lay just south of Mt. Carmel, reported to the *Tribune-Herald* that "the music and the noise . . . sent his Brahman hybrid cattle into frenzied stampede, tearing down fences and running down into the nearby river bottoms where he can't get to them. . . . Helicopters spook the cattle, putting stress on them which makes them lose weight. Ranchers sell their cattle based on weight."

Inside Mt. Carmel, "the noise was an annoyance. It was hard to get any sleep, except when you were completely exhausted," Clive Doyle remembers. From time to time, the public address system also broadcast messages, warning the residents to stay indoors, for example, but the effect was often lost. "They had one set of speakers out front, and another in the back, and sometimes they sort of canceled each other out. What we heard sounded like somebody talking underwater," Doyle recalls. Schneider reported that some of the men inside wanted to shoot holes in the Bureau's speakers, but Koresh nixed the idea: indeed, no gutshots were fired by parties on either side until the last moments of the siege.

The audio blasts that began March 9 were paired with yet another harassment technique, control of Mt. Carmel's electric lines. At the onset the blackouts were timed to allow residents to listen to the Bureau's daily press briefing, and on March 11, a continuing electric supply was held out as an inducement to successful talks. "We had a very good dialogue last night. The electricity will not go off tonight because we've had a very good dialogue this evening," a negotiator promised Steve Schneider. But half an hour later, the lights went off for good.

The residents weren't entirely without defense. They had two dozen lanterns and two gasoline-powered generators, one of which worked. Twice during the standoff they cranked the generators to running speed—to provide power for jam sessions! They also tried recharging several batteries under generator power, with mixed success. But Mt. Carmel's best defense was its austere lifestyle. Most of its residents, as Kathy Schroeder noted during the San Antonio trial, were only mildly inconvenienced because they had no personal appliances.

The chief kink that lack of electricity put into the community's lifestyle was that it forced a reduction in water usage. As survivor Jaime Castillo explained in a letter, "We had the artesian well which supplied us with water. The water was pumped from the well to the 1500-gallon water tanks. Prior to the assault the water tanks were kept full . . . . But when the assault took place the water tanks got riddled with bullets, which handicapped our water supply. Even though the water tanks got shot, they were still capable of holding about one to two hundred gallons. What happened is that Greg [Sommers] got some army men out of the kids' toys and melted them in the water tanks to cap the holes, which worked for a while."

Clive Doyle, assessing the same situation, says that Sommers was able to make his repairs only on the building's side of the tanks, and because his patches did not last, by mid-March—despite warnings from the FBI that they'd be treated as targets—residents were going outside during rainfalls, collecting runoff from the roof in buckets and pans. Bathing was restricted, and when Louis Alaniz emerged on April 17, he reported that the residents were existing on a water ration of two 8-oz. ladles per day.

On March 14, the Bureau, perhaps inadvertently, added a new dimension to its psywar campaign, turning on banks of stadium lights that it had erected around Mt. Carmel. "It's a purely defensive thing to do," spokesman Dick Swensen explained the following day. " . . . By shining those lights, we are hoping to make less of a target to all of the people in the compound. . . . We just don't want them seeing us back there." He then quipped, " . . . in addition to protecting the agents they're amazingly annoying."

Just as Swensen said, the residents could not see figures who stood and moved around behind the lights, but in the absence of electricity, the Bureau's candlepower was more of a benefit than a hindrance. "The lights weren't much trouble to us, because you could put a blanket over a window and keep them out," Clive Doyle explains. Indeed, the tactic enabled some of the residents to conserve lantern fuel, reading by the light from outside. "On the night of April 18 and 19, I was transcribing some tapes of David by the light that came in," Doyle says.

"We are trying to reinforce to them we are in charge of the situation, that the compound is in complete control of the government. It is, in fact, no longer their compound," declared FBI press spokesman Al Cruz, explaining the psywar campaign. The agent overdrew the results he claimed. When David Koresh preached to agents on the phone, followers gathered around, taking notes on the theology he imparted, as they had always done. Even after March 26, when G-Men began lobbing flash-bang grenades at anyone who ventured outdoors without permission, stealthy residents emptied pots of night soil, fed the chickens, and brazenly, in groups and in broad daylight, came outside to catch rainfall. David Jones, who had always stepped outdoors to puff on cigarettes, now did his smoking on the rooftops, sometimes in view of the G-Men.

The major achievement of the psywar battle came in mid-March, in a diversion aimed at influencing the public, not the faithful of Koresh. On March 11, from a radio broadcast by commentator Paul Harvey, David Koresh first learned of an astronomical phenomenon that the press quickly dubbed the "Guitar Nebulae." Steve Schneider was excited by the reported sighting, which he and others hoped was a sign from God: after all, Revelation's text on the Sixth Seals says (6:13), "And the stars of heaven fell unto the earth, even as a fig tree casteth her untimely figs, when she is shaken of a mighty wind." When negotiators offered to tell him more about the sighting, Schneider called David Koresh to the telephone. A Bureauman read to him a *Houston*

Chronicle story entitled "This Is One Hot Guitar: Neutron Star Is Moving Darn Fast Through Our Galaxy."

Koresh listened warily, found fault with data in the report, and was generally unimpressed. When the negotiator offered to send in copies of reports about the event, Koresh turned him down. Later he explained to his expectant followers that the star wasn't moving fast enough to be one of the celestial chariots that they hoped would save the day. But the Bureau's payoff came a few days later, when a reporter inquired about the Guitar Nebulae chat. Koresh "gave us an indication with regard to certain astrological things that were going on," spokesman Bob Ricks declared. "I won't be more specific than that, but if these things came to pass, we're talking in terms of days, not weeks." The Bureau's spokesman, in an unchallenged statement, had pictured Koresh as a stargazer, waiting perhaps for Jupiter to align with Mars.

Neither straight talk, nor unorthodox tactics, nor psywar waged on the public was producing the resolution that the FBI sought, and its agents were ill at ease in Waco, just as was the press. The some 720 lawmen who were in town—250 from the Bureau, 150 from the ATF, a scattering of other federal agencies, and the Texas Department of Public Safety—had to be housed, along with an average of nearly 1,000 members of the press. The problem went beyond cost: there was a shelter shortage. The town's first- and second-rate hotels were bulging with guests, and when the federal police agencies went looking for forty housing units, they found that Waco's apartment occupancy rate was at 90 percent before the siege began. Because the agencies were short-handed and living quarters were scarce, the lawmen assigned to work in Waco worked in two- and three-week shifts, piling up overtime—and longing to return to their far-flung homes.

Early in March, the Tourism Division of the Texas Department of Commerce postponed a series of television ads, on the theory that nobody would want to visit the state any time soon, and town residents, tired of the bad jokes and quips about "the wackos in Waco" began affixing to their cars stickers that read: "WACO PROUD." As each day passed, pressure built inside and outside the ranks for a speedy end to the standoff.

In late March, FBI commanders on the scene began sketching plans for a tear-gas assault. The plan worked its way up to Washington, where on April 12 it was presented to Janet Reno, the nation's new Attorney General. It called for easing the residents out of Mt. Carmel by injecting tear gas into first one, then another sector of the building, narrowing its zone of habitability over a period of two days. If this measure failed, the field commanders proposed another, one whose strategic wisdom was unassailable: If there is no Mt. Carmel, its logic said, no one can become a fugitive there. In its report on the affair, the Justice Department, perhaps with calculated irony, says that it had no plan to destroy the building. "While it was conceivable that tanks and other armored vehicles could be used to demolish the compound, the FBI considered that such a plan would risk harming the children," it states. Just what would constitute demolishing the compound isn't explained, but the report does note that if the tear-gas effort failed, "walls would be torn down to increase the exposure of those remaining inside." When walls are leveled a point is soon reached at which there is no "inside"—but that was a point too deep for the review's assessment. The Bureau's Jericho plan was not the simple dream of officers in the field: among those who discussed it with Reno were FBI director William Sessions and acting Assistant Attorney General Webster Hubbell, a figure in the Arkansas scandals that were dogging the new President.

Reno was not an easy sell. According to the Justice Department's report, she declared that she wouldn't approve the scheme until she was assured that CS, the type of gas that the planners proposed to use, would not cause serious harm to pregnant women and young children. The Justice report says that two days later, at a briefing also attended by Sessions, Hubbell, and other Justice Department brass, a Ph.D. from a Maryland Army research center assured her that "although there had been no laboratory tests performed on children relative to the effects of the gas, anecdotal evidence was convincing that there would be no permanent injury." The Justice report also says that her adviser told her that CS gas could not cause a fire.

CS is the common name for orthochlorobenzalmalononitrile, a white powder that manufacturers and vendors classify as a "lachrymator irritant," i.e., a substance that causes the shedding of tears. It is, however, a bit more noxious than its designation implies. Named for two Americans who first concocted it in 1928, B. B. Corson and R. W. Stoughton, it is listed in OSHA manuals as causing "irritation of eyes, skin and respiratory system," and as corrosive to aluminum and magnesium besides. More than one hundred nations, including the United States, have banned it for use in warfare, though governments are free to inflict it upon their own citizens. Manufacturers of CS gas warn against its use indoors, in part because heavy exposures have been cited as causes of death in a report by Amnesty International. "Generally persons reacting to CS are incapable of executing organized and concerted actions," a U.S. Army manual on civil disturbances points out, "and excessive exposure to CS may make them incapable of vacating the area." When burned, a manufacturer of the CS cautions, its particles can give off lethal fumes.

Though her reservations about tear gas had been laid aside, Reno remained wary. She held another meeting in which she suggested a new tack: How long could Mt. Carmel's water supply last? The state of the Bureau's information was recorded in a March 20 log, which noted that "An analysis of available information on water in the compound indicates most probably a limited supply to begin with, and reserves are very low. Replenishing the supply seems to be accomplished through techniques such as capturing rainwater."

But Reno's Washington advisers told her that they doubted the report, and at her request, on April 15 the Bureau ran a check. It sent an airplane loaded with spy gizmos over Mt. Carmel by night. ". . . The rear water tank now appears to be full. . . . This determination was based on the thermal image of the warm water in the tank," the agency's log stated.

Reno's point was tactically apt, the spy plane's report notwithstanding. In the unlikely case that the water tanks were full, they weren't bulletproof, as the February 28 assault had already shown. They could have been pierced again. The water pump upon which Mt. Carmel relied was located outside the building; tanks could have sheared its pipes, which were above ground. Nature would have been on the Bureau's side had it decided to wait for a dwindling water supply. Summers in Waco are relatively dry: only half an inch of rain had fallen in August 1992 and in 1993 no rain would touch the area in July. But Reno let her rainfall strategy go by the wayside, apparently convinced by the FBI's argument that "Koresh was rationing water to ensure discipline."

The U.S. Attorney General requested a written proposal from the Bureau, and after perusing it on April 17, gave her approval for an assault that would begin on April 19 and extend over a period of forty-eight hours. "The action was viewed as a gradual, step-by-step process," the Justice Department's report maintains. "It was not law enforcement's intent that this was to be 'D-Day.' "

Chapter 28

D-DAY

"You can tell your commanders that they can run the building over. They can set it on fire. . . . Seriously, that's not where you're going to reach the minds of these people."
—Steve Schneider

". . . Some religious fanatics murdered themselves."
—President Bill Clinton

Janet Reno's 48-hour plan for gassing Mt. Carmel lasted about five minutes. At 6:02 A.M., on Monday, April 19, FBI logs show, combat engineering vehicles, or CEVs—M6OA1 tanks modified for demolition duty—began punching holes in Mt. Carmel, and through them, injecting CS gas into the building. This much was according to plan. But at 6:04 A.M., the Bureau's logs say, people inside Mt. Carmel fired upon the armored CEVs.

A clause in the written plan that the Bureau had presented to Reno called for an escalation if the tanks drew fire. The Justice report notes: "Under the operations plan, as approved by the Attorney General, 'If during *any* tear gas delivery operations, subjects open fire with a weapon, then . . . tear gas will immediately be inserted into all windows of the compound utilizing the four BVs. . . .' "—a reference to Bradley armored vehicles, ordinary combat tanks.

267

Reno, watching the assault by television and special wire hook-ups in Washington, was apparently taken by surprise. The nation's Attorney General, the Justice Department report indicates, "did not read the prepared statement carefully, nor did she read the supporting documentation. . . . She read only a chronology." Like a naive used-car buyer, she hadn't checked the fine print on the contract that the Bureau's salesmen placed before her.

The significance of the Bradley escalation turned on the kind of esoteric detail that only chemists and Bureau veterans—not newly minted Attorney Generals—could have known. The Bradleys were not equipped with hydraulic booms, as the CEVs were. They could not deliver gas as the CEVs did, from cylinders containing a mixture of carbon dioxide and CS powder, mounted near the tips of their 30-foot booms. Bradley drivers were able to deliver tear gas only by shooting football-sized metal or plastic canisters, called ferret rounds, out of a small port in their front sides. CS powder was suspended in the ferret rounds, not in carbon dioxide, but in a different chemical, methylene chloride, a petroleum derivative.

Standard chemical reference books say that methylene chloride in its liquid state is practically non-flammable. But their texts do not picture the chemical as harmless. One reference, for example, reports:

HEALTH HAZARDS: Eye, skin, and respiratory tract irritant. Toxic. Harmful if inhaled or absorbed through the skin. Narcotic in high concentrations. Metabolized by the body to form carbon monoxide. Products of combustion may be more hazardous than the material itself.

FIRE AND EXPLOSION HAZARDS: No flash point in conventional closed tester, but forms flammable vapor-air mixtures in larger volumes. May be an explosion hazard in a confined space. Combustion may produce irritants and toxic gases. Combustion by-products include hydrogen chloride and phosgene.

Phosgene, says the *Encyclopaedia Britannica* "is a colourless, extremely poisonous gas. . . . It first came into prominence in World War I (1914-18), being used as an offensive poison gas. . . . "

In a word, methylene chloride, used in a confined space, threatened to create conditions conducive to fire, explosion, and death by poison gas. Manufacturers of CS powder warn against its use indoors because their chemists and attorneys know the dangers of both CS and methylene chloride. So do most street-smart SWAT team operatives.

The effect of shooting ferret rounds into buildings has for twenty years been an item of cop lore. At least two incidents in FBI history point out the danger of their use. In 1974, police officers and G-Men surrounded a house at 1466 E. 54th Street in Los Angeles, occupied by members of the Symbionese Liberation Army, notorious for its kidnapping of heiress Patty Hearst. In their book on the SLA, *The Voices of Guns* (1978), Vin McLellan and Paul Avery provide the following account of the events that brought on the demise of the occupiers of the house at 1466 East 54th:

"When the LAPD ran short of tear gas (some 100 canisters of CS and CN gas were lobbed into 1466 during the gunfight), the FBI asked if its own SWAT team could lend a hand. Approval was given, reluctantly. Seven agents spent the next half-hour shooting tear gas (sixteen canisters) and bullets . . . at the house." The SLA suspects were largely impervious to the effects of the tear gas itself because, like the adults at Mt. Carmel, they were equipped with gasmasks; no gasmasks are manufactured in the United States for children. "At 6:40 a Team Two SWAT man," McLellan and Avery continue, "tossed a couple of Federal 555 riot-gas canisters into a window on the east side of 1466. A minute later black smoke could be seen pouring out windows at the rear of the house. Within another minute flames started shooting up through the roof. . . . In less than four minutes the whole of the rear of the house was aflame and fire was spreading throughout the small structure." None of the six people inside survived.

On December 9, 1984, FBI agents cornered a right-wing fugitive named Robert Matthews in a house in Washington State. A contemporary newspaper account reports: "Earlier in the evening, a SWAT team twice stormed the house but was repulsed by automatic gunfire from inside, said FBI spokesman Joseph Smith in Seattle. That followed a barrage of tear gas from authorities that lasted more than three hours. 'At about 6:20 P.M., agents assaulted the house with illumination devices and for some reason the house caught fire,' Archey said."

The FBI assault force at Waco, in preparation for the Bradley/ferret option of its plan, had stockpiled some four hundred CS canisters. About ninety minutes after the first canister was fired, the agency's logs show, the supply was nearing its end. The Bureau put out an emergency call for more rounds, though the forty-eight additional rounds that it received on a flight from Houston were apparently not used: about twenty minutes after the last of the ferrets was fired at Mt. Carmel, at 11:40 A.M.—long enough for vapor to form—the building went ablaze. In half an hour, Mt. Carmel was a smoldering ruin from end to end.

In order for fire to exist, three elements are necessary: oxygen; a combustible material, such as Mt. Carmel's building of salvaged wood, soaked with methylene chloride, its air powdered like that of a grain silo with CS particles instead of dust; and an ignition source, a match, an overturned lantern, or a Molotov cocktail for hurling at a tank. FBI spokesmen, Janet Reno, and even the President would afterwards insist that the occupants of Mt. Carmel had set fire to their home; in line with that presumption, most reporting about the cause of the fire has focused on ignition, not on the volatility of its combustible material.

The facts give off the fumes of irony: both the FBI and Mt. Carmel's spokesmen had expected the standoff to end by fire; Steve Schneider had even discussed the possibility with the opposing team.

After the ATF withdrew on February 28, David Koresh had turned the secular side of his mind to predicting the government's next move. "You're going to smoke bomb us or you're going to burn our building!" he declared in a conversation with the feds. Having examined the bullet holes in the front door, and those he attributed to helicopter fire at several spots inside the building, Steve Schneider announced in early March that a fiery finish was in the interest of the federal besiegers: it would get rid of evidence that credited the Carmelite version of the siege. "If you people don't burn the building down . . . it wouldn't surprise me that they wouldn't want to get rid of evidence," he told a negotiator on March 6. "If anybody wanted to come here and burn the place down, kill all the people, what evidence would be left?" he asked on March 10. Three days later, he ventured that "They may want to burn the building down, they want to destroy the evidence, because the evidence from the door will clearly show how many bullets and what happened. . . ." "You don't know the whole story yet," he once admonished. ". . . If this building stands, and, and the reporters and the press get to see the evidence, it's going to be shown clearly what happened and what these men came to do. . . . So if you guys want, you can even be involved with them in burning this place down. . . ." The negotiators, of course, denied any such intention.

Late in the siege, on April 13, Schneider mentioned to a negotiator that the residents were reading by candle and lantern light. Defense attorney Zimmermann would later note that "almost every room had a Coleman lantern." Bales of hay, brought from storage in the gymnasium, had been stacked against walls which faced outside, as protection against renewed gunfire. Schneider's negotiator recognized a hazard and asked, "Do you have any fire extinguisher systems?" Schneider wasn't sure how many of the devices were on hand, and at the negotiator's request sent a resident to do a count. Schneider reported that only one extinguisher was found. "Somebody ought to buy some fire insurance," his negotiator said.

The residents of Mt. Carmel were not unnerved by the specter of a fiery finale. If God wanted to save them from the flames, they believed, He would find a way. Judy Schneider reminded the FBI that the Book of Daniel reports that God saved Shadrach, Meshach, and Abednego from the flames of a fiery furnace, and on March 27, while discussing means of persuading the residents to leave, Steve Schneider entered into the following dialogue with a negotiator:

SCHNEIDER Well, you know what I think would work—well, I better not say that.

FBI Go ahead, it's your dime.

SCHNEIDER I was just going to say, throw a match to the building, people will have to come out.

FBI No, we're not going to do something like that.

SCHNEIDER . . . Sometime when you have the chance, read Isaiah 33 about people living in fire and walking through it and coming out surviving.

271

Schneider's citation was to one of the Bible's 587 references to fire and flames. So plentiful is the biblical tool kit that a Dallas–Fort Worth area researcher, James Trimm—with the endorsement of theologian Phil Arnold—has been able to build from it, complete with citations from Houteff and Lois Roden, an ostensibly plausible theory about the start of the fire.

On the morning of April 19, Trimm postulates, David Koresh ignited the fatal fire at Mt. Carmel as a means of closing the Fifth Seal and ushering in the Sixth. Key to Trimm's theory are two passages from the scriptures, Ezekiel 10:2 and Zechariah 2:5, neither of which played a role in Koresh's usual message, but both of which, like almost all other lines in the Writ, were known to him. Ezekiel 10:2 reads: "And he spake unto the man clothed with linen, and said, Go in between the wheels, even under the cherub, and fill thine hand with coals of fire from between the cherubims, and scatter them over the city." Zechariah 2:5 says: "For I, saith the Lord, will be unto her a wall of fire round about, and will be the glory in the midst of her." The Trimm-Arnold theory holds that Koresh may have scattered coals over his city, Mt. Carmel, building a "wall of fire" that he believed would be harmless to its inhabitants, but death to intruders. And indeed, on March 7, Koresh did cite the "wall of fire" text in a chat with the FBI.

On April 18, a listening device that the FBI had placed within feet of the front door captured snatches of conversation in which unidentified residents were discussing scriptures related to fire. "They can't destroy us unless it's God's will they do," one of the faceless speakers says on tape. "Haven't you read Joel 2 and Isaiah 13, where it says He's going to take us up like flames of fire. . . ?"

But when Jaime Castillo read transcripts of these conversations, he explained them by saying, "A fire was expected, it was and is, but not that we of our own will could bring about such an event. God will eventually bring about that event. . . . " Livingstone Fagan attributes a similar meaning to the conversations. "They were just reviewing scriptures," he writes, "regarding what happens when we are delivered and the Kingdom is set up"—an event that, Mt. Carmel's survivors believe, still lies in the future. In the same way, the biblical instruction

272

to scatter coals is clearly not an order given for execution on earth: cherubim do not live here. And it is God, not David Koresh, Yashua, the Messiah, or Jesus, who is to be the wall of fire mentioned in Zechariah 2:5.

Bureaumen listened to the discussions of fire relayed by the bugging devices on April 18, and presumed that the talk referred to plans for arson. But on the morning of April 19, the Bureau did not surround Mt. Carmel with fire trucks, as would have been appropriate. Instead, the agency launched a fixed-wing aircraft equipped with forward-looking infrared radar, or FLIR, capable of determining when and where fire broke out. The purpose of the film that the FLIR equipment made was apparently to show that if any fire did break out, the Bureau didn't ignite it.

The government's fire expert, Paul Gray—whose wife now works for the ATF's Houston office—finds in the FLIR tapes evidence that the fire broke out at 12:07:04 P.M., on Mt. Carmel's second floor. He and his assistants also claim that the tapes show three separate points of ignition in quick succession—an almost certain sign of arson.

But independent fire examiners have found that the first blaze spotted by the FLIR rig began at 11:59:16 A.M., not on Mt. Carmel's second floor but in its gymnasium, as a tank backed out of the room. The second-story fire was captured by the cameras at Satellite City and broadcast around the globe. The gym fire, clearly evident on the FLIR tapes, made from overhead, was out of the scope of television lenses. Rather than multiple fire points, what the tapes show, FBI critics argue, is that the holes that the tanks had knocked into Mt. Carmel acted as flues, sweeping the gymnasium blaze down Mt. Carmel's hallways.

The controversy over ignition points almost always proceeds into another series of arguments, about the sensitivity of FLIR equipment, the content of smoke clouds, the likelihood of multiple ignition points, the speed of the fire's spread, and other technical, and unverifiable, details. Government reports worthy of the Warren Commission consistently blame the residents for their own demise, but critics respond with doubts as devastating as those that challenged the "Magic Bullet" theory in the JFK case.

273

To this stirring mix of speculation are added interpretations of nearly unintelligible bugging tapes made early on the morning of April 19 from beneath the floor of Mt. Carmel's lobby. Transcripts of the murkily transmitted voices show residents saying things like, "Spread the fuel" and ". . .fire around back." One transcript by a forensic audio specialist renders the latter phrase as part of a longer one, "I want a fire around the back," while another records it as, "There's a fire around the back." The dark spots of memory that remain with the fire's survivors, both loyal followers of Koresh and one government witness, Marjorie Thomas, do not resolve the discrepancy, around which a new industry has grown: Just as ATF agents have sued the *Waco Tribune* and Jim Peeler's employer for allegedly causing death and mortification on February 28, survivors of those who perished are suing the FBI for having sparked the April 19 blaze.

Whether or not, for theological reasons, David Koresh thought he had orders to burn Mt. Carmel to the ground, as some of his accusers maintain, he recognized a tactical and wholly mundane use for flames. "Those tanks are not fireproof, you know," he had warned the FBI on March 19. If, on April 19, Koresh decided to repel the monstrous vehicles that had tormented his flock for fifty days, he did not have to send anyone outside—and into camera view—to fling Molotov cocktails. They presented themselves as targets, by barging indoors.

About three minutes before the ferret rounds began breaking windows, tanks started crashing through Mt. Carmel's walls. Bureau spokesmen declared that the entries were made, not to destroy the building, but to inject gas into its inner recesses and to provide openings through which the inhabitants could escape. During the fifty-day siege, Mt. Carmel's two telephone lines had been reduced to one, which the FBI had connected, not to the overhead lines that once served the building, but to a land or ground line that the FBI men had tossed in to resident technicians. They, in turn, had connected it to an instrument in the building's lobby. The Bureau's spokesmen told the world that Steve Schneider had cut off communication by throwing the telephone outside when the tear gassing began, but television footage and even the Justice Department's internal investigation indicate that a tank's steel tracks severed the line, leaving Mt. Carmel out of touch with even the negotiators. Transcripts of conversations picked up by listening devices show that Steven Schneider wanted to ask the Bureau to withhold its assault so that Koresh could finish writing his interpretation of the Seven Seals.

Rather than creating escape routes, the tanks that rammed Mt. Carmel closed them. They demolished the stairways connecting the building's first and second floors, and also pushed debris over a trapdoor leading to a buried school bus, whose exit opened to the fresh air outside. The bodies of six women were found within feet of the trapdoor, dead of smoke inhalation; they apparently took their last breaths while racing toward the newly blocked underground passage. During an entry at high noon, one of the CEVs went into Mt. Carmel's cafeteria, where some three dozen women and children were huddled in a concrete room at the base of the residential tower. Though the Bureau's spokesmen and the press called it a "bunker," the room had been built in Ben Roden's day to house Mt. Carmel's printshop, and in 1993, the community's walk-in refrigerator and store of guns sat inside.

The CEV's boom apparently struck high on the wall of the room's western side, sending chunks of concrete tumbling onto the heads of those cowering below. Though most of them were wrapped in wet blankets and towels—to protect the children from tear gas—six of the mothers and children died from what the Fort Worth coroner's office termed "blunt force trauma." Coroner Rodney Crow says that these victims were crushed and suffocated "from the falling concrete in the bunker than fell on them." But, in tune with the passions of the hour, several newspapers interpreted "blunt force trauma" as an indication that the victims were bludgeoned to death by their peers.

It is apparent from the accounts of survivors that some of those inside Mt. Carmel preferred death to surrender, even death for their children. Some two dozen of the eighty-five people inside died by gunshot wounds, including David Koresh, Steven Schneider, and David Jones. Clive Doyle says that as smoke and flames circled, Wayne Martin came into the chapel, slid down one of its walls, and removed his gasmask. "Somebody asked him something like, 'What do we do now?' " he recalls. He sighed or coughed and said something like, 'Well, I guess we wait on God,' or, 'I guess we have to trust in God.' " Doyle and

275

three others left the chapel, but Martin, either overcome or determined, died there, his autopsy report says, of smoke inhalation. Among the chemical traces found in his body was cyanide, a by-product of many house fires—and also of burning CS particles.

Government witness Marjorie Thomas, who suffered third-degree burns over half of her body, was not one of those who preferred martyrdom to the risk of dishonor. In a deposition for the San Antonio trial, she described the final moments of Mt. Carmel:

> . . . The whole entire building felt warm all at once, and then after the warmth, then a thick, black smoke, and the place became dark. I could hear—I couldn't see anything. I could hear people moving and screaming, and I still was sitting down while this was happening. Then the voices faded.
>
> . . . I was making my way out of the building, because it began to get very hot, and my clothes were starting to melt on me. . . . Before the fire had started, Sheila [Martin] Jr. was sitting on the step . . . I couldn't see her. I was making my way towards getting out, and I trod on her, and I said, "I'm sorry," and her voice was very faint, and I couldn't see her, and I could feel the flames . . . I saw a little bit of light. I made my way towards the light, and on doing so, I could see where it—it was one of the bedrooms. I could—the window was missing. I looked out. I don't like heights, but I thought . . . "I stay inside and, and die, or I jump out of the window," so I put my head—my hands over my head and leapt out of the window."

While the tanks were rudely bringing down Mt. Carmel, FBI chief negotiator Byron Sage and an assistant were attempting to calm those inside. Over the public address system that had earlier given voice to Nancy Sinatra and Alice Cooper, the two were broadcasting a new message. "This is not an assault. This is not an assault," the message said. "We will not be entering the building."

Surviving residents say that in making their entries, the tanks knocked over lanterns and cans of fuel, and crushed a pressurized tank filled with liquified propane gas, a volatile heating and cooking fuel. About the time that the fire got under way, transcripts show that the Bureau's broadcasters began to ad-lib, adding to their prepared text exclamations like, "David, you have had your fifteen minutes of fame," and, "Vernon is finished. He's no longer the Messiah!" Television footage shows that after the conflagration began devouring Mt. Carmel's densest structures, CEV tankers, instead of merely standing by, may have used their bulldozer blades to push debris and remaining sections of wall into the blaze—destroying bits of evidence, as Steve Schneider had said they would. Ultimately, the heat was so intense that it ignited Mt. Carmel's flag, 25 yards away atop a steel mast. By the time that fire trucks had chilled the building's ashes, a new and victorious banner was flying in its place—someone had hoisted the flag of the ATF.

Unnoticed, and sometimes uncounted among the dead, were two fetuses, one full-term, the other seven months. Both are believed to have been born as the result of an evolutionary reflex, instants after their mothers, Aisha Gyarfas and Nicole Gent, expired. Gyarfas was the victim of a gunshot wound; Gent of the crashing concrete. The deaths of their infants, who would have been viable had they experienced normal births, were the omega of the day whose alpha was the seemingly innocuous tear-gas raid.

Chapter 29

JUSTICE

"When we heard all that testimony, there was no way we could
find them guilty of murder. We felt provocation was pretty evident."
—an anonymous juror, quoted by the *San Antonio Express*.

"I'm very happy with the decision."
—ATF Special Agent Davy Aguilera

"The government was successful in convincing the court to ignore
the jury's findings."
—defense attorney Mike DeGeurin.

The San Antonio federal courthouse is a drum-shaped, three-story
building of pale brick, erected as a movie theater for a 1968 exposition
called the HemisFair. After the exposition closed, this theater-in-the-
round was squared into courtrooms, with paneled walls, carpeted floors,
and fluorescent lighting. In one of these spaces, in January 1994, the
government brought eleven former residents of Mt. Carmel to trial:
Norman Allison, Renos Avraam, Brad Branch, Jaime Castillo, Graeme
Craddock, Clive Doyle, Livingstone Fagan, Paul Fatta, Woodrow Kendrick, Ruth Riddle, and Kevin Whitecliff.

The San Antonio venue was a product of negotiation. The defense attorneys were a baker's dozen recruited from across North, South, and East Texas, most of them by Dick DeGuerin, whose client was dead. The successor attorneys had originally been content to go to trial in Waco, located just east of the center of the state. But during the siege, the town's attitude toward religious nonconformists changed from one of indifferent bemusement to one of loathing and fear. The "Davidians," as Waco's residents also now called the residents of Mt. Carmel, had brought infamy and inconvenience to town. Waco's chamber of commerce, for example, had scheduled its annual banquet for April 19, but canceled the fête after Mt. Carmel went up in flames.

After the conflagration, ATF sympathizers erected billboards all over town, thanking Wacoans for their support of law and order, and that act showed more gratitude than the press or the religionists had displayed. Ruling that Mt. Carmel's house fire victims had been participants in a "civil disorder," even the Red Cross had hardened its heart, denying Sheila Martin and her surviving children cast-off clothing and second-hand furnishings. The defense attorneys concluded that their clients were viewed as witches who'd hexed Waco's middling good luck, and they asked that the trial be moved elsewhere.

The defense hoped for its setting in liberal and largely Protestant Austin, 100 miles away and nearer the center of the state. But Judge Walter Smith, Jr., couldn't find an ample courtroom there, and chose instead San Antonio, a largely Catholic and military city about 200 miles south. San Antonio wasn't the best venue in Texas to defend a group of Protestant heretics, but the other cities in Smith's jurisdiction—Midland, San Angelo, and El Paso—were too far away from the attorneys' homes to be attractive. Two of the defenders lived in San Antonio. It was within an hour's drive for three others, and was a half-hour's distance by air from Houston and Fort Worth, where five of the others lived. The shift was not without its cost—most of the lawyers had to rent apartments in San Antonio, and one, from the Waco area, petitioned to be relieved of his public appointment because, he said, he could not pay commuting or rental expenses from his public defender's fee. Most of those who stayed on the case took it on a pro bono basis, though they estimated that it would cost them about $25,000 each. "I had one talk with my client, Clive Doyle," declared Houston attorney

Dan Cogdell, "and I decided, 'This is why we go to law school.' This was a case about the abuse of authority."

It was not, however, political or religious sympathy that motivated the defense team. The attorneys were not Constitutionalists, gun-rights advocates, or devout Christians. As a group, the men on the defense team, including the professorial Mike DeGeurin, brother to the flashy Dick DeGuerin (despite different styles and spellings of the family name), were well known in the cities where they lived. But their names weren't household words. Some of them wanted the publicity that accompanies notorious clients, and some were attracted by the lure of team play. "You know what this case reminds me of?" Fort Worth attorney Tim Evans confessed. "It reminds me of when we were back in high school, and we'd get a bunch of guys together some weekend, and pool five or ten dollars for gas, and drive down to Acuña and go to Boys' Town"—a reference to the tradition by which Texas men were once introduced to sex, in Mexico's red-light districts.

Judge Smith, a red-faced, balding, and portly figure, fifty-four, was a part of the Waco establishment, and that worried the defenders. He was a graduate of Baylor Law School, who in 1984, when Ronald Reagan appointed him to the bench, had been defeated at the polls after a term as a state jurist. He was also chairman of the McLennan County Republican Party. The *Dallas Morning News*, in a thumbnail profile, reported, "Formal in courtroom proceedings, he . . . has a reputation among defense lawyers as pro-prosecution. He is known even among prosecutors as harsh in sentencing." But challenging Smith's fairness to hear the case was not an option that the defenders took seriously. The consensus of the group is probably summarized by Corpus Christi attorney Douglas Tinker, who says, "When you get in federal court, the cards are stacked against you, anyway."

In the trial before them, Tinker's argument was more than grousing. The defendants were charged, among other things, with conspiracy to murder federal officers, attempted murder of federal officers, aiding and abetting the murder of federal officers, murdering federal officers, and various gun charges. Had the prosecution chosen to try the case in the state courts, under the terms of the Texas Penal Code, it could have

280

sought the death penalty on the murder charge. But the defendants could have sought protection in a section of the Code stipulating that the use of deadly force to resist an arrest or search is justified "if, before the actor offers any resistance, the peace officer . . . uses or attempts to use greater force than necessary to make the arrest or search. . . ." No similar language protects suspects against abuses by federal officers. "The government's position is that if they have a badge and gun," Dan Cogdell declared, "you're supposed to take the bullet and let your survivors sort out the legalities."

The Justice Department had assigned a half-dozen U.S. Attorneys to prosecute the case. They were headed by Ray Jahn, fifty, a tall man with intense blue eyes and a mustache, who had gone from San Antonio to Washington as special counsel to FBI director Sessions; and by his wife, LeRoy Jahn, a specialist in procedural law. Assisting the Jahns were two federal prosecutors from the Waco region—Bill Johnston, thirty-four, a tall, lanky, and aggressive figure; and John Phinizy, forty-six, dumpy, and receding. Motivation was the prosecution's strong suit: Johnston had participated in planning the February 28 raid, and Ray Jahn had taken part in planning sessions for the April 19 tear-gas attack. Seated at the table with the attorneys, dressed in a suit and sporting a fade haircut, was bronze-skinned Davy Aguilera, author of the flawed search warrant. Also at the table was Ray Cano, who headed the team of Texas Rangers that gathered evidence for the case. If for LeRoy Jahn, John Phinizy, and Ray Cano, prosecuting the defendants was a matter of professional duty, for Ray Jahn, Bill Johnston, and Davy Aguilera it was also matter of professional self-justification.

Judge Smith showed his sympathy for the prosecution early, in several ways. He nixed motions to sever the cases of the defendants, whose circumstances were in many ways unalike. Saying that "the government is not on trial," he also discouraged defense moves to subpoena planners and other behind-the-scenes figures important to the raid. In December and early January, Smith pared the jury pool himself. He sent questionnaires to prospective jurors, then decided which of them to strike, winnowing a panel of seventy-eight to forty-one before giving the legal teams a chance to conduct voir dire examinations. This measure was accepted by the defense both because it is common in federal trials today, and also because a thorough jury selection would have taken two weeks: time is money in the lawyer's trade. Attorney Cogdell confessed that to finance a long stay in San Antonio, he'd sold a Rolex and a Mustang, and the bearded Tinker—a picture of Ernest Hemingway in his latter years—sighed that he'd bounced a check to the IRS. If the defense attorneys didn't like the moves that Smith made, they said little because they couldn't say much: the judge had placed them under a gag order to keep them from making their case in the press.

Judge Smith also declared that the identity of the jury panel would be kept secret. To ensure secrecy, he put a gag order on the jurors, too, and arranged for them to report to a military base each morning, where they boarded a bus that took them to the federal courthouse under armed escort.

The judge's moves were publicly protested by local supporters of an organization called the Fully Informed Jury Association (FIJA). The unifying principle of FIJA, a group that claims a Texas membership of five thousand, is the belief that citizens have the right, and duty, to nullify bad law from the jury box. Brochures that the organization publishes cite nineteenth-century Justice Oliver Wendell Holmes as having opined that "The jury has the power to bring a verdict in the teeth of both the law and fact," and quote a 1972 appellate finding that "The pages of history shine upon instances of the jury's exercise of its prerogative to disregard instructions of the judge; for example, in acquittals under the fugitive slave law." Especially in controversial trials, members of FIJA accost members of juries and jury panels, offering them literature that extols the juror's power to acquit. When Judge Smith announced that the San Antonio jury would be anonymous, FIJA state leader Larry Dodge complained in a letter to the *San Antonio Express*: "If the public cannot know who is on the jury, what's to keep the government from packing it with ATF or FBI agents?"

Each morning FIJA members and other protesters gathered outside the courthouse, holding placards and banners in the view of passing motorists and the TV crews who haunted the courthouse steps. Unable to reach the jurors by leafleting, protesters displayed placards along the route of the jury bus. When he learned of FIJA's action, Judge Smith ordered the jury—eight women and four men, most of them Mexican-Americans—to avert its gaze when protesters were in view. So the FIJA activists obtained a copy of the jury wheel list—a roll of the hundreds of people from which the panel had been selected—and mailed brochures to everyone it named. Smith told the jurors to bring such propaganda to him, unopened, and the FBI began investigating the mailing, though nothing illegal had occurred.

The government's chief case against the eleven was the conspiracy charge, which hinged on Mt. Carmel's theology, though the prosecution tried to avoid saying so. Ray Jahn opened the trial on January 12, 1994, by telling the court, "In order to place the story in perspective, we are going to have to get into some of the teachings of David Koresh. . . . One thing we need to make clear right now . . . this is not a trial about religion. . . . The theology comes in only to place in perspective the existence of a conspiracy. . . . What did David Koresh teach? We anticipate that the evidence will show that David Koresh's theology was the theology of death."

Jahn's object was to picture the religion of Mt. Carmel as a conspiracy to make war. Koresh's followers, he said, held certain beliefs about prophecy, and when faced with a situation which they thought confirmed their beliefs, they had acted in accord with those beliefs, defying the law: at that point, theirs "was not a religious message." The trial that was opening was not a heresy trial, because the defendants were not charged with holding prohibited religious beliefs—none being prohibited—but with practicing what they held sacred. "This is a story or a trial about the physical acts that the individuals undertook," Jahn proclaimed, as if beliefs that don't lead to actions were worthy of the name.

In closing arguments Jahn's assistant, Bill Johnston, made it clear that from the government's point of view, even passive behavior proved the guilt of the defendants. ". . . Merely an implied understanding to do something against the law can be a conspiracy. That's it, there is nothing weird about it," he declared. The defendants were guilty, he explained, of membership in a revolutionary organization. "Each one here, each defendant," he pointed out, "decided to belong to this group." In early 1992, the assistant prosecutor went on, "there was talk of war—talk of war, that these people would be involved in a literal war, and they stayed." Members of the group bought numerous weapons, converted them to automatic fire, he argued, "and a person not wanting to be involved in such a thing had a choice to make, and they stayed." "Once they had joined the conspiracy," Johnston had already told the court, "they are liable for every act in furtherance of it."

In order to give the conspiracy a name, the prosecution relied on a bob-tailed version of an allegation from Marc Breault, without calling him as a witness or presenting any other evidence that the charge was true. "It was part of the conspiracy that in order to prepare for the 'war' with the United States," the indictment and charge to the jury read, "Vernon K. Howell, also known as David Koresh, would and did establish a unit among his followers which he called the 'Mighty Men.'" This group, the prosecutors alleged, engaged in preparations for civil war. All of the male defendants in the dock, it said, were members of the "Mighty Men" corps.

The term "Mighty Men" is used in eighty-four Bible verses. Marc Breault alleged that one of its uses—as the name of a group whose duty was to guard a ruler's bedroom antics from discovery—was the one adopted by Koresh. But no record of such a citation exists, and if such a group existed, its military training was perfunctory. One of the male defendants at San Antonio, Graeme Craddock, had in a statement to the Texas Rangers confessed to learning all that he knew about weapons while living at Mt. Carmel. He described an instance in which Mark Wendell, who died on April 19, allowed him to fire ten rounds from a pistol, and another occasion when Koresh called him to the rifle range, handed him a semi-automatic rifle, and supervised while he fired five to ten rounds. Trainees even in Third World armies fire a hundred times as many shots with each small arm in which they're schooled. Craddock told the Rangers that he had been issued an AR-15 rifle, and also a 9mm pistol, without ammunition, because Koresh believed that loaded guns in the hands of greenhorns were dangerous. Defendant Jamie Castillo, in his statement to the Rangers, confessed that he, too, had an AR-15, but that it had been issued without ammunition, for the same reason.

The Mighty Men may have been daring commandos in David Koresh's fantasies about Camaros, *chanteuses*, and hot guns. Their real identity was made clear when the prosecution introduced into evidence the videotaped deposition of government witness Marjorie Thomas. During cross-examination by attorney John Carroll of San Antonio, who represented defendant Renos Avraam, Thomas endorsed the meaning assigned to "Mighty Men" by other survivors of the affair.

CARROLL   And very briefly, on the Mighty Men, the Mighty Men were the men who had believed the message; isn't that right?
THOMAS   Yes.
CARROLL   And it could have been a weak, physically weak man, right—
THOMAS   Yes.
CARROLL   If he was strong in his faith?
THOMAS   Yes.
CARROLL   A paraplegic could have been a Mighty Man?
THOMAS   Yes.

Marc Breault, in the memoir he wrote of his days with Koresh, had pictured the Mighty Men as only half a conspiracy whose other component was the "House of David," a grouping that he said was composed of Koresh's concubines. In order to show their status, members of the House of David, Breault said, sported medallions in the shape of the star of David. Like the "Mighty Men," the House of David is a designation of biblical origin; 103 verses mention the entity. But the scriptures do not refer to it as an institution of concubinage, and the prosecution chose not to allege that Ruth Riddle, the only female defendant, had been a concubine of Koresh, perhaps because Breault's medallion story had already been debunked: Bonnie Haldeman wore a star of David, as did Wayne Martin and Steve Schneider.

The government's definition of conspiracy ran counter to common sense—were the cowering women on the second floor also conspirators?—and Gerry Morris of Austin, Woodrow "Bob" Kendrick's attorney, in his closing speech, argued that it stretched the law as well. ". . . When the government argues conspiracy," he told the jury, "they make it sound like getting involved in a conspiracy is about like catching a cold. You walk through Mt. Carmel a couple of times, get exposed to a little preaching and, wham! you've got it, and once you've got it, you can't get rid of it. Whatever happens from then on is your fault. . . . In order to convict any of these folks . . . not only must you find that they engaged in a conspiracy, but you must find that they entered into that agreement . . . with intent to murder, the same intent that they would have to have to be guilty of murder if they acted alone."

Though the government hoped to convict all of the defendants of conspiracy, most of them were charged with murder and other crimes. The murder accusation was based on the belief that Mt. Carmel's residents had laid in wait and ambushed the ATF raiders, an accusation that seemed to preempt the very idea of self-defense. But the prosecution had wrested no confessions to murder from the defendants, it had no eyewitness testimony to any ambush from anyone inside Mt. Carmel, and only one of the surviving raiders claimed to recognize the resident who shot at him.

The strongest case was against defendant Brad Branch, thirty-four, a beefy aviation mechanic from Waco. In his five years as a follower, he had more than once moved back into town, found a job, and resumed his rounds at honky-tonks and topless bars. On the morning of February 28, witness Marjorie Thomas testified, Branch had come to the second floor of Mt. Carmel and had run from "room to room" carrying a weapon that Thomas described only as "a brown one," presumably an AK-47 rifle. During the fourth week of the trial, the prosecution would bring Victorine Hollingsworth from England to testify that while the firefight was hot, she heard Branch blurt, "He nearly got me!" and, "I got one!" ". . . The evidence shows Branch killed 'Steve' Willis," prosecutor Johnston would conclude at the end of the trial. "Why? As you look at the front of the compound there, the green and white van, Willis' position, the shot came from the upper . . . left. Who was the only one we know was firing from the upper left, that is, the second floor? Who was the only male on the second floor shooting, and who is it said, 'I got one'? Brad Branch killed 'Steve' Willis."

The argument was weak, for several reasons. No one, either inside or outside Mt. Carmel, came forward to say that they saw Branch shoot anyone. No testimony was brought to show who might have been firing from the residential tower—above, and to the left of Willis—though several of the ATF agents said that they'd seen shooters there. No ballistics tests matched any bullet that felled Willis with any weapon found inside Mt. Carmel, and Hollingsworth's testimony about Branch was placed in doubt by its similarity to what she reported about Livingstone Fagan. Hollingsworth had told the court that Branch had bragged that "He nearly got me and I got one," or, "One nearly got me and I got one." But she also said that she heard Livingstone Fagan make reference to one of the agents outside by saying, "He nearly got me, but I got him first." It was as if the barfly and the theologian had used the same choice of words.

The other murder that the prosecution detailed involved the death of Robert J. "Rob" Williams, the agent who was killed while providing cover fire to the roof raiders. Evidence for the charge came only from convicted dope dealer Bradley Rogans, twenty-three, who claimed to have struck up a long jailhouse friendship with defendant Renos Avraam, a Britisher, twenty-nine years old. Records introduced by the defense would show that Rogans had been in jail only one day with Avraam, not weeks, as he claimed, and the testimony that he gave was anything but convincing.

PHINIZY Did he talk to you about anything that he did specifically on February 28, that being the day that there was a shooting with ATF?

ROGANS He did, I guess.

PHINIZY Did he tell you where he hid?

ROGANS Yeah, behind a safe, I think he said. It was behind a safe or something like that.

PHINIZY And when he said that he was behind the safe, did he tell you anything about shooting?

ROGANS Nothing that was like incriminating. . . . I asked him about—that was just a main curiosity—I said, you know, "Did you shoot?" or something like that, and he would say, "No," and then kind of laughed and said, "Well, I'm not a bad shot," . . . something along that line. . . ."

Yet in making the prosecution's closing argument, Bill Johnston would argue that "Renos Avraam shot 'Rob' Williams. And how do I come up with that? Renos Avraam apparently states to this kid something about hiding behind a safe, and he's a pretty good shot. There was someone hiding behind a safe and was shot on that side, and that was 'Rob' Williams." Johnston's oral reconstruction moved the safe that Avraam mentioned from inside Mt. Carmel, where he hid, to the outdoors, where Willis was taking cover—behind another strongbox. Among the more than 2,500 charred items that investigators salvaged from inside Mt. Carmel was the safe that Avraam hid behind, duly registered, photographed, and filed in an FBI inventory.

Jaime Castillo, twenty-four, prosecutor Johnston argued, was guilty of attempted murder because he had shot agent Ballesteros in the thumb. "How did I come up with that?" the prosecutor asked the jury. "Castillo, by his own admission, is at the front door and his rifle jams. Does a rifle jam just holding it, or does it jam while the action is going and he's at the front door?" Johnston derived his conclusion from a statement that Castillo gave the Texas Rangers: "Castillo stated that he never fired a weapon during the initial raid, nor on the day of the fire. Castillo admitted to having a rifle that became jammed when attempting to load it. . . . Castillo stated he tried to chamber a round in his rifle, but that it jammed." Guns can jam, and do jam, while being loaded, and Ballesteros, if he was struck by a bullet from inside Mt. Carmel—rather than by friendly fire—may have been wounded by one of Castillo's companions at the door.

The prosecution also sought to prove that Kevin Whitecliff was guilty of attempted murder. Following the February 28 shoot-out, the government's star witness, Kathy Schroeder, told the court that at the instruction of Koresh, she and other women had penned statements about what they'd seen. After she'd collected the women's accounts, she began recording statements from the males, which she entered into a computer. All of these records were lost in the fire, but during her courtroom appearance on February 2, Schroeder recalled that Kevin Whitecliff, thirty-one, a hulking former prison guard from Hawaii, had told her that he'd shot at the helicopters that flew overhead. Prosecutor Johnston used Schroeder's report as the basis for a conclusion that "Whitecliff shot the helicopters, by his own admission," and perhaps he did. In his closing argument to the jury on behalf of Whitecliff and the other defendant he represented, attorney Steven "Rocket" Rosen said that "Kevin Whitecliff and Livingstone Fagan relied on the most basic instinct of survival, and that in defending their loved ones. . . ." Whitecliff, he maintained, "did what he had to do to defend himself and the two children of Mr. and Mrs. Fagan and the rest of the family in that home."

But whether or not Whitecliff fired the first shot of the war or returned fire to the helicopters was an issue that was sidestepped at trial. Testimony showed that three helicopters were used in connection with the raid, two civilian-sized Apache models, and a larger Sikorsky Blackhawk, piloted by Warrant Office Jerry Seagraves of the Texas National Guard. In eliciting direct testimony from Seagraves about weapons, prosecutor Johnston walked lightly around the question that was key:

JOHNSTON   And when any law enforcement people are involved in riding in your aircraft, are there certain rules that apply to them?

SEAGRAVES   Yes, sir, there are.

JOHNSTON   What are the rules concerning weapons in the aircraft?

SEAGRAVES   The rules concerning weapons, that you cannot have any chambered rounds in the weapon while you're in the aircraft, and no weapon will be discharged from the aircraft.

The prosecutor did not ask if the rules had been broken or ignored, or if anyone had made a check of any weapons that were bought aboard. Attorney Mike DeGeurin, defender of Paul Fatta, raised the issue as best he could.

DEGEURIN   You had some—do I understand, you had one ATF agent aboard?

SEAGRAVES   No, we had approximately eight.

DEGEURIN   Eight armed agents?

SEAGRAVES   They were armed. . . .

DEGEURIN   All right. And what were they supposed to—what were they going to do with their guns?

SEAGRAVES   They were administrative personnel. Our understanding of the mission was once, the compound—or Mt. Carmel was secure and it was deemed secure, then we were to land with those people and they were going to be admin people to start processing the folks that were there.

DeGeurin   I was just wondering, what were they going to do with their guns, if they are processing. Do you know?

Seagraves   I don't know.

The prosecution's most prized evidence of attempted murder pointed to Livingstone Fagan. Not only did Victorine Hollingsworth report having heard him boast that "He nearly got me, but I got him first," but his alleged victim, Special Agent Eric Evers, had picked Fagan from a photo line-up. In court on January 19, during an acrid cross-examination by attorney Rosen, Evers gestured toward Fagan and blurted, "I know that man over there shot me. It's—everything is etched in my—my brain until the day I die, because of that incident. There's no doubt in my mind that man shot me." But the facts, Rosen insisted, placed the identification in doubt.

In the wake of February 28, Evers had told the Texas Rangers that two whites and one black male had pinned him down. He gave no description beyond the racial/sexual designations. A fellow Special Agent, also hemmed in near the tornado shelters with Evers, had described for the Rangers a black male taller than the diminutive Fagan, a man who was wearing goggles. Survivors say that Fagan spent the hours of the firefight praying in the cafeteria, but he refuses to profess any personal innocence because, he says, "We were all of the same spirit in there, so why should I talk about differences about what we did in the flesh?"

Fagan suffered a handicap beyond theology, too. As attorney Rosen pointed out, he was the only black male to leave Mt. Carmel during the siege, and because of his spokesman's role, the only one whose face was frequently broadcast on television. Of the eleven black male residents at Mt. Carmel, only two survived the siege, Fagan and Derek Lovelock, who was not charged and did not give any testimony in the case.

Though Evers picked Fagan out of a photo line-up that Texas Rangers showed him months after the incident, during cross-examination a startling revelation was made about his pick. Saying, "Right is right,"

Ray Cano, the Texas Ranger assigned to the prosecution team, rose to show the court the original card of photos from which Evers had made his choice. Cano said that he'd run across the card just minutes before, while rummaging through the files on the prosecution desk. In compliance with judicial rules requiring prosecutors to disclose evidence, Fagan's attorney had been given a photocopy of the original. But the photocopy, unlike the original, did not bear a telling notation, written in the hand of the Ranger who presented Evers with the line-up. It said: "unsure if I.D.ed from TV or the shooting." The prosecution's accusation against Fagan rested on tainted evidence and impeachable witnesses.

The aiding and abetting charge was leveled chiefly at the defendants who could not have killed anyone. Paul Fatta, for example, with his fourteen-year-old son Kalani, had been in Austin on February 28, 100 miles from Mt. Carmel. Norman Allison and Bob Kendrick, also charged, had been at the auto shop and, since no lawmen had been killed in the shoot-out with Michael Schroeder, were also patently innocent of actual murder.

"In this case, I think there are a couple of textbook example of aiding and abetting," prosecutor Johnston said in his closing. "One is Ruth Riddle handing her firearm to another, being totally foreseeable that the firearm could be used. And the second one is Paul Fatta being conveniently miles away, while all of his ammunition and firearms are being used to kill."

No evidence was ever brought showing that Fatta had converted any weapons to automatic fire, or was aware of their conversion. Attorney Mike DeGeurin argued that Fatta bought and owned many things that he did not control. In his conversations by telephone with the FBI, Koresh had estimated the cost of operating Mt. Carmel at $15,000 a month, or about $125 for each person there, including children. Fatta, a wealthy heir, may have paid most or all of that price. DeGeurin told the court that his client provided $60,000 as a down payment on a home where group members stayed in California, $12,000 for a church bus, some $20,000 for auto shop equipment. Fatta also bought fifteen to twenty go-karts and dirt bikes for the children. In a word, he purchased anything that Koresh thought he needed. Paul Fatta's job at Mt. Carmel was making and supplying money, not managing the goods that money bought.

The prosecution accused three of the defendants—Doyle, Castillo, and Craddock—of starting the April 19 fire, even though Doyle's daughter, Shari, nineteen, had died in the blaze. ". . . When the fire was finally set, ladies and gentlemen" the chief prosecutor told the jury, "we anticipate showing that it was set virtually simultaneously when a tank, FBI tank was inside the building." Setting such a fire in self-defense was not a mitigation in the prosecution's culpability scheme, but instead was an act of attempted murder. The basis for its accusation, the prosecution would show, was that traces of accelerants, or petroleum derivatives, were found on the shoes of the three defendants. Defense attorneys argued that yes, their clients had spilled fuel on their shoes, while refilling motors and lanterns inside Mt. Carmel during the siege.

Witnesses for the prosecution, besides testifying to points of the accusations, tried to bias the jurors on wider grounds. When Special Agent Bernadette Griffin told the court how she had extracted the wounded Kenny King from the courtyard of Mt. Carmel, she alleged that defendant Jaime Castillo, usually known as Jamie Castillo, had stood watch in a doorway, a gun at the ready. "And I heard someone," she told the jury, "I'm not exactly sure, but someone saying to me to bring my black ass out so that they could see me. . . ." Griffin had not mentioned the racial remark to the Texas Rangers who'd interviewed her shortly after the events, and the claim was hardly worthy of belief.

Jamie Castillo is a bronze-skinned, soft-spoken young man, who was a musician at Mt. Carmel. Born in Texas, he'd spent his childhood and adolescence in the Los Angeles area, where, after his father, a musician, abandoned the family, his mother had made ends meet on welfare. As a child, Jamie says, his greatest thrill had been listening to his father's voice on a couple of recordings of songs in the ranchera genre, and he wanted to succeed where his dad had failed. But as he grew up and came into an understanding of his circumstances, his hopes dimmed. An older brother fell into drug use and gang activities, and Jamie narrowly missed the same fate. He slid through high school,

292

then found a day job as a courier, working as a drummer and guitarist at night. He had discovered groupies while playing in bands, but these sexual encounters left him with feelings of guilt. After joining a Pentecostal church, in 1988 he placed an ad in a newspaper, asking for a spot in a Christian band. David Koresh answered the notice, and after a few jam sessions and theology sittings, in 1989, Jamie Castillo had come to Mt. Carmel, a place where racial doctrines, though not unknown, were not taken seriously. Castillo denies that he said anything about Griffin's "black ass," and recalls that when he told her "to get where I could see you," standing at his shoulder were Steven Henry and "Dabo" Thomas, both black Englishmen, and both, at the time, armed with rifles.

But if the prosecution had difficulty in making much of its case, on one issue the trial was easy going all the way. More than a week of the court's time was consumed by the introduction of weapons, carted to an evidence table in wooden and cardboard boxes, each gun wrapped in a plastic bag. Investigators had found some 300 guns in and around Mt. Carmel, a few still in firing order. In addition, they found dummy grenades, parts of exploded grenades, and the remnants of what were alleged to have been a half-million rounds of ammunition, before they "cooked off" during the fire; almost all of this weaponry, the defense argued, had been bought for resale. The prosecution's heaps of evidence also included what appeared to be illegal, homemade silencers for rifles, and forty-eight semi-automatic rifles that had been converted to automatic fire. The armory did not, however, contain any .50-caliber machine guns, as even a correspondent for National Public Radio had reported from the trial. Nevertheless, the display of hardware was impressive, and the prosecution drove hard on the point. ". . . Firearms training, yeah, every church does that, that's not unusual," prosecutor Johnston said with sarcasm in his closing. "Let's get the Methodist men and the Knights of Columbus together and go out and shoot some machine guns. It's ridiculous."

The defense countered that most of the guns had been bought as investments, and when the prosecution brought gun dealers to the stand, attorney DeGeurin exacted from them admissions that the armaments that Koresh and Fatta owned had more than doubled in value since the date of their purchase. But the defenders did not deny—and could not have denied—that someone inside Mt. Carmel had illegally converted some of the weapons. Koresh had practically admitted that much himself. On March 7, discussing the search warrant's charges with FBI negotiators, Koresh had confessed that "Yes, I have some things maybe I shouldn't have. I mean, hey, if Vatican can have its own little country, can't I . . . ?" The prosecution did not introduce that statement into evidence, perhaps because the prosecution's aim was to implicate all of Mt. Carmel's residents in illegal arms activity.

On February 14, 1994, after calling 120 witnesses, the prosecution rested, and a debate began in the defense camp. Its initiators were the accused, some of whom, led by Livingstone Fagan, wanted to be put on the stand. They wanted to talk about their religion, but their attorneys preferred that they remain silent: praising Koresh, they thought, would be a liability. After tense meetings with their clients and among themselves, the defenders called attorney Jack Zimmermann to testify about what he saw in Mt. Carmel during the siege. The defense also subpoenaed a couple of residents from the Waco area, who swore that they'd seen Koresh outside of Mt. Carmel in the weeks before the assault, and it called gun dealer Karen Kilpatrick, who spoke of Aguilera's unwillingness to meet with the preacher. But none of the defendants took the stand and the defense presentation lasted less than two days. Afterwards both sides adjourned to wrestle with Judge Smith over the charge, or instructions, that he would issue to the jury.

The briefs that lawyers write, cluttered as they are with thick language and references to obscure precedents, do not ordinarily make good reading and, indeed, are often unintelligible to laymen. But in the San Antonio trial, Terrence Kirk, an assistant to Joe Turner, Ruth Riddle's attorney, found a way to speak to Judge Smith's background as well as his jurisprudence. The attorney's object was to persuade Smith to allow the jurors to consider self-defense as a motive for the defendants' acts. "To tell a Texan," Kirk argued in a brief that read like a manifesto,

> or any citizen of this country, that he must forfeit his life, or if
> he survives, risk conviction for defending himself where he rea-

sonably believes a federal agent is unlawfully trying to kill him
. . . well, Defendant does not believe this Court will say that to
our citizens. Such a ruling would lead, for example, to the
absurd result that both a federal officer and an innocent citizen
could be prosecuted where the officer unlawfully tried to kill the
citizen, and the citizen dared to defend himself: the officer for a
civil rights violation, and the citizen for assaulting a known federal agent. . . .

When he came out of his deliberations, Judge Smith accepted the
argument. "If a defendant was not an aggressor, and had reasonable
grounds to believe that he was in imminent danger of death or serious
bodily harm from which he could save himself only by using deadly
force against his assailants, he had the right to employ deadly force in
order to defend himself," the judge instructed the jurors.

At the prompting of the defense, Judge Smith also granted a manslaughter option for the murder charge. Smith defined manslaughter as
appropriate if a defendant "unlawfully killed in the sudden heat of
passion caused by adequate provocation." The difference between firing shots in self-defense and firing with "adequate provocation" was
nearly lost in legalese, and indeed, it derives from doctrines and traditions as opaque as any that Koresh ever preached. Jurors concluded
that manslaughter was an offense that would carry a lighter sentence
than the same acts punished as murder.

On Wednesday, February 23, after the prosecution presented the
closing argument of the trial, Judge Smith called the jury into the courtroom and read them sixty-seven pages of instructions on how to proceed
in rendering a verdict. He also gave them copies of his exposition. In
deliberations that afternoon, the jurors quickly divided, says jury forewoman Sarah Bain, who, along with another juror, Jeanette Felger
(they'd been Panelists 182 and 16, respectively) identified themselves
after the verdict was delivered. The jury, which included schoolteach-
ers, housewives, civil servants, and a retired banker, was split, 9–3,
schoolteacher Bain says. Its majority leaned toward acquittal on all
charges, while a minority favored conviction on the conspiracy count.
Their disagreements were revived on Thursday and Friday, but Sat-

urday morning, with a shortened weekend already in view, the twelve hit on a compromise. The jurors found all eleven defendants not guilty of the murder and conspiracy accusations, and three of them—Clive Doyle, Norman Allison, and Woodrow Kendrick—innocent of all charges. The jury also found seven defendants guilty of aiding and abetting in the voluntary manslaughter of federal officials, five of them additionally guilty of carrying a firearm during the commission of a crime of violence, and two defendants, Paul Fatta and Graeme Crad- dock, guilty of other arms violations. Judge Smith dismissed the jury, and then called the attorneys to the bench. Sighing deeply, he began explaining a problem that some of them had already noted.

The jury's verdicts had not been in line with the instructions that the judge had given them, nor were they internally consistent. In Smith's instructions, the conspiracy charge was referred to as "Count One," the murder charge as "Count Two." The third count in the instructions was "using and carrying a firearm during and in relation to the com- mission of an offense." The judge instructed the jurors that "for you to find the defendants guilty of this crime, you must be convinced that . . . the defendant under consideration committed the crime alleged in Count One . . . I instruct you that 'Conspiracy to Murder Officers and Employees of the United States' is a crime of violence." In effect, the judge had told the jurors that Count Three was a left shoe, of value only if worn with the matching right shoe, a Count One or conspiracy conviction. The jurors had come out of their deliberations wearing only one shoe.

"The guilty finding as to Count Three will have to be set aside," Smith told the lawyers. "That portion of the verdict simply cannot stand." There was no point, he explained to the disappointed prose- cutors, in sending the verdict back to the jurors for rectification, since "the only decision they could have made was to change that finding to not guilty. . . ." His last words on Count Three were that "the court"— meaning himself—"will set that finding aside." Then he recessed the trial until sentencing.

Woodrow Kendrick and Clive Doyle walked out of the courtroom as free men. Norman Allison, who had been acquitted of all charges, and Canadian Ruth Riddle, who'd been found guilty only of the mooted

296

Count Three, were held over the weekend for processing by the Immigration and Naturalization Service, which suspected them of overstaying their visas. Once outside, Kendrick and Doyle shed tears on camera for the seven comrades who faced imprisonment, and prosecutors Jahn and Johnston tried to put a victorious face on the verdict, declaring that it proved that assaults on federal officers could not go unpunished. But in the bar of the nearby Fairmount Hotel, the defense team uncorked bottles of champagne. Had their clients been handed the life sentences that accompanied conviction on the murder or conspiracy charges, by the usual standards of calculation, they would have faced a total of 440 years in prison, or 40 years each. The maximum terms that now faced the seven who were still in jeopardy totaled only 70 years—about 16 percent of the sum that the prosecutors had sought. As the attorneys and a few well-wishers passed out congratulations, an announcement was made over television that the full footage of a commentary on the verdict by Janet Reno would be aired at 10:00 P.M. that night. "Hell, by then we'll all be drunk!" attorney Dan Cogdell exclaimed.

On Monday morning, February 28, Judge Smith ordered the release of Ruth Riddle. She and Norman Allison were transferred to a San Antonio immigration facility, and were standing in line, awaiting processing, when the judge sent a new message, ordering that Riddle be arrested again. Two hundred miles away in Waco, he'd changed his mind, after reading a brief by procedural expert LeRoy Jahn. Her research showed that in a case that set precedent in the federal Fifth Circuit, the appeals court that oversees Smith, an inconsistent verdict had been allowed to stand. By the time he ordered Riddle's detention, Judge Smith was preparing a decision in favor of the government.

Jury forewoman Sarah Bain, after learning of the judge's decision, felt compelled to explain to him what the jury had done. The group had mistakenly believed, she said in a letter, that the "using and carrying a firearm" charge, or Count Three, could be matched with the charge of aiding and abetting manslaughter. The decision reflected a compromise, and leniency, Bain said. "After we had delivered our verdict to the court and prior to its being presented to the public," she wrote, "we jurors discussed what most of us felt was the possibility that

297

with the consideration of time already served by the defendants, none would be facing severe penalties. Even five years is too severe a penalty for what we believed to be a minor charge." In effect, she said, the jurors had found the defendants guilty of using firearms to commit a rash but not murderous act.

But the judge had another perspective in mind, breathtaking in scope. On June 17, 1994, he revealed it while sentencing the eight defendants who remained in custody. Standing the jury's intent on its head, Smith declared that since the jurors had found the defendants guilty of carrying a firearm during the commission of a crime, they had therefore found them guilty of that crime—conspiracy—as well. "These defendants, and other adult Branch Davidians," he wrote in his order, "engaged in a conspiracy to cause the deaths of federal agents. It was a part of the beliefs of the Branch Davidians, expressed and taught by their leader. . . ."

Going beyond that, he also found that on February 28, "the first shots were fired from inside the front door of the compound"—a finding that many raiders couldn't confirm—and that the survivors of the raid had set the April 19 blaze. "Finally, by a combination of suicide and murder inflicted by Davidian upon Davidian, all but a handful of the Davidians were killed," he concluded.

In a few words, Judge Smith had rewritten the jury's findings. He reinstated charges that he'd vowed to dismiss, and he imposed guilt where a jury had found none. The judge justified his dubious findings on a principle unknown to most of the citizenry. At trial, the government must prove its charges beyond the shadow of a reasonable doubt, but at sentencing, a federal judge may use a different and less demanding standard called "the preponderance of evidence." Even though the jury had not found the defendants guilty of conspiracy, or of killing their loved ones and peers, Judge Smith, by applying a lower standard of decision, in effect did just that.

So confident was he of his legal maneuver that most of Smith's sentencing opinion was devoted to an essentially auxiliary issue. The prison terms mandated by federal guidelines for carrying weapons during the course of a crime are drawn on a sliding scale. Sentences for using automatic weapons are "enhanced," or longer than those for using semi-automatic and single-shot weapons. Trial testimony had established that most of the defendants had possessed weapons during the assault and siege, but did not establish what type of guns they carried. Drawing from the snake-filled basket of drug law precedent, Smith ruled that since automatic weapons were present in Mt. Carmel, everyone inside enjoyed "constructive possession" of them, and was therefore liable to the stiffest penalties provided for in the sentencing guidelines.

After announcing these decisions, Smith handed forty-year sentences to five of the defendants who had been at Mt. Carmel on February 28. Because Australian Graeme Craddock had in a grand jury hearing provided most of the evidence used against him, Smith limited his prison term to twenty years. He set Ruth Riddle's term at five years, perhaps because she was female, and perhaps because testimony had shown that she had not fired her weapon during the siege. Paul Fatta, having been away from home on February 28, had not been found guilty of Count Three. Judge Smith could not punish him with a life term, but sentenced him to fifteen years instead. The upshot of Smith's rulings was that the eight convicted defendants would serve a total of 240 years, an average of 30 years each. In addition to prison terms, each of the eight was sentenced to pay $1.2 million in restitution to the ATF and FBI. In the hands of Judge Smith, the prosecution had won 75 percent of the punishment that it had sought.

After the judge had read his sentencing order, each of the defendants was given a chance to address the court. Livingstone Fagan, who had spent much of the trial leafing through a Bible at the defense table, spoke first and, in many ways, spoke for the group as a whole. ". . . There is no doubt in our minds that we are innocent . . . ," he told the judge. "There is no doubt in my mind that the actions that we were forced to take were justified. . . ."

Noting that the judge, in an aside, had complained of receiving hundreds of telephone calls and fax messages urging leniency upon him, Fagan drew a comparison. ". . . This reminds me of a situation . . . that goes back to 2,000 years ago regarding Christ," he said. ". . . It kind of reminds me of that woman that came to . . . Pilate and said something to the effect, 'Have nothing to do with this just man.' "

Much in the style of the disciples of earlier days, Fagan explained that he and his peers "serve a God who sits on a throne like you, a judge. He's got a book in his hand, sealed with Seven Seals. . . . As you have judged," the apostle warned, "so, too, will you be judged." The Judgment that Mt. Carmel's survivors prophesy will come, of course, at the End Time, when Christ returns to the earth in glory. When He does, Fagan and the others say, Judge Smith, the prosecution, and the rest of the living will recognize Him as David Koresh.

A NOTE ON PUBLISHED SOURCES

Determining what happened at Mt. Carmel in February, March, and April 1993 is a task that requires resort to conflicting sources of information: the researcher must weigh both a government and an anti-government point of view.

The government makes its essential case in print in two volumes. The *Report of the Department of the Treasury on the Bureau of Alcohol, Tobacco and Firearms Investigation of Vernon Wayne Howell, also known as David Koresh* is available from the U.S. Government Printing Office in Washington, D.C. This volume covers the planning and execution of the February 28, 1993, raid.

The second volume, covering the subsequent fifty-one-day siege and the FBI's actions, is the *Report to the Deputy Attorney General on the Events at Waco, Texas, February 28 to April 19, 1993, Revised Version*. It is also available from the Government Printing Office.

Several books, all essentially supportive of the government's positions, were published by commercial houses in the wake of the April 19 fire. These include *Inside the Cult*, by Marc Breault and Martin King; *Massacre at Waco*, by Clifford Linedecker; *Mad Man in Waco*, by Brad Bailey and Bob Darden; *See No Evil*, by Tim Madigan; and a more scholarly treatment, *Prophets of the Apocalypse*, by Kenneth Samples, Erwin de Castro, Richard Abanes, and Robert Lyle. Available from the *Waco Tribune-Herald* is a bound volume of the stories that its reporters penned during 1993 and 1994.

In attempts to counter the government's version of events, four books were published by their authors, and one by an organization: *Sinister Twilight*, by Ron Cole; *Blind Justice*, by Ken Fawcett; *The Waco Whitewash*, by Jack DeVault; *Bushwacked by Bushmasters*, by Ronald Davidson; and a draft of *The Massacre of the Branch Davidians*, by Carol Moore. Moore's book, in a revised form, is available from Gun Owners of America; the other three are of limited distribution. In addition, television station KPOC of Ponca City, Oklahoma, produced six volumes of documents related to the controversy, and *Soldier of Fortune* magazine covered the affair closely through 1995.

Pro-government works on the Waco events mainly presume that gun ownership is a privilege; anti-government writings presume that it is a right. A scholar's attempt to bring this controversy to ground is *To Keep and Bear Arms*, by Joyce Lee Malcolm.

As important as any chronicle of events is the theology that stood behind the standoff. My interviews with survivors of Mt. Carmel convinced me that Ellen G. White's writings are the best guide to what David Koresh believed. Dozens of books by White are still in print; most are accessible through a four-volume index, available, as the works themselves are, through any bookstore operated by the Seventh-Day Adventist Church. For my work, I drew on *The Adventist Home* (AH), *Christ's Object Lessons* (COL), *Counsels on Health* (CH), *The Desire of Ages* (DA), *Education* (Ed), *Early Writings* (EW), *The Great Controversy* (GC), *Life Sketches* (LS), *The Ministry of Healing* (MH), *Patriarchs and Prophets* (PP), *Prophets and Kings* (PK), *Testimonies* (T), and *The Spirit of Prophecy*. (The last is not accessible through the White index.)

Several other works, also available at church bookstores, helped bring me up to date on the doctrine of today's Seventh-Day Adventists. These included *The New World Order*, by Russell Burrill, *The Antichrist and the New World Order*, by Marvin Moore; and *It's Your Money, Isn't It?*, by Edward Reid. A church periodical, *Adventist Today*, devoted its first issue to the Waco affair. The SDA also published a forty-year-old, four-volume work, *The Prophetic Faith of Our Fathers*, which is useful in tracing the history of intepretations of the Seven Seals.

The fundamental scholarly works on Ellen G. White and her following are *Prophetess of Health*, by Ronald L. Numbers, and *The Disappointed*, edited by Numbers. Neither is to be found in church bookstores: the University of Tennessee Press published both. The journal *Spectrum* devotes itself to scholarly and semi-scholarly commentary on Adventism, chiefly by believers.

Most of the writings of the founder of the Davidian movement, Victor Houteff, are available in two books, *The Shepherd's Rod Series*, and *The*

Symbolic Code Series, both from Mt. Carmel Center in Salem, South Carolina. Most valuable among them, to those researching Koresh, are the articles in the "Timely Greetings" (TG) series, a part of *The Shepherd's Rod*.

The innovations to Davidianism wrought by Ben and Lois Roden, Koresh's predecessors, are known largely through the memories of their followers, some two dozen pamphlets and perhaps as many audiotapes. The tapes and pamphlets are out of print, though heirs to Lois Roden's Living Waters Branch of Righteousness are publishing new material in Gadsden, Alabama.

The nineteenth century's Cyrus Teed, whose theology in some ways anticipated David Koresh, left behind too many works when he died. His *Cellular Cosmogony* remains in many libraries, as does a novel, *The Great Red Dragon*. More useful to understanding his theology, and available in some libraries, are *Koreshanity*, by his disciple Augustus Weimar, and *The Immortal Manhood* and *Interpretation of the Book of Revelation*, both by Teed himself. Copies of his movement's newspaper, *The Flaming Sword*, are in the Library of Congress, and provide the best information regarding his dalliance with the Seven Seals. America's expert on the seer, R. L. Rainard of Tidewater Community College, from time to time produces academic papers on Teed.

A dozen Palestine-era audiotapes and a half-dozen letters, including an explanation of the First Seal, are David Koresh's sole doctrinal legacy. A disciple, Livingstone Fagan, has begun to pen brief works from jail, as has an elderly follower, Catherine Matteson. Their writings, and some of the Koresh materials, are currently available only by E-mail from Mark Swett, 74073.3573@compuserve.com.

Transcripts of the San Antonio trial of the eleven Mt. Carmel conspirators are available through the Western Federal District Court in Waco, Texas, where most files from the case are stored. Other important documents in government hands—transcripts of FBI conversations with Mt. Carmel during the siege, for example—may not be released until the year 2000.

Several contemporary works of broader scope contributed to my understanding of the topics in this book. These include *The Pursuit of the*

303

Millennium, by Norman Cohn; *A Noble Death,* by Arthur Droge and James Tabor; *From the Ashes,* a survey of scholarly opinion edited by James Lewis; and *Harper's Bible Commentary.* Most helpful of all, however, was the King James Version of the Good Book itself.

INDEX

INDEX

White, Ellen G. (Sister White)
(*cont.*)
evolutionism of, 56
on heretics, 89–90
on "innumerable worlds," 94–95
Koresh as successor to, 98
on Orion constellation, 96
persecution expected by, 56
present truth doctrine of, 56–57
as prolific writer, 52–53
on Revelation, 103, 105
visions of, 52, 53, 54, 56
White, E. T., 60
Whitecliff, Kevin, 127, 278, 288–289

White House Recruiter, The (Houteff), 95
Wilkerson, Denise, 77
Williams, Robert J. (Rob), 154, 287–288
Willis, Steve, 158, 159, 286–87, 288
women's dormitory, Mt. Carmel, 48

Yair, Eleazar ben, 217
Yardbirds, 153

Zechariah, 272, 273
Zimmermann, Jack, 134, 142, 145, 252, 255, 271, 294
Zion, Mt., 93–94, 116, 205